P9-AQR-740

Advances in Contemporary Educational Thought Series
Jonas F. Soltis, Editor

TECHNICAL COLLEGE OF THE LOWCOUNTRY
LEARNING RESOURCES CENTER
POST OFFICE BOX 1288
BEAUFORT, SOUTH CAROLINA 29901-1288

ANSWERING THE "VIRTUECRATS"

A Moral Conversation on Character Education

ROBERT J. NASH

Teachers College, Columbia University
New York and London

TECHNICAL COLLEGE OF THE LOWCOUNTRY
LEARNING RESOURCES CENTER
POST OFFICE BOX 1288
BEAUFORT, SOUTH CAROLINA 29901-1288

Published by Teachers College Press, 1234 Amsterdam Avenue, New York, NY 10027

Copyright © 1997 by Teachers College, Columbia University

All rights reserved. No part of this publication may be reproduced or transmitted in any form or by any means, electronic or mechanical, including photocopy, or any information storage and retrieval system, without permission from the publisher.

Some portions of Chapters 8 and 9 first appeared in Nash, R. J. (1997). "Fostering Moral Conversations in the College Classroom." *Journal on Excellence in College Teaching, 7* (1). The material appears with the permission of the Publisher.

Library of Congress Cataloging-in-Publication Data

Nash, Robert J.
    Answering the "virtuecrats" : a moral conversation on character education / Robert J. Nash.
        p.   cm. — (Advances in contemporary educational thought series : v. 21)
    Includes bibliographical references and index.
    ISBN 0-8077-3670-8 (cloth : alk. paper) — ISBN 0-8077-3669-4 (paper : alk. paper)
        1. Moral education—United States.   2. Character—Study and teaching—United States.   3. Postmodernism and education—United States.   I. Title.   II. Series.
    LC311.N27   1997
    370.11'4—dc21   97-23123

ISBN 0-8077-3669-4 (paper)
ISBN 0-8077-3670-8 (cloth)

Printed on acid-free paper
Manufactured in the United States of America

04 03 02 01 00 99 98 97   8 7 6 5 4 3 2 1

To Madelyn, as always;
and to my parents, James and Myrtle Nash

Contents

Foreword

Many in America today believe we are living in an era of moral decline. Not only are our streets unsafe and violence an everyday occurrence, but holders of public office are charged with serious breaches of ethics, young people abuse drugs and vandalize, television and the movies celebrate violence and sex, and even ordinary courtesy and civility are hard to find in our public spaces. Many feel that a pervasive relativism and an ultra-liberal view of morals, a belief in the absolute right and freedom of the individual to choose his or her own lifestyle, have eroded the best of what a more traditional view of ethics and values once provided.

One answer to this perceived state of affairs has been the call for "character" and "virtues" education in American schools and colleges. Popular books by the likes of William Bennett, Marva Collins, and William Kilpatrick on virtues, civic morality, and character education have almost become a cottage industry, often ending up on best-seller lists. To reflect this state of affairs, the first version of this book was tentatively titled *Merchants of Morality*. The new title, *Answering the "Virtuecrats": A Moral Conversation on Character Education*, better reflects the seriousness and solidity of Robert Nash's thoughtful and thorough treatment of contemporary ideas about teaching morality.

Unlike most other books on the topic, this book does not present a single point of view, one sure solution to the perceived problem of moral decay. It offers hope; it offers direction; it offers perspective; but most of all it offers critique, in the best sense of the word. Drawing on the work of many contemporary writers, whom he metaphorically calls "ministers of morality," Nash characterizes their positions as either neo-classical, communitarian, or liberationist. He then examines each approach to moral education by first attempting to understand it sympathetically, then by pointing out both its strengths and weaknesses, and finally by formulating the problems and issues uncovered in his analysis. He ends with his own version of a postmodern "patchwork" pedagogy of moral conversation.

His scholarly critique excels in understanding, clarity, and sensitivity. Readers will find much that is appealing in this book, not the least of which is Nash's strong and wise personal voice weaving many years of practical teaching experience into the fabric of his scholarship. He invites the reader to join in on a continuing moral conversation using "a non-foundational, multifunctional, and nonexclusionary public moral language." He provides a way for individuals to develop their own moral language by respecting the ideas of others who speak different moral languages. He offers what he calls a "postmodern alternative": the cultivation of democratic dispositions and virtues strong enough to stand up to the challenges of postmodernism. He repudiates the postmodern tendencies toward moral relativism and nihilism as well as traditional moral dogmatism, absolutism, and indoctrination. He offers a way for ordinary people to manage their moral lives in the discordant reality of our contemporary pluralistic, secular, democratic society. He speaks equally well to the concerns of parents, politicians, and educators. This book truly is an advance in contemporary thought about moral education in a postmodern world.

Jonas F. Soltis
Series Editor

Acknowledgments

The great theologian Karl Barth once called morality a terribly thin covering of ice over a sea of primitive barbarity. In another place, he referred to morality as a meeting place between the human and divine. As a long-time teacher of applied ethics and moral education, I, too, oscillate between such outrageous extremes whenever I consider the uses to which morality has been put in recent years, on the one hand, by certain infamous politicians, clergy, and educators, and, on the other hand, by the fine, ordinary people who come to my classes every semester. This book is my attempt to make some sense of the role that moral education plays in people's personal and professional lives, including, not least, in my own. I am grateful to the following persons for helping me to find a sense of proportion in my work as a moral educator and for inspiring me to put into words what, in my saner moments, remains ineffable.

I simply could not have written the book without the assistance of my wife, Madelyn. For months, during the course of putting words to paper, I tried out virtually every idea on her during our early-morning walks. While she does not agree with everything I have said here, her willingness to indulge my pleas for "just one more dialogue" about moral education sustained and invigorated me when the writing was most difficult. Her perspective on the topic as wife, mother, and school guidance counselor was invaluable.

I want to express my deepest gratitude to Jonas Soltis, William Heard Kilpatrick Professor Emeritus, Teachers College, Columbia University, and editor of the *Advances in Contemporary Educational Thought Series*, for his continuing support of my work over the years. He is one of the most unselfish scholars I have ever met and a wonderful benefactor. At the Press, too, I am once again indebted to Susan Liddicoat, acquisitions editor, for her meticulous attention to my manuscript. She makes my books better than they otherwise would be. And I am grateful to David Blacker who took my work seriously enough to disagree with me at times and to suggest several changes that improved the manuscript.

Without the enthusiastic students who have signed up for my courses over a 29-year career at the University of Vermont, I am convinced I would have written a far less informed and less interesting book. Whatever its ultimate worth, the book owes much to the insightful contributions that students have made through the years in my seminars on applied ethics, philosophy of education, and moral education. I am particularly grateful to five former students for their assistance and inspiration, even though they may not philosophically agree with the interpretations and applications of their work in this book: Constance Krosney, for providing me key materials on the liberationist perspective; Joshua P. Armstrong, via conversations and his thesis, for helping me to think more deeply about the religious possibilities in postmodernism; Kathleen Knight, for sharing her doctoral dissertation with me on the topic of building community in a public high school; and Karen L. Warren for her thesis that defends a liberationist agenda for higher education administration. I am also indebted to Christopher Foley who in a casual conversation helped me to think about the four virtue perspectives as actually comprising distinct moral languages.

Finally, I wish to thank my parents, Myrtle and James, for being the most important moral educators in my life as I was growing up. They taught me by their example how pivotal a simple moral decency can be in living a fulfilling life. I only hope I have been as successful in my own parenting of two terrific daughters, Mika and Kayj.

CHAPTER 1

Ministers of Morality:
Past, Present, and Future

Knowledge and religion are the supports of a republican government. The means of education, and moral and religious instruction, ought therefore to engage our serious and vigorous attention.
—Thomas Sparhawk, July 4th Oration, Boston, 1798, in Hersh et al. 1980
I believe that the moral education centers upon this conception of the school as a mode of social life, that the best and deepest moral training is precisely that which one gets through having to enter into proper relations with others in a unity of work and thought.
—John Dewey, My Pedagogic Creed, *1897/1959*
There is nothing deep inside each of us, no common human nature, no built-in human solidarity, to use a moral reference point. There is nothing to people except what has been socialized into them—their ability to use language, and thereby to exchange beliefs and desires with other people.
—Richard Rorty, Contingency, Irony and Solidarity, *1989*

I can always count on getting the most passionate reactions from students whenever I teach a course on moral education. Twenty-five years ago in my classes, many students wondered why such courses were necessary, especially when they might already have attended a workshop in their school districts on values clarification or on Kohlberg's stages of cognitive moral development. Today, although less skeptical, students still harbor serious doubts about the content and ultimate efficacy of university offerings on moral education. For example, recently two high school teachers had the following conversation after the first class meeting of a course I was teaching on character education. One said:

How can this guy expect me to teach children to be good? He reminds me of the politicians who sound like they know everything when they constantly harp on family values. As a classroom teacher, I can only do so much, you know. Doesn't morality begin at home? Years ago, teachers knew what they had to do, and

I'll bet it wasn't shaping up kids morally. Wasn't that left to the parents and churches? I wouldn't even know where or how to begin to shape character or what morality to teach. Besides, aren't the school years too late in a child's life to start forming character?

The other teacher remarked:

Yes, but I liked it when he said that whether we know it or not, we are always teaching morality. He's right. All of education is moral education. We're always shaping character, and, as far as I'm concerned, it's never too late to do this. Your morality sticks out like a sore thumb, just as mine does. Why not at least acknowledge your values openly instead of sneaking them into your teaching? In our school, we have been working hard to get students and staff to respect each other, to be fair and honest, and to accept responsibility for their actions. Last year we held three schoolwide assemblies in an effort to create the best moral environment for our kids. And this year, one of our guidance counselors has started a mediation program for students based on the values of mutual respect, sensitive listening, and peaceful conflict resolution. I'm hoping I can pick up some additional information about character education in this class.

Unappeased, the first teacher responded:

I'm not questioning *your* school's commitment to character education, but as far as I'm concerned few of *my* colleagues are qualified to teach students how to be better human beings. Teacher, heal thyself, I say. Besides, the best character education is by example not by imposition, isn't it? Frankly, I'm tired of the so-called experts from the university and the various foundations coming into my school to hustle their particular agendas. Let me teach what I'm trained to do. Let the hustlers go elsewhere.

The other teacher got the final rejoinder before her ride arrived:

Come on; give this guy a break. Don't we all "hustle" our own little agendas? When it comes to teaching morality, who really knows what's ultimately right and wrong anyway? Why don't you chill a little bit and give the class a chance? Do what I do; take what you can use, and forget the rest. After all, it's not like there's a God present to tell us the "right" answers, or to check up on us when we teach. Why did you decide to take this course anyway, if you're so skeptical? I, for one, am tired of handing over my responsibilities to be a character educator to MTV, the advertising industry, and Hollywood. I'll take help wherever I can get it.

CLASSICAL QUESTIONS ABOUT VIRTUE

At that early point in the semester, little did these two teachers know that their conflicting views on character education had been circulating for at least 2,400 years, dating as far back as ancient Greece. Socrates, Plato's legendary teacher, was the first Western educator to express an interest in teaching children to be good human beings, and these questions have continued to plague educators ever since, right up to the present day, as the above interchange illustrates. In Plato's (1956) dialogue *Meno,* a young Thessalian nobleman, Menon, asks Socrates: "Can you tell me, Socrates— can virtue be taught? Or if not, does it come by practice? Or does it come neither by practice nor by teaching, but do people get it by nature, or in some other way?" (p. 70). Socrates' initial answer to Menon is brusque: "My good man, you must think I am inspired! Virtue? Can it be taught? Or how does it come? Do I know that? So far from knowing whether it can be taught or can't be taught, I don't know even the least little thing about virtue; I don't even know what virtue is" (p. 70).

Throughout most of his dialogues, Plato explores a variety of highly generalized answers to these difficult questions, at one time claiming that virtue is knowledge and, thus, it can be taught, and another time asserting that it is not knowledge, and, therefore, it cannot be taught. Although, in his writings, Plato is more than willing to have Socrates name the "cardinal" virtues as courage, temperance, justice, and reason, he seems far less interested in exploring practical educational questions regarding the teaching of these virtues. He is more concerned with raising fundamental metaphysical questions about the nature and content of what he calls the pure "Forms" and their possible relationship to individual moral virtues. At the end of *Meno,* finally, in answer to Menon's queries, Socrates asserts:

But if we have ordered all our enquiry well and argued well, virtue is seen as coming neither by nature nor by teaching; but by divine allotment incomprehensibly . . . we shall only know the truth about this clearly when, before enquiring in what way virtue comes to mankind, we first try to search out what virtue is in itself. (pp. 67–68)

For Aristotle, Plato's pupil, virtue has more to do with practical considerations and the skills of everyday living than with the "divine allotment" of something considered good "in itself." Eschewing Socrates' ironic "ignorance" on the subject of virtue, Aristotle confidently enumerates a list of "intellectual" and "moral" excellences claiming that virtue is a set of unique dispositions, a state of character, a "knowing how to like and dislike the proper things" that makes a person good and leads ultimately to happiness. In the *Nichomachean Ethics*, Aristotle (1976) sounds remarkably like Menon as he asks in Book One how people can learn to be happy: "Is happiness something that can be learnt, or acquired by habituation, or cultivated in some other way, or does it come to us by a sort of divine dispensation, or even by chance?" (p. 80). Aristotle's answer to these questions, unlike Socrates', is that happiness results from the acquisition of particular virtues acquired through training, habituation, and lifelong character development. God has little to do with the appropriation of moral character. Rather, the happy person is "one who is active in accordance with complete virtue, and who is adequately furnished with external goods, and that not for some unspecified period but throughout a complete life" (p. 334).

THE CURRENT REVIVAL OF VIRTUE

At the present time, an increasingly powerful, highly visible group of educational thinkers are attempting to answer Socrates' and Aristotle's questions in their own unique ways. These late-twentieth-century "character educators" are urging America's schools and colleges to take the lead in the formation of moral character in our nation's youth. Less convinced than Socrates that it is essential to know what "virtue is in itself" and, like Aristotle, highly skeptical that virtue "comes by divine allotment, incomprehensibly," these thinkers believe unequivocally that virtue *can*, indeed *must*, be taught in the schools and colleges, and they manage to appear with increasing regularity on key television talk and news shows to make their appeals. In fact, today, books, articles, and workshops on character education have become something of a growth industry in the publishing field. The likes of William Bennett (1993, 1995), Marva Collins (1990), William Kilpatrick (1992), Thomas Lickona (1991), and Edward Wynne and Kevin Ryan (1993) deplore what they consider to be the "moral decline" both in society and in the schools and colleges. What these thinkers, and others like them, have in common is the belief that there are desirable states of moral character—*virtues*—that youths need to cultivate; that they learn these traits mainly through example, exhortation, training, and the reading of special stories that dramatically exemplify the desired virtues; that they need to practice these qualities until they become second nature; and that besides the home and church the best place for virtue inculcation is in the school.

These authors mourn the widespread disappearance of civility, patriotism, discipline, intellectual rigor, and respect for law and property throughout the culture, and especially in America's schools and colleges. The virtues these writers mention most frequently as worthy of educators' sustained attention and enactment are diligence, civility, responsibility, self-restraint, prudence, honesty, self-respect, reverence, and compassion. Astonishingly, many books on the topic of moral character today become immediate best-sellers, a sure thing along with books on angels, low-fat diets, and new political paradigms designed to eliminate "welfare as we know it." For example, there are currently more than 2.5 million copies of William Bennett's *The Book of Virtues* (1993) and *The Moral Compass* (1995) in distribution; and William Kilpatrick's *Why Johnny Can't Tell Right from Wrong* (1992) has sold in the hundreds of thousands in hardcover and paperback editions.

In 1990, the conservative, African American, inner-city principal, Marva Collins, reissued her 1982 *Marva Collins' Way,* and it soon became another moral-character best-seller, even making some top-ten educators' booklists. In the popular press, the *USA Weekend* magazine (November 1995) devoted an entire issue to character education for the moral edification of its 39.1 million readers; and the august *New York Times Magazine* (April 30, 1995) had as its lead article, "Who'll Teach Kids Right from Wrong? The Character Education Movement Thinks the Answer Is the Schools." Even the political left has made its voice heard on the virtue front: In the last few years liberal authors such as Kenneth A. Bruffee (1993), Lisa Delpit (1995), Herbert Kohl and Colin Greer (1995), Deborah Meier (1995), George W. Noblit and Van O. Dempsey (1996), and Judith Renyi (1993) checked in with their own works extolling particular virtues associated with "collaborative learning," "reacculturation," diversity, and equality in schools across the United States.

It is my contention that many of the more celebrated, conservative character educators—and several others of a more liberal and radical ilk who are not as well known to the public, and whose work I will discuss in the following pages as well—have become "ministers of moral character." And because their moral strictures strike a responsive chord with people throughout the United States, millions of readers are taking their preachments very seriously. These highly committed proponents of a "traditional [or progressive] morality" know how to impart their quasi-religious messages with extraordinary perspicacity, being particularly adept at passing on their special virtues to schools and colleges throughout this country. Some, like William Bennett and Thomas Lickona, have even become "ministers plenipotentiaries," "lay cardinals" invested by their peers with the fullest power to proclaim their moral truths. Their publications and media proclamations on behalf of virtue, rigorous curricula, and discipline have had a tremendous impact on a number of diverse religious, political, and educational constituencies. In fact, to apply another metaphor, in its June 17, 1996, issue on the "25 most influential Americans," one of *Time* magazine's choices was the "virtuecrat," William Bennett, whom it called "the virtual C.E.O. of what might be dubbed Virtue Inc."

A BRIEF HISTORICAL CONTEXT FOR CHARACTER EDUCATION

Obviously, there is nothing ipso facto wrong with being a successful minister of morality in a country that has always prided itself on being religious, even while it takes very seriously the constitutional principles of separation of church and state and religious freedom. Moreover, imparting morality to our nation's educational institutions is a venerable, near-missionary undertaking, dating back to the sixteenth century, and as American as apple pie and baseball.

The nation's Founding Fathers called for the schools to forge a kind of civic virtue rooted in religious and moral instruction, the necessary requirements of democratic life. During the seventeenth century, character educators who believed their divine purpose was to shape a child's demeanor in accordance with the Puritan ethic pushed such virtues in the schools and colleges as piety, loyalty, industry, and temperance. The *New England Primer*, for instance, featuring such religiously overt assertions as "In Adam's fall, We sinned all," first appeared in the public schools in 1690 and sold in excess of 3 million copies over a period of 150 years (Rippa, 1992). As much as two centuries later, in the Boston public schools, such "readers" as the 1808 *The Boston Primer, Child's Companion,* and *Beauties of the Bible* emphasized the virtues of religious devotion and deference to authority (Hersh, Miller, & Fielding, 1980). In Massachusetts, the first schooling law was the 1647 "Old Deluder Satan Act," and it required that students be taught how to avoid Satan's snares (Kirst, 1984). Moral education in the seventeenth and eighteenth centuries was actually a type of religious instruction, and in the New York public schools character education was almost catechetical in tone, enjoining students not to lie, steal, or swear and to be acutely aware that God "sees and hears" everything they do (Hersh et al., 1980). Later, the McGuffey Readers, first published in 1836 and actually used by more than 200 million school-children from 1900 to 1940, were blatantly moralistic. According to Kirst (1984), in these readers, "in story after story good children are rewarded, while bad ones are punished with equal celerity. Honesty and industry are the leading values, closely followed by courage, kindness, obedience, and courtesy" (p. 28). Town, city, and country schools in the eighteenth and nineteenth centuries were primarily concerned to impart those virtues that would best equip students for active involvement in the worlds of politics, work, and family.

In the mid- to late nineteenth century, the common school movement opened America's schools to everyone—immigrant, urban resident, and rural dweller alike. Common school educators sought to instill the virtues of egalitarianism and majoritarianism, and under the leadership of Horace Mann, the schools embarked on their mission to incorporate children from all socioeconomic classes and ethnic groups (Kirst, 1984). According to Kirst, nineteenth-century educators were primarily character educators who "considered the school superior to the home as a source of values and moral training, and superior, certainly, to society at large, which offered the young the temptations of the street" (p. 30). The teacher taught by example, and the textbooks emphasized the moral precepts of a "pan-Protestant morality and a politically neutral form of republican virtue" (pp. 30–31).

In the late nineteenth century, Kate Wiggin and G. Stanley Hall ushered in the child-centered movement in moral education, with an emphasis on "health, emotions, growth, and heredity" (Hersh et al., 1980, p. 19). For Wiggin, children "have a tolerably clear sense of right and wrong needing only gentle guidance to choose the right when it is put before them" (quoted on pp. 18–19). And Hall, something of a Rousseauian, expressed great faith in the natural proclivities of the child, echoing the opening lines of *Emile* in saying that "childhood, as it comes fresh from the hands of God, is not corrupt . . . there is nothing else so worthy of love, reverence, and service as the body and soul of the growing child" (quoted on p. 19). The romantic approach of Wiggin and Hall tended to glorify the child's natural virtues while resisting the stringency of Puritan and "melting pot" training.

Out of the child-centered movement came the twentieth-century reform known as progressive education, whose originating impulse and commanding presence was John Dewey. Dewey resisted the character-education trend of teaching particular virtues as being too "goody-goody" (quoted in Hersh et al., 1980, p. 21). In general, progressive educators rejected the inculcation of Puritan virtues in favor of such democratic "habits" as sociality, instrumentalism, practicality, and coop-

eration. They believed that when children worked together to solve problems and participate in democratic processes, then they were actually
living the moral virtues they were learning intellectually. For the first 50
years of the twentieth century, Dewey's approach to moral education was
dominant, characterized by a flurry of experimentation in schools
throughout the country with group work, laboratories, projects, and
community-involvement activities. By the mid-1950s, however, progressive education was on the wane, in part because Dewey's ideas were tragically misunderstood and misapplied by his disciples, in part because the
times were changing, and in part because Dewey's writings were often
exasperatingly dense, never clearly defining such key terms as *experience,
growth,* and *democracy* (Rippa, 1992).

   With the Soviet launching of *Sputnik I* in the 1950s, character education took on a new look: The celebrated virtues in America's schools became rigor, discipline, and scientific mastery as the nation mobilized to
restore its economic and military supremacy in the face of the Russian
challenge. Technical and scientific training supplanted character education, an area now considered "soft" by certain economic and military
standards (Ravitch, 1984). By the late 1960s and throughout the 1970s and
1980s, in a period of major social upheaval featuring a series of tragic
political assassinations, the Vietnam war and its aftermath, a wide range
of social justice and liberation movements, and an increasing ethnic and
racial pride on the part of disenfranchised groups, the preferred virtues
for the schools had become tolerance, social justice, fairness, diversity,
and interdependence. It was not so much that character education was
now being seen as a panacea for the social ills of modern times; rather,
educators experienced it cautiously as a way to make the ideal of social
justice a reality by helping students to understand the enormous complexities of pluralistic living and democratic decision making (Ravitch,
1983).

   Today, in reaction to the "moral declivity" that many character educators believe is threating the very foundations of American life and
schooling, the "declinists" call for fostering such virtues as respect, responsibility, diligence, prudence, and chastity, or in Wynne's and Ryan's
(1993) shorthand language, "character, academics, and discipline." And
so, at this time, Americans have appeared to come full circle in the pursuit
of a moral education appropriately suited to the period in which they
live, and character educators are still playing the role of quasi-ministers.
In actual practice, the American educator, like the classical thinker, has
always been concerned with fostering particular moral virtues in the nation's schools. And like the two teachers in my course who engaged in a
heated exchange earlier in this chapter, educators for the better part of

three centuries in this country have wrestled with the same perennial virtue questions that manage to haunt us even today—questions that in various forms will appear in the pages ahead:

- What exactly is virtue, and how do we become virtuous people? Is the concept of personal virtue actually an anachronism in a secular pluralist America with its insistence instead on laws, rules, principles, individual and group rights, and entitlements?
- Should the schools and colleges teach virtue? And, if so, which virtues? How can secular schools and colleges avoid imposing particular religious and political agendas in teaching virtue?
- What special dispositions, abilities, and understandings should teachers of virtue possess? Is it necessary that we expect teachers to know the good, à la Plato, before we ask them to teach what is good? Or is it enough that we require teachers to do the good in order to exemplify what is good, à la Aristotle?
- What are the best ways to teach virtue? What pedagogical methods and materials are likely to be the most effective (Chazan, 1985)? To what extent is character formation a product of systematic classroom instruction? How much is the attainment of virtue actually a product of conditioning or training? Is moral indoctrination ever justified in the classroom, and, if so, under what conditions? Or are imitation, inspiration, and persuasion more effective in the shaping of moral character?
- Is self-esteem a virtue, and, if so, is it the business of schools and colleges to foster such a quality? Should the schools and colleges be about the task of setting such "extracurricular" goals as self-fulfillment, happiness, a caring ethic, social justice, gender equity, and democratic responsibility? If so, how can these institutions achieve these purposes without diluting their more strictly educational responsibilities, and without duplicating or preempting the work of the family, therapists, social service agencies, government, and church organizations? In what senses are these other "helping" institutions "educating," virtue-fostering institutions in their own right?
- What is the relationship between moral reasoning and moral action, between moral cognition and moral character (Chazan, 1985)? Should the schools and colleges teach moral character as a cognitive process or as an ethical content, as a way of thinking or as a way of acting? Or both?
- To what extent, if any, should character education be political education? How should the schools and colleges interact with the state? Should the schools and colleges fulfill the needs of the state, or should they challenge and transform those needs? Do the schools and colleges

have a political purpose, and, if so, is this purpose to indoctrinate, train, and form citizens, or is it to encourage subversive questioning in order to bring about social change (Frost, 1962)?

A POSTMODERN CRITIQUE OF CHARACTER EDUCATION

Surprisingly, there has been very little methodical criticism of the late-twentieth-century version of character education, and what critique there is has been mostly ad hoc and eclectic, coming from a few extremists on the religious right and political left. The time is right, I think, for a serious, systematic analysis of the character-education movement by a philosopher of education. In a nutshell, I believe that, in spite of its many worthy qualities (some of which I will discuss and even defend), character education—as it is currently being promoted by various ministers of morality—is deeply and seriously flawed, as are two of its more laudable alternatives, communitarian and liberationist education, which I will also explore. In the extreme, much character education is unnecessarily apocalyptic and narrow in its cultural criticism, inherently authoritarian in its convictions, excessively nostalgic and premodern in its understanding of virtue, too closely aligned with a reactionary (or a radical) politics, anti-intellectual in its curricular initiatives, hyperbolic in its moral claims, dangerously antidemocratic, and overly simplistic in its contention that training and imitation alone are sufficient for instilling moral character.

Furthermore, I will attempt to make the case that while character education is strong on prescription and exhortation, it has yet to develop an effective praxis. Pedagogically, character educators do one of two things. Either they advocate assigning traditional readings rich with virtue implications and assume that students will somehow get the moral message and miraculously emerge from their studies as more virtuous people. Or else they create prepackaged moral-character handbooks designating predetermined outcomes—complete with checklists, charts, simulations, and role-plays—which educators can use to teach virtue by the numbers. Or, as is the case with some of the more political virtue educators (the liberationists), they end up preaching, debunking, accusing, and rebuking, all the while assuming that making people feel guilty for being morally retrograde in some way will transform vicious behavior and liberate the "oppressed."

In my estimation, too many contemporary character educators (of all political and philosophical stripes) resemble John Stuart Mill's (1859/1982) "moral police," who "encroach on the most unquestionably legitimate liberty of the individual" (p. 152). In pushing a kind of moral conformity on the schools, character educators blissfully ignore the fact that modern, constitutional democracies must continually find new ways to resolve the inevitable clash of values that is the heart and soul of democratic living. In today's world, moral and political absolutes are ephemeral (there are no more universal "sacred texts"). Pluralism frequently gives rise to unruly public disagreements and intractable divisions. And people more than ever need the skills and dispositions to deliberate effectively together in order to reach political compromise and achieve consensus. In contrast to the more traditional virtue programs finding their way into the schools today, I will present in the chapters to come an alternative philosophical rationale for character education, and I will develop an argument for a general virtue curriculum whose main purpose is to foster the "democratic dispositions." In brief, I will assert that educators should commit themselves to the cultivation of a "democratic character" among citizens, one that effectively predisposes people to engage in collective decision making; respect liberty, autonomy, and political equality; and reach consent through careful deliberation.

Moreover, I will argue that educators must understand that, beyond mere rote knowledge of laws, constitutions, and political institutions, certain virtues are necessary for democratic citizens to become truly self-governing. What citizens require is a certain liberality of character, marked by the virtues of self-discipline, obligation, civility, tolerance, fairness, and generosity.

In the last two chapters, I will submit that, in the classroom, educators and their students are more likely to learn the "democratic dispositions" necessary for productive and mutually respectful living in a diverse, robust, secular pluralist society when they learn to carry on conversations and read texts in the spirit of certain postmodern virtues. Among these virtues are a sensitivity to the postmodern realities of incommensurability, indeterminacy, and nonfoundationalism; dialectical awareness; empathy; hermeneutical sensitivity; openness to alterity ("otherness"); respect for plurality; a sense of irony and humor; a commitment to civility; a capacity for fairness and charity; compassion in the presence of suffering, with an antipathy toward violence; and humility in the face of shifting and elusive conceptions of reality, goodness, and truth. I take the position, inspired by Richard J. Bernstein (1993), Shaun Gallagher (1992), Stanley J. Grenz (1996), Andrew C. Thiselton (1995), and David Tracy (1994), that postmodernity need not be nihilistic and destructive, or even antireligious. In fact, I will argue that it is only when we learn to communicate with each other without the need to impose traditional moral certitudes (the putative foundation for much character education) that we can be more open to genuine reconciliation amidst the differences (the ruptures) that currently separate individuals and groups in a troubled, contentious world.

I will propose that one way college and high school educators (and philosophers of education in particular) can model the democratic dispositions in their teaching is by encouraging a type of postmodern classroom discourse on a number of past and present educational "great books," placed in strategic opposition to each other. By way of creating an alternative moral-character pedagogy, I will present a "virtuous" way of analyzing and talking about these inspirational books, grounded in a type of democratic discourse—a "moral conversation"—that I have been employing in my own teaching for more than a quarter of a century. I have found this type of discourse to be an excellent in-class preparation for helping students to confront the discordant realities of a secular pluralist society like the United States.

Because William Kilpatrick (1992) and William Bennett (1993, 1995) currently occupy elite status among the ministers of morality, I will use their work, as well as some of the writings of their like-minded colleagues, as a kind of lodestar in the next chapter to guide my inquiries into virtue education. My main purpose will be to expose some deficiencies in their neo-classical thinking from my own reconstructed postmodern perspective, one that repudiates both moral nihilism/relativism *and* moral dogmatism/indoctrination of all stripes. I will also examine and critique other important work being done in the name of character education, including representative writings by communitarians and liberationists, each of whom has a particular bag of virtues to impart to America's schools and colleges.

It is important to note here that I do not intend to spend any time examining such moral-education initiatives as values clarification or Kohlberg's stages of moral development because I believe their impact on contemporary character education in the late 1990s has largely dissipated. Highly popular throughout the 1970s and 1980s, but in serious decline today, these "movements" represent a kind of anachronism to my current students, most of whom have never even heard of them. Moreover, a number of powerful criticisms of these movements have already been published, and I refer the reader to three of the better ones—Barry Chazan (1985), Betty A. Sichel (1988), and Christina Hoff Sommers (1984). In this current project, I prefer to concentrate my efforts exclusively on the *virtue* writers of the last two decades, the 1980s and 1990s: the neo-classical character educators and two of their more notable rivals, the communitarians and the liberationists.

My way of presenting each "intitiative" in Chapters 2–7 will be as follows: In Chapters 2, 4, and 6, I develop the *philosophical* and *historical* bases for each virtue "initiative" in a relatively straightforward way. Also in Chapters 2, 4, and 6, I describe the distinctive *educational* aspects of each initiative, emphasizing its general goals, the role of the school and college, the curriculum, and instructional methods (Gutek, 1988), in a relatively straightforward way. In Chapters 3, 5, and 7, I reflect on the strengths and weaknesses of each initiative from a more personal, postmodern perspective, and from my own vantage point as a moral educator. And I point out the special relevance of each initiative for forming a genuine "democratic character." Finally, Chapters 8 and 9 are considerably more speculative and prescriptive, as I attempt to delineate more fully the features of my own virtue initiative.

CONCLUSION

I intend for *Answering the "Virtuecrats"* to be more than merely a series of rancorous or detached scholarly reactions to those authors whose ideas may be fundamentally different from my own. Frequently, via what I hope is a judicious practice of personal narrative, I will share experiences in my own teaching whenever I think they might illuminate a particular philosophical or pedagogical point I wish to make. I will also express many self-doubts, because, even at its best, I am convinced that character education is an uncertain and humbling activity. The postmodernist asks (and I agree): Who, in an age of moral pluralism, indeterminacy, and incommensurability, knows for sure what is good or *a fortiori* how to make others good? And while it is true that I will be critical of certain points of view throughout the book, I will always be respectful of, indeed grateful for, these views and for the opportunity they present to engage in a lively conversation with thinkers whose ideas I take very seriously—some of which I actually admire. As someone who has been teaching courses in ethics, moral education, and philosophy of education for almost 30 years, I have learned a great deal from each of these thinkers.

On a related point: I have written elsewhere on the *applied ethical* implications of this project (R. J. Nash, 1996), and so I will have little to say about that topic here. In my previous book, I talked mainly about what I *do* as an applied ethics professor. Here, I develop what I *believe* as a moral educator.

For definitional purposes, I think of *moral character* as a designation that sums up the total of a person's *virtues*. Virtues include dispositions, behaviors, habits, likes, dislikes, capacities, traits, ideals, ideas, values, feelings, and intuitions (Angeles, 1992; R. J. Nash, 1996). *Moral character, therefore, is all about virtue, and character education has a great deal to do with the formation and practice of personal virtues and the avoidance of particular vices.* Most of the thinkers I will look at consider the role of formal schooling at all levels to be immense in effecting this formation and practice of virtue and avoidance of vice.

From a technical, *philosophical* perspective, I will be vitally interested in the *languages* of each of these virtue initiatives as they relate to matters of culture, social construction, hermeneutics, and narrative, and how these languages reach ultimate moral expression in the complex, multifaceted interaction of an individual's thoughts and actions, dispositions and desires, beliefs and behaviors. I make the assumption that the language of each of the virtue initiatives represents a fairly consistent belief and meaning system. Thus, in the final chapters, I will refer frequently to neo-classical language, communitarian language, liberationist language, and postmodern language as embodying/communicating well-defined worldviews that constitute distinct hermeneutical frameworks—particular philosophical vantage points from which to interpret educational realities.

I must emphasize that the "ministers" of each of these initiatives, with their own unique languages, do not differ that drastically from one another in the *specific virtues* they would advocate for schools and colleges. In fact, in many cases, their designated virtues are very similar, as we shall see in the pages ahead. I do contend, however, that because these "ministers" use very different, and often *very dogmatic,* virtue languages to preach their "gospels"—languages that represent clashing worldviews—they run the risk of intensifying, instead of diminishing, the moral confusion of the postmodern world. I believe this moral confusion, this postmodern politics, to be the inevitable consequence of what literary theorists and philosophers attribute to the presence of *alterity* (difference, otherness) in a secular pluralist society. On the one hand, I hold that alterity can be a virtue in an increasingly monochromatic mass culture, making life richer for us all. On the other hand, I know that when people celebrate a kind of radical alterity (e.g., a pluralism of "identity politics") for its own sake, as a viable alternative to democracy with its common public goods and moral consensuses, then separation, alienation, divisiveness, and, ultimately, psychological and physical violence can sometimes be the devastating results.

In my estimation, despite their several strengths, neo-classical, communitarian, and liberationist virtue languages are each, by themselves, inadequate for the task of preparing students to live with the uncertainties of an emerging, increasingly secular, and increasingly pluralist democracy. When each one is pushed on people as the ineluctable, final (moral and political) vocabulary, these languages can only end up harming us as we search for more effective ways to live together, in order to pursue our own projects individually and collectively without violence or interference. In a postmodern America, I will argue in the closing chapter, we are less in need of ministers and more in need of what Rorty (1979) calls conversationalists.

Furthermore, I am also highly sensitive to the several technical objections that philosophers have raised regarding the relevance of virtues in the late twentieth century (for example, see Jorge L. A. Garcia in Robert Audi [1995, pp. 841–842]). Among Garcia's concerns are that virtues are anachronistic, because they are dependent on an obsolete conception of human nature; reactionary, because they buttress the sociopolitical status quo; unintelligible, because definitions of virtues and right actions tend to be circular; irrelevant, even arbitrary, because there is today no universal moral standard to evaluate their worth; impractical, because too many virtues are in conflict with each other; egoistic, because they divert moral attention to the self rather than to others; and, ultimately, fatalistic and deterministic, because, as Aristotle believed, virtues are too closely linked to chance (*fortuna*, L.)—to wealth, family background, training, and intelligence. At times in the pages ahead, all of these more technical, philosophical issues will concern me as well, even though they may not be central to my particular educational purposes in the text.

Finally, a student once opined to me in class that moral character is "who we are in the dark." I suppose this was her way of saying that when all the artifice, intellectuality, and publicity are stripped away, moral character is really about who we are when nobody is around to look at us, or even to care. If she is right, I shudder at the enormity of the task we teachers have in trying to produce in people such a distinctive, impervious, and enduring moral core—one that survives even "in the dark" when nobody is there to observe it. If, indeed, it is true, as I think it is, that each of us has *three* moral characters—the one we exhibit, the one we actually possess, and the one we think we possess—then I believe it is essential that we take very seriously the authors whose works I examine in the coming chapters. It is my conviction that, despite many of my critical concerns, each writer has something extremely important to offer in helping us to locate and, when necessary, to refine the actual moral character we, and others, do *in fact* possess.

TECHNICAL COLLEGE OF THE LOWCOUNTRY
LEARNING RESOURCES CENTER
POST OFFICE BOX 1288
BEAUFORT, SOUTH CAROLINA 29901-1288

CHAPTER 2

The Character Education Initiative: The Neo-Classical Virtues

If we want our children to possess the traits of character we most admire, we need to teach them what those traits are. . . . So the question is: How does education form character?
— William J. Bennett, Our Children & Our Country, 1988

There are values all American citizens share. . . : honesty, fairness, self-discipline, fidelity to task, friends and family, personal responsibility, love of country, and belief in the principles of liberty, equality, and the freedom to practice one's faith. . . . How do we teach these values? . . . . It is by exposing children to good character and inviting its imitation.
— William J. Bennett, The De-Valuing of America: The Fight for
Our Culture and Our Children, 1992

Children need to learn what the virtues are. We can help them gain a grasp and appreciation of these traits by giving them material to read. . . . There are many wonderful stories of virtue and vice with which our children should be familiar.
— William J. Bennett, The Book of Virtues: A Treasury
of Great Moral Stories, 1993

Stories help to make sense of our lives. They also create a desire to be good. Plato, who thought long and hard about the subject of moral education, believed that children should be brought up in such a way that they would fall in love with virtue. And he thought that stories . . . were the key to sparking this desire.
— William Kilpatrick, Why Johnny Can't Tell Right from Wrong:
Moral Illiteracy and the Case for Character Education, 1992

I chose these stories [Aesop's Fables, Grimms' Fairy Tales, La Fontaine's Fables, *Leo Tolstoy's* Fables and Fairytales] *because they teach values and morals and lessons about life. Fairy tales and fables allow children to put things in perspective—greed, trouble, happiness, meanness, and joy. After reading these stories, [students] have something to think over and discuss.*
— Marva Collins, Marva Collins' Way, 1990

While the character-education project in teaching virtue in the schools and colleges is flourishing at this time, educators in the United States have actually had a 300-year tradition of instilling a particular kind of moral character, one typified by some of the same qualities mentioned in the excerpts that introduce this chapter. Character educators such as William Bennett, Allan Bloom, Marva Collins, William Honig, William Kilpatrick, Thomas Lickona, Edward Wynne, and Kevin Ryan, whose ideas I will emphasize in this chapter, are basically in concert with the founders of the common schools: If Americans are to be people of "good character and sound morality," then schools "must be charged with the mission of moral and civic training, training that finds its roots in a ground of shared values" (Bennett, 1988, p. 72). But, unlike the founders of the common schools—whose main purposes in advocating "character" education were based on an optimistic, political, and humanitarian agenda for extending a free, state-subsidized public education to everyone (admittedly, a liberationist critic, Michael Katz [1968], would disagree with this rosy story)—contemporary character educators are "declinists." They believe American culture, and education in particular, are in a period of grave, near-catastrophic moral decline and in desperate need of a massive virtue infusion to save them.

THE CULTURAL DECLINISTS

According to William J. Bennett (1992), former U.S. secretary of education, America has been tragically "devalued" and there is a "battle" raging "for our culture and our children" between the forces of good—those who hold traditional values and believe in the worth of the Western heritage—and the forces of evil—"entrenched bureaucracies, belligerent lobbies, a recalcitrant Congress, a hostile academy, and a skeptical press" (p. 11).

William Kilpatrick (1992) also speaks of "skirmishes" to be fought, and "cultural wars to be won" (p. 13). Like Bennett, he sees the "battle for the culture" as being fought over who is going to define what is permissible and impermissible in speech, conduct, politics, music, art, literature, television, and films. Among Kilpatrick's "enemies" are drug and sex educators in the public schools; such "modernist" philosophers as Jean Jacques Rousseau, Friedrich Nietzsche, and John Dewey, who, he believes, had nothing but "contempt" for traditional values; "cultural relativists"; left-wing university faculties in the humanities, education, and social sciences; and radical feminists.

And Edward A. Wynne and Kevin Ryan (1993) present much alarming trend data, represented in a series of graphs, that, since 1940, youth homicide, suicide, out-of-wedlock births, number of arrests, student drug and alcohol use, and in-school violence have risen precipitously, reaching epidemic proportions today. Although they acknowledge that the causes of youthful disorder are socially complex, Wynne and Ryan indict the following educational culprits: too many elective courses in the high schools and colleges, historical revisionism, moral relativism in literature and social studies, more "democratic" classrooms, lessening the importance of patriotism, and "deemphasizing the importance of character as a goal of education" (p. 17).

For the declinists, character education in the public schools is the only way to reverse the erosion of moral standards in America, because there are certain traits of character that all children need to know and, if children are to learn how to become virtuous human beings, only practice of these dispositions will make perfect. In answer to the question "How should the schools make a student virtuous?" the declinists answer as Aristotle (1976) did: "A man becomes kind by doing kind acts. He becomes brave by performing brave acts" (pp. 91–92).

The educational imperative in all the declinist writings is that teachers must stress "traditional moral values" if the schools are "to be put back on track." For most declinists, the traditional moral values are to be found mainly in stories, myths, poems, biographies, and drama (Kilpatrick, 1992), and declinist educators tend to highlight the motivations, aspirations, and moral conflicts of a variety of characters who appear in "inspiring" books of virtue. They believe it is mainly by reading these books that children can find the proper heroes to emulate in reclaiming, and learning, the traditional moral values. According to William Honig (1987), "Great literature can create that sense of empathy, of shared values, of belonging to a civilization with a common history and common concerns . . . it has the power to show us what moral and immoral characters look like" (pp. 65–66).

THE CLASSICAL WORLDVIEW AND THE ROLE OF VIRTUE

As upholders of "traditional moral values," the declinists are self-declared "neo-classicists" who extol the traditional virtues of Western civilization, especially those embodied in the cultural legacy of the ancient Greeks. Declinist writings abound in laudatory references to the educational ideals of Plato and Aristotle. For example, in Bennett's highly popular *The Book of Virtues* (1993), there are a dozen entries alone on the "moral stories" of Plato and Aristotle, more attention than is given to most other authors, including Shakespeare. Kilpatrick (1992) refers to Plato and Aristotle a whopping 22 times in a book devoted exclusively to an analysis of *contemporary* education. And Marva Collins (1990) speaks frequently of the ancient philosophers—particularly Plato and Aristotle—both in her more general analysis of the education of ghetto children and in the personal account of her actual, day-to-day teaching in a private, inner-city elementary school. She cites Plato and Aristotle, and a variety of other ancient authors as well, at least 50 times in a relatively short volume aimed at the general reader.

What exactly is this "classical perspective" that character educators share? Although he has a tendency to draw his contrasts too sharply, making Plato look like a metaphysical absolutist and Aristotle something of an early postmodernist, Richard Tarnas (1991) has insightfully pointed out that the classical worldview is actually an interplay of two "partly complementary and partly antithetical sets of principles" (p. 71). One set is grounded in a "metaphysical idealism" dramatically expressed in much of Plato's work, particularly in the *Republic.* The other set, typified by a "secular skepticism," finds expression in Aristotle's writings, especially in his *Ethics, Politics,* and *Metaphysics.* Most character educators tend to lean toward Plato's "metaphysical idealism" in their overall view of human nature and society and toward Aristotle's "experiential" approach in their understanding and teaching of virtue.

Thus, on the one hand, Plato, the poet, can believe in an "essential human nature" that all people possess which is virtually unmodifiable; a cosmic moral order that is static, immutable, and eternal; a realm of well-defined moral "truths" (essences) that are both abstract and universal and can only be deduced by worldly beings after extensive study of a reasoning process called the dialectic (Hare, 1982). And on the other hand, Aristotle, the physician and scientist, can reject a transcendent realm of ideas in favor of a this-worldly, empirical approach to truth. He can hold that nature is knowable to the human intellect and that its secrets can be readily grasped by human reason and scientific observation. There is little use for mythological or supernatural explanations of natural reality, given the scientific fact that the systematic study of particulars is able to yield all the knowledge that human beings need to understand the world. The search for truth must always be self-critical, relativistic, and revisable. And human beings become virtuous mainly by imitating adult moral exemplars in a life devoted to action (Barnes, 1982). Among today's neo-classical character educators, some are clearly Platonists (Bennett, 1988, 1992, 1993; A. Bloom, 1987; Collins, 1990; Honig, 1987), and some are Aristotelians (Kilpatrick, 1992; Wynne & Ryan, 1993). But what they all share, to some extent, is an attachment to the ancient worldview.

Despite their temperamental and philosophical differences, Aristotle and Plato are both products of the ancient world. Thus they are likely to agree, rather than disagree, on important moral fundamentals. Concerning the role of the dispositions in creating good and happy human beings, both would concur that virtues are necessary to live a harmonious moral life; that human beings are always moving to achieve a specific *telos* (end or purpose), and virtues enable them to realize that end. Virtues that frequently appear in the classical literature are fortitude, temperance, justice, *sophia* (theoretical reason), and *phronesis* (practical wisdom). Whether Platonists or Aristotelians, contemporary character educators are in essential agreement with these classical virtue fundamentals, although they frequently give them a modern twist, as we will see in the educational sections below.

NEO-CLASSICAL CHARACTER EDUCATION

Neo-Classical Educational Goals

Perhaps Allan Bloom, at the university level, best captures the spirit of neo-classical educational goals. In his surprise best-seller of 1987, *The Closing of the American Mind*—a book that is still selling briskly more than a decade later—Bloom ruefully asserts that relativism is the philosophy of choice for young people today and that its primary moral virtue is "openness." This ubiquitous disposition toward openness has caused youth to reject all moral absolutes save one—individual freedom. Thus they consider the only "moral" villain today to be the person who refuses to be "nonjudgmentally" open to all kinds of people, lifestyles, and ideologies. Bloom mourns the modern loss of faith in "natural rights," "essential being," and "religion," whereby people once found a "fundamental basis of unity and sameness" (p. 27). The tragic consequence of the dissolution of this "basis of unity," for Bloom, is that with all the progressive and forward-looking "openness" and "respect for diversity" prevalent in the American university today, shared goals and a vision of the public good have virtually disappeared. The Enlightenment idea of the social contract is no longer possible or even desirable, and, sadly, when people do come together today, they can agree on only one thing—to disagree.

   In 380 pages of highly technical philosophical and political analysis, Bloom goes on to show how a classical sense of virtue has little or no meaning for most of today's college and high school students. Sadly, according to Bloom, a belief in relativism—young people's all-pervasive perspective on the world—has "extinguished the real motive[s] of education" (p. 34): the search for truth in life and how to live a morally decent existence. Morality has become synonymous with mere lifestyle. And values have become personal preferences, beyond the reach of any kind of "objective" moral assessment. No longer do the young believe that wise people in other places and times have anything to teach them about life's truths, because there are no truths, certainly none that are absolutely binding. At best, truths are relative to the particular cultures that spawn them, so why should youth bother to seek a universal wisdom where there is only the stark reality of "historicism" ("the view that all thought is essentially related to and cannot transcend its own time" [p. 40]) and "interpretation"?

In his less somber moments, Bloom looks to a classical formulation of the liberal arts in order to recapture the fundamental moral purpose of the contemporary American university: to help students determine what kind of life is worth living and what manner of human beings they should become. For Bloom, it is mainly through the study of such authors as Plato, Aristotle, and Shakespeare that students can participate "in essential being and [forget] their accidental lives" (p. 380). Bloom is unabashedly candid in his love of Plato's *Republic,* which for him is *"the"* book on education and virtue. The *Republic* brooks no compromise regarding what should be the essential purpose of education at all levels— the establishment of a community of virtuous "friends" who are dedicated foremost to the search for truth, to discovering their rightful place in the social order, and to the pursuit of a moral life.

In the public schools, the neo-classical character educators echo Bloom's goals for education. Generally, they believe in an essential human nature that conduces all children everywhere, regardless of class, ethnic, racial, and gender difference, to want to know the truth and to lead the morally good life. They stress the importance of the Western cultural heritage in embodying this universal truth and the responsibility of the schools to transmit this truth to all children. For the character educators, the generic goal of a neo-classical education must be to stem the moral erosion in the culture by fostering the virtues of wholeness, excellence, and integrity wherever schooling occurs in this country. Like Socrates and Plato—who battled the nihilism of the original relativists, the Sophists— the character educators attempt to discover and transmit a moral core that is universal and unchanging. And like Aristotle, they strive to find the most effective ways to inculcate the virtues.

In a phrase, character educators believe that the major purpose of education is to transmit "character, academics, and discipline"—the educational triad that incorporates the "traditional moral values" (Wynne & Ryan, 1993). Like Aristotle, character educators advocate the importance of exemplification, imitation, and habituation in the formation of moral character. Thus, for them, the transmission of character, academics, and discipline is most likely to occur when the schools stress intellectual rigor and academic achievement, insist on stringent codes of personal moral conduct, and provide heroic role models and committed classroom teachers and educational leaders; and when teachers use their subject matter to impart the information, values, and skills necessary for forming good character. These educational themes predominate throughout the writings of today's character educators, and nobody summarizes these ideals as passionately as William Honig, past superintendent of public instruction in California. His *Last Chance for Our Children* (1987) was a best-seller in both its hardcover and paperback editions.

Honig (1987) believes that the "schools must uphold, even celebrate, the ideal of the virtuous life—because ethical behavior is learned" (p. 39). For Honig, the central purpose of schooling is to encourage the full moral flowering of each child's "humanity." In order to do this, Honig maintains that the schools must strive to help students balance the "core" individualist virtues of liberty, individuality, personal initiative, and self-reliance with the "core" cooperative ideals of justice, tolerance, honesty, magnanimity, compassion, and the willingness to sacrifice for the common good. Traditional values are actually "civil values," according to Honig, and when students can show respect, consideration, friendship, and mercy toward each other, then society itself becomes a better place for all. Educators are most likely to transmit these traditional values when education is "traditional," when classrooms are orderly and purposeful, when mutual respect is the norm, when teachers are clearly authority figures, and when high moral and academic expectations are the ideals held up for all to achieve.

The Neo-Classical School/College

Character educators conceive of the school as a place to preserve and transmit the cultural heritage in such a way as to foster the virtues. The school's central task should be both intellectual *and* moral rather than social or psychological, and competent teachers ought to provide the systematic intellectual and moral experience, training, and practice that students need to become good human beings. For Allan Bloom (1987), the university ought to be a place where "permanent dialogue" occurs among people who come together in community to read, and to discuss, "wonderful stories" about the "nature of the good," in order to become good human beings. For neo-classical public school educators, the school should mainly be a place where people interact with each other around academics in order to become better-informed citizens, more virtuous human beings, and "happier" individuals.

It is important to note that, in theory, character educators think of "happiness" in Aristotelian, not psychological, terms. For Aristotle (1976), *eudaimonia* (happiness) is "an activity of the soul in accordance with excellence" (p. 87). Happiness is an "activity," and human beings "flourish" when they *do* things in contrast to being in a particular state of mind. Happiness, therefore, is never to be construed as a state of bliss. Neither is it simply the achievement of a therapeutically induced self-esteem. To flourish, according to Aristotle, requires strenuous, disciplined engagement throughout the course of a person's life in intellectual, moral, and practical pursuits. Character educators stress both intellectual and moral excellence, as does Aristotle, as the only route to happiness, and all of them are likely to identify his virtues as highly worthy of cultivation in the late twentieth century: knowledge, good judgment, and practical wisdom, along with courage, generosity, and fair-mindedness. *Eudaimonia*, therefore, is the goal of all human beings, their natural end or purpose in life, and the schools' primary goal is to promote "happiness" in this Aristotelian sense.

Thus, for Wynne and Ryan (1993), schools must be places whose foremost duty is to teach "character," rather than a "dead-end" self-esteem (which they regard as "selfishness") or "happiness" in the modern sense of "feeling good about oneself." Self-esteem is something to be earned, not given, and, according to the authors, the teaching of "diligence" is the only alternative to a "corrosive form of pupil narcissism" (p. 105). Diligence is the cardinal virtue. Schools, therefore, should articulate clear and specific instructional goals, be tuned into pupils' "developmental limitations," establish strong learning incentives, encourage hard work, assess measurable learnings, and publicly reward success while "rebuking" failure. The authors advocate "prosocial conduct"—community service, teamwork in competitive sports, membership in performing groups, fund-raising, and miscellaneous extracurricular activities. These activities teach students how to live together in a spirit of mutual assistance, how to compromise, exhibit initiative, act courageously by accepting difficult responsibilities, and defer to adult authority.

For Thomas Lickona (1991), the school should be a place where students can learn how to be both "smart *and* good" (p. 6). Lickona maintains that "wise societies since the time of Plato have made moral education a deliberate aim of schooling" (p. 6). Lickona believes that because children live in a democracy, they must understand and be committed to the moral ideals of democracy: respect for individual and group rights, regard for law, a willingness to participate in public life, a passion for justice and equality, and a dedication to furthering the public good. Lickona is deeply troubled by what he sees as a "moral decline" among youth, characterized by increasing incidents of violence and vandalism, stealing, cheating, disrespect for authority, peer cruelty, bigotry, bad language, sexual precocity and abuse, declining civic responsibility, and drug abuse. The school's role, along with the home and the church, in reversing this "moral decline," according to the author, is to provide a moral education that answers two questions: "How can we live with each other?" and "How can we live with nature?" (p. 21). In answer to the first question, Lickona looks to the school to foster such civic virtues as honesty, civility, responsibility, and loyalty.

The Neo-Classical Curriculum

Character educators conceive of the curriculum as a body of disciplines and activities that are basically intellectual and moral in nature (Gutek, 1988). In the public schools, the character-education curriculum is a kind of hierarchy, with history and literature ranked the highest—because students can most successfully mine these disciplines for the moral values and exemplars conspicuously missing in the modern world. In the university, the disciplines of philosophy, theology, history, literature, and art potentially provide students with the richest sources for Western culture's highest moral ideals, although character educators deeply regret the turn toward a "nihilistic" postmodernism in these disciplines during the last decade (Bennett, 1992; A. Bloom, 1987; Kilpatrick, 1992). In the past, a university curriculum in the humanities, arts, and sciences was a rich repository of the funded wisdom of the Western heritage, and, consequently, it served as a source of well-defined intellectual inspiration and character emulation for youth of college age (Bennett, 1988; Pelikan, 1992). Now, according to Allan Bloom (1987), the college curriculum is really "an anarchy . . . there is no vision . . . of what an educated human being is. . . . The student gets no intimation that great mysteries might be revealed to him, that new and higher motives of action might be discovered within him" (p. 337). Bloom yearns for the retrieval of a "great-books" curriculum "in which a liberal education means reading . . . classic texts, just reading them, letting them dictate what the questions are and the method of approaching them . . . trying to read them as their authors wished them to be read" (p. 344).

Marva Collins (1990), a self-professed Platonist who believes in a world of timeless truths and an invariant moral order, is harshly critical of "curriculum experts" who are obsessed with "relevance." As both a founder and principal of a Chicago private school, Westside Preparatory, and as someone who has taught there for more than 20 years, Collins, an African American, believes that a "relevant" curriculum serves only to undermine the fundamental purpose of education: to "expand children's horizons."

> Children do not need to read stories that teach "street smarts." They learn enough on their own. What they need are character-building stories. They need to read for values, morality, and universal truths. That is my reason for teaching classical literature. (p. 156)

Collins's well-publicized success at Westside Preparatory School, with its 250 inner-city children, begins with her beliefs that teachers must always set the highest intellectual standards for every single child and that they must see themselves foremost as character educators. Collins has children in her classes as young as 3 and 4 years old reading classical Greek myths, memorizing edifying proverbs from the Bible, and quoting from Plato, Shakespeare, and Tolstoy, so that they might learn core "values and morals and lessons about life" (p. 52).

Wynne and Ryan (1993) contend that every curriculum is actually a "moral educator." For them, a curriculum "includes all of the events and activities experienced by the students during their school years" (p. 135). Thus they are more interested in what they call the "hidden curriculum" (incidental, covert content) and the "null curriculum" (what is left out of the formal curriculum) of the school than they are in the formal academic curriculum. About the latter, they actually have little to say, except when they recommend particular narratives in history and literature as a way for students to learn about "heroes and villains." Instead, they direct their attention to the school's general "ethos" ("the shared attitudes, beliefs, and values of a community" [p. 99]; the overarching spirit of the community) as the most powerful "curriculum" of all and the one most in need of transformation.

Every school "curriculum," according to the authors, should reflect the universal "moral facts of life," those transcendent precepts crucial for people to live in harmony and peace with others. Some of these "moral facts" include an emphasis on kindness, love, and loyalty to parents, friends, and families; a sense of honesty and responsibility in social relationships; an obligation to help others and to respect property rights; and an awareness that some actions are always immoral (e.g., treachery, betrayal, and physical violence toward innocent people). Moreover, the authors urge teachers and administrators to create a school ethos characterized by eight "ethical ideals" that "seem to reside in the human condition and are universal" and are embedded in the "Judeo-Christian heritage" (pp. 140–141): prudence, justice, temperance, fortitude, faith, hope, charity, and duty. Throughout the closing chapters of their "handbook,"

Wynne and Ryan recommend a number of concrete "symbols, rites, and ceremonies" that they believe can foster a sense of community and collegiality in schools everywhere.

Bennett (1988) and Honig (1987) are two character educators who believe that "citizenship" virtues must be fundamental to curricula in both the elementary and secondary schools. Honig aptly quotes Thomas Jefferson on the subject of a virtuous citizenry: "If there is not virtue among us, if there be not good, then there is no form of government that can render us secure" (p. 38). Bennett (1988) speaks often of the need for American children to understand the nature of "freedom," "fairness," "enterprise," "equality," "our common culture," the writings of the "founding fathers," American history, the American Constitution, the need for a "common language," and the glories of "Western Civilization." And Honig (1987) makes the cultivation of citizenship one of the central purposes of the curriculum. He, too, talks of the necessity for all students to speak English, know the history and nature of democracy, understand the civic responsibilities of an active citizenry, and recognize the centrality of free, rational inquiry in a democracy.

For Bennett and Honig, school curricula at all levels must foster an understanding and love of individual freedom, along with the realization that the only political system capable of securing that liberty for everyone is a democracy. As neo-classical character educators, Bennett and Honig recognize that there is a troubling paradox at the center of democracy: On the one hand, Americans have always revered the virtues of personal liberty, individuality, initiative, and self-reliance. Historically, the schools have emphasized these dispositions throughout the seventeenth to early twentieth centuries, and both authors believe they must, of course, continue to transmit these qualities even today. Nevertheless, both are aware, as were Plato and Aristotle (two radical skeptics on the subject of democracy), that self-interest alone can never be the motive force for binding a society together. A set of cooperative dispositions—fairness, tolerance, civility, compassion, a willingess to make sacrifices, liberality, a commitment to the common good—are also pivotal in creating and sustaining a democratic way of life. Even though striking a balance between the individualistic and communitarian virtues is both difficult and tenuous, Bennett and Honig know that students need to find that middle ground if they are ever to become functional, democratic citizens, as concerned with the welfare of others as with their own.

Neo-Classical Instructional Methods

For all of the above writers, the ideal character educator is one who strives to be at the center of the student's learning—a virtuoso blend of moral exemplar, "great-books" enthusiast, firm but gentle disciplinarian, inspiring homilist, and living, enthusiastic embodiment of the wisdom contained in the Western cultural heritage. Although some will employ the Socratic method of questioning to help students discover the perennial truths and morals in a great work of literature, all will attempt to be mimetic in their pedagogy, attempting mainly to model or exemplify the highest virtues of the culture and inviting students to imitate them (Gutek, 1988). These teachers will encourage students to read the "great books," either alone or in the company of others, and then make it a point to get out of the way in order to let the books work their mysterious moral magic on their own. A character educator like Lickona (1991), however, takes a somewhat more active, psychological/sociological approach, conceiving of the teacher's role as "caregiver," as a kind of instructional strategist whose main purpose is to create "democratic communities" in the classroom.

The major role of character educators is to help students discover the "moral core" that transcends particular times and places and promises to restore a sense of moral direction to a "rudderless," out-of-control, secular world. This "moral core"—a "traditional" set of principles and virtues that help human beings achieve wholeness and excellence—can be found in such disciplines as history, literature, religion, and philosophy (Gutek, 1988), in the timeless religious teachings of churches and synagogues, in such political documents as those framed by America's Founding Fathers, and in the traditions handed down through generations of families. Instructionally, the character educator attempts to adopt teaching methods that, at once, impart, transmit, and "indoctrinate" these permanent truths, while striving always to be an archetype of those special virtues that represent the most noble dispositions of human beings everywhere, regardless of time or place.

Once again, Allan Bloom (1987) effectively captures the neo-classical spirit in his sentiments regarding college teaching. For him, it is only when professors insist that students study the "classical texts," in a way that encourages genuine dialogue among discerning "friends," that the university will be able to rise above what is merely trendy and popular in the disciplines today—for example, deconstructionism ("the denial of the possibility of truth" [p. 379]). When presented well, the study of Aristotle or Kant or Shakespeare, for example, can lead a student to ask the "permanent questions" and, in some instances, even find how to go about answering them. "Programs based upon judicious use of great texts provide the royal road to students' hearts" (p. 344).

For Bloom, professors of humanities must go back to their original task: "interpreting and transmitting old books, preserving what we call tradition, in a democratic order where tradition is not privileged" (p. 353).

Time and again, Bloom suggests that the best instruction for the development of moral character at the college level happens when knowledgeable, "friendly," "lively" professors gather to tell "wonderful stories" about the meaning of their lives. They do this through a Socratic approach to the "great books," and, when successful in their mutual questioning, professors and their students create something far more enduring than the political simulacra of community so fashionable on campuses today in the name of "diversity" and "multiculturalism." They create a "true community of knowers" where a commitment to truth and goodness, instead of to a narrow careerism or to a bogus form of egalitarianism, is what links a few special people together in their pursuit of the virtuous life. It is only in this kind of community, according to Bloom, "that the contact people so desperately seek is to be found" (p. 381).

The belief that exposure to good books alone can sometimes be the best instructional methodology for teachers reverberates throughout Bennett's and Kilpatrick's writings. For Bennett (1993), books "speak" about virtues and how important it is for young people to "live" them. Simply "reading [a] book with or to children can deepen . . . a [child's] understanding of life and morality" (p. 14). Bennett's enormous best-seller, *The Book of Virtues* (1993), is intended to help parents and teachers primarily to "train the heart and mind" of the young "toward the good" (p. 11). And, to this end, he provides a huge compendium of stories, poems, and essays from history and literature to illustrate the virtues in action. The book is organized around 10 cardinal virtues—self-discipline, compassion, responsibility, friendship, work, courage, perseverance, honesty, loyalty, and faith—and Bennett asks that parents and teachers read the stories aloud whenever children "need reminding of some virtues more than others" (p. 15).

Kilpatrick (1992) agrees with Bennett that "good books do their own work in their own way" (p. 268). Thus "it is not necessary or wise for adults to explain the 'moral' in each story" (p. 268). Kilpatrick, too, encourages parents and teachers to read the stories aloud, but not in a manner that "treat[s] books like doses of moral medicine" (p. 268). In his last chapter, Kilpatrick spends almost 50 pages in compiling a list of "great books for children and teens," and throughout the main body of his book, he also includes a number of inspirational films for youth to view.

In his chapter entitled "What Schools Can Do" (pp. 225–244), Kilpatrick mentions a number of programs around the country that teach character in ways he enthusiastically approves. Although he never explicitly describes them anywhere in his book, Kilpatrick especially likes "direct methods of teaching character" (p. 238) whereby teachers actively define the virtues in classrooms, stimulate discussions about the virtues, study people past and present who have demonstrated a desired virtue, and suggest concrete ways of putting a virtue into practice. At one point, he supports a program in which 35 faculty attended a three-week institute to study Plato's *Republic* and Aristotle's *Nicomachean Ethics,* as well as selections from the Bible, in order to have a "classical" foundation for their work with students.

He also spends the better part of the same chapter reiterating Wynne and Ryan's (1993) strategies for bringing "virtue and character" back into the schools. He, too, speaks of "ethos," and many of his specific recommendations are provocative: He calls for an ethos of "pride, loyalty, and discipline," based on a military esprit de corps. At one point, he even advocates all-male schools, because boys are more "aggressive" than girls, and thus they need stricter discipline. He advocates a return to frequent assemblies, dress codes, behavior codes, and high academic standards. He urges educators to be "unapologetically authoritarian," making rules and enforcing them, "policing bathrooms, playgrounds, corridors, and lunchrooms," and demanding respect at all times from students (p. 229).

Finally, Collins (1990) is considerably more detailed than most character educators in explicating her classroom teaching methods for imparting the virtues at Westside Prep. Throughout *Marva Collins' Way,* she gives innumerable concrete examples of how she inculcates virtues in her classroom. She is a peripatetic dynamo, in the tradition of Socrates, in the way she relates to children, continually asking questions that lead her pupils to the answers she seeks; pacing up and down each aisle, complimenting as well as touching, chiding, goading, and challenging each student. She is the master of the appropriate proverb, the key aphorism, the fable that will teach the important moral lesson at just the right time. She is as likely to quote from Plutarch as from Aesop, from Homer's *Odyssey* as from *Charlie and the Chocolate Factory.* Everything Collins does in the classroom is calculated to teach her poor, inner-city children the virtues of "self-reliance and self-respect . . . to teach them the importance of learning, of developing skills, of doing for themselves" (p. 54). Her overarching mission is to "develop a child's character, to help build a positive self-image" (p. 58).

CONCLUSION

In the next chapter, I depart from the descriptive format of the above in order to look more critically at what I have been calling the "character-education initiative" in imparting the "neo-classical" virtues. I make the argument that, while the neo-classical approach to character education has much to commend it, its weaknesses are, nevertheless, considerable. Certainly, as the above authors have shown, habit, training, and modeling are important educational elements in any school program that intends to impart the virtues. And they are also right, I believe, to challenge the domination of self-esteem, values clarification, and cognitive-developmental approaches to moral education in schools and colleges. But, for the most part, I believe that character educators go too far in separating moral reasoning from moral conduct. The result is to foster an ethos of compliance in the schools wherein indoctrination and rote learning replace critical reflection and autonomous decision making. In the end, I submit, the loser is democracy, because, if Socrates is correct—that only the *examined* life is worth living—how much more true is the axiom that the only democracy worth having is the one that invites its citizens to be autonomous, informed, articulate critics.

CHAPTER 3

Imparting the Neo-Classical Virtues: A Morality of Compliance

Teaching students how to defend democracy and to reason about our political disagreements is no less essential to developing moral character than instilling the less intellectual virtues of fidelity, kindness, honesty, respect for law, diligence, and self-discipline.

—Amy Gutmann, Democratic Education, *1987*

Within this [neo-classical] educational philosophy, relations of power are implicated in the distribution and legitimation of particular forms of knowledge . . . [this philosophy] accepts the virtues of passivity, obedience, and punctuality as normal and desirable. Subjection to a particular type of authority and rule become normalized, so to speak, through the daily routines of school organization and classroom learning.

—Henry A. Giroux, Schooling and the Struggle for Public Life: Critical Pedagogy in the Modern Age, *1988*

As the authors of the above excerpts charge, neo-classical educators foster a morality of compliance in schools and colleges. For the neo-classicals, character education is mainly about complying with various kinds of authority, with looking to a canonical *telos,* a text, an individual, a rule, or a principle for ultimate moral guidance and validation. At its best, a morality of compliance supports such dispositions as respect (especially for tradition) and responsibility, self-discipline, a capacity for hard work, and a concern for excellence. At its worst, a morality of compliance encourages submission, conformity, and docility. Madelyn A. Nash (1996), a public school educator and counselor, aptly describes a morality of compliance with reference to Thomas Lickona (1991), a character educator I talk about in the previous chapter:

> [Lickona] does not seem to help the teacher go beyond interpersonal dilemmas to those that affect the community or our country. His morality is one of compliance. . . . He wants to address the moral decline in America by making people aware of the ways in which our culture perpetuates this decline. What he does not seem to question is whether and in what ways de-

mocracy or capitalism contribute to the problem. He also does not question the traditional format of most schools with the teacher as the ultimate authority. [This is] antithetical to giving students experience in democracy. (p. 3)

At one point or another, I have used all of the books I discuss in the previous chapter in my moral-education course. The one text that students continually find helpful and inspiring is in some ways the most unyieldingly rigid (and morally compliant) in its philosophical and instructional approach to character education, *Marva Collins' Way* (1990). In contrast, regardless of their particular views on the benefits of character education, many of my students find the works of Bennett, Bloom, Kilpatrick, and Wynne and Ryan to be somewhat less useful and uplifting. In fact, these latter authors occasionally stir up such angry resistance among students, even among those who are the "true believers" in character education, that their constructive messages tend to get obliterated. I vividly remember one student, a sex educator, getting so furious at Kilpatrick's (1992) *Why Johnny Can't Tell Right from Wrong* that she burst out in class with something like the following:

> Even though Kilpatrick has almost convinced me that what I do as a sex educator is counterproductive in many ways, I'd never admit it to him, nor would I ever change anything I do. He's far too self-righteous and closed-minded for me to take seriously what he says. I think he's got a religious agenda he's pushing, but he won't come right out and admit it. He's probably right about kids' getting messed up if they have sex before marriage, but he's also wrong. He might know in principle what's best for kids, but he doesn't really know kids. And he certainly doesn't know me, and what I have to face every single day in the classroom.

I suspect most students respond favorably to Collins as a character educator in part because she is a self-made, African American woman who is struggling in her own way to put her ideals into practice in an inner-city school and because she always seems to have the best interests of her children at heart. She appears to my students to be a doer, not some "Platonic theorist" who views the "real" world from the safe distance of the academy, and they are willing to forgive her somewhat imperious attitude that she alone has the answers her students need to be successful in a white world (e.g., the "phonics method" as the *only* way to teach reading). Even though she is not as intellectually polished as most of the writers we read, Collins tends to come across as the most genuine, the most concrete, and the most trustworthy of the group.

Does this suggest, then, that effective character education has more to do with personal style than with moral substance, more to do with the day-to-day battle to implement one's ideals in the actual classroom against all odds than with the mere philosophical elucidation of these principles? I believe the partial, most obvious answer to this question is "yes." But the full truth is far more complex and elusive than that. My students are actually of many minds regarding neo-classical approaches to character education, and this dichotomy finds expression in which authors they embrace, and which they reject, and why. What I will present in the following paragraphs are some of the underlying reasons I believe character education elicits such mixed reactions as the above. I will highlight several interrelated themes that often show up in the writings of character educators: cultural decline; classical worldview, democracy, and the virtues; books of virtue, pedagogy, and postmodernism.

CULTURAL DECLINE

Much of what the character educators say assumes a precipitous moral decline in the culture. In truth, cultural decay (what some televangelists call "moral rot") in the United States does seem self-evident, and this element of the character-education agenda usually elicits strong initial assent in my classroom. For my students, the entertainment industry has become nothing more than a purveyor of sexual exploitation and gratuitous violence. Professional and amateur sports figures (quadrennial Olympics excitement notwithstanding) in this country have grown increasingly self-aggrandizing, strung out on drugs, alienating, and rude. Politicians get caught in one compromising situation after another, leaving the impression that corruption and scandal are ubiquitous and inevitable. Organized religion in America is fractured from within, as contesting intradenominational factions wage bitter war over doctrinal and lifestyle differences that threaten to tear apart the fabric of any semblance of denominational unity. Moreover, if media coverage is accurate, clerical misbehavior and hypocrisy in some of these churches have become almost epidemic. And all the human service professions, including business, health care, and education, have experienced a serious loss of public credibility in the wake of rising costs, managed care, corporate downsizing, and a spate of highly publicized incidents involving individual incompetence, greed, and malpractice. The sad truth is that professionals are no longer considered society's "trustworthy trustees." Certainly, whenever we take a media-generated look at society, students tend to agree with the character-education hypothesis that American culture is in perilous moral decline.

Moreover, at least on the surface, the declinists seem especially convincing in their diagnosis of disturbing youth trends, especially in the areas of violence, vandalism, self-destructive sex and drug use, and diminishing civic responsibility. Also, it is difficult for anyone in America today to ignore teenagers' growing insolence toward authority figures both in schools and in a variety of other institutions throughout the country. At first glance, it does appear that America is a crumbling moral edifice and that young people seem to be both the source and reflection of so much that ails this country today. At the outset, the declinists seem to be on to something, and they effectively capture my students' attention with their convincing cries of moral alarm, especially where gang violence, teenage pregnancy, and drug abuse are concerned.

On closer reflection, however, after we have done some initial reading and discussing, students start to raise a number of skeptical questions: Is the character-education assessment of the moral erosion in contemporary America an accurate one, or is it merely self-serving? Are *all* institutions and professions in this country really in such calamitous moral decline? Are no other interpretations possible for what troubles America? For example, the liberationists I examine in Chapter 6 claim that capitalism, and the inequality and oppression the free-market system seems to spawn, is the primary culprit in the "decline" of American democracy. And yet not one neo-classical thinker even mentions, let alone indicts, the huge concentration of wealth and power in the multinational corporations and the frenzied pursuit of influence, profit, and perquisites that accompany the monopoly of capital. This type of "decline," according to the liberationists, affects the quality of moral life of *all* Americans, including the devolving middle class. Finally, a few of my students always ask this type of question: Are things really so unprecedentedly bad in this country, or is this generation of moral catastrophists simply the latest in a long line of Jeremiahs who lament the evils of their age as being unparalleled in the history of civilization?

At times, the declinists remind us of Patrick Devlin (in Hart, 1983), a British jurist, who propounded what has come to be known as the "social disintegration thesis"—the belief that social institutions have both a right and a duty to enforce "traditional morality" for the sake of "social cohesion," even if the toleration of such acts as "homosexual sodomy," abortion, and divorce are the law of the land. For Devlin, moral decline signals the "beginning of the end" of a society, and only a return to "traditional values" can save a culture. H. L. A. Hart (1983) criticized the "social cohesion" thesis on the grounds that it tends to reduce the cause of a society's integration to one element—its dominant morality. Also, it assumes that the dominant morality alone is capable of maintaining order—an empirical thesis that, for Hart, history is simply unable to vindicate. Hart argued that societies are complex entities, and their *moral* component, though unarguably significant, is hardly the sine qua non for maintaining order or measuring overall societal well-being. Other social institutions, such as the media, recreation, law, politics, education, families, religion, government, and economics, for example, are also necessary for sustaining order and for assessing the degree to which a society is flourishing or declining.

Moreover, I suspect that character educators might be one of the main groups whom one contemporary cultural analyst has in mind when he charges that youth have become the "scapegoat generation" in America's "war against adolescence." Mike A. Males (1996) notes that trend data and cultural-indicator studies of the Bennett and Wynne/Ryan ilk are, at best, ambiguous and, at worst, extraordinarily misleading. On the subject of adolescent misbehavior, for example, Males challenges some of the statistical findings of the declinists, concluding that in many areas—illegitimacy, delinquency, alcohol abuse, stealing, and vandalism—the trend line has barely changed in decades. Furthermore, the cultural-indicator studies fail to tell *who* among America's youth is guilty of "delinquent" behavior, nor do they tell how such "disorderly youth" are different from youth in previous decades. According to Males, the allegation that America is in the midst of a dramatic "character decline" needs more substantial documentation than the usual cultural survey data that the media circulate from time to time. The point of Males's critique is that adults in this country need to face squarely their own moral deficiencies, as well as their own role in contributing to cultural decline, instead of scapegoating adolescents.

On a related note, I believe that if these same researchers were ever to emphasize *positive* cultural indicators, the reverse of cultural decline might prove to be true: They could conceivably postulate that America is in the midst of a "character *incline*," given the rise of volunteerism and community service among youth (Barber, 1992; Coles, 1993); the number of young people going on to college in order to improve themselves and develop a "philosophy of life"; the increasing number of youth interested in entering the "helping professions," where sufficient financial remuneration is not always guaranteed; the trend toward monogamous, long-term, mutually respectful relationships among some young people; the choice by a growing coterie of youth to abstain from alcohol and drugs; and the increasing turn toward spirituality, environmentalism, and peace studies (Roof, 1993). (Many of these trends are reported in "Attitudes and Characteristics of Freshmen" [1995].)

What I think the character educators tend to ignore (or obscure) is the striking reality that only a tiny percentage of adolescents actually exhibit "delinquent" behavior, while the vast majority of young people are busy with the perennial tasks of growing up, having fun, forming relationships, getting an education, working, making do with diminishing resources, and coping with life's vagaries, all while trying to retain some modicum of personal dignity in their everyday lives. The widely heralded nihilism of "Generation X" (Sacks, 1996) is largely a media-generated myth, once Americans get beyond the sensationalized headlines and into everyday reality where most youth tend to live. Character educators resolutely refuse to consider the possibility that, in truth, *few* young people today might need the schools to teach them right from wrong or to mold their moral characters. It could be that, in general, as many communitarians (even those who are themselves declinists of sorts) might argue, families, neighborhoods, churches, synagogues, and even some peer groups are still doing quite well in this respect. In fact, the likelihood that these institutions are still morally functional is good to excellent, all the conventional nay-saying "wisdom" of the neo-classicals and expedient politicians notwithstanding.

But even if the declinists are entirely accurate in their cultural analysis, they still have not satisfactorily answered the tantalizing question that both Plato and Aristotle asked about character formation: "Who can tell whether virtue is acquired by teaching or practice, or if by neither teaching nor practice, does it come by nature or by some other way?" It is precisely this question that continues to haunt most of my students today, even though many are at least subliminally convinced of the need for some kind of "countercultural" moral instruction, however mild, in the schools and colleges. They wonder if educational institutions are truly the best places for cultivating good character—those moral dispositions and ethical standards that make up the inner nature of a person. "Who, after all, is able to transform the 'inner nature' of a person?" they ask.

In response to the last question, many character educators appear well-meaning but simple-minded, even a bit naive, to my students. Someone like Kilpatrick (1992), for example, evinces a moral hubris that many students find arrogant and insulting. It is one thing, they believe, for educators to discuss ethical issues with students, either incidentally or systematically, and then to explore with them some ways that people who hold different points of view might adjudicate conflicts and reach agreements in a civil, reasonable manner. But whenever educators like Kilpatrick urge the schools to move into the character-building vacuum created by what they see as "morally deficient" or "neglectful" families and churches, and by a culture falling headlong into what they perceive to be moral decline, then they begin to sound both presumptuous and patronizing to students, even though their culture critiques might be accurate.

As if to confirm Allan Bloom's (1987) charge that they are obdurate relativists, many students tend to reject outright the analysis of any "experts" who come across as sounding arrogant and absolutistic in their moral judgments. But even though some of their reactions are barely concealed *ad hominem* arguments, I believe students still raise compelling questions: Exactly why, and in what ways, are these educational critics more qualified to shape character than families and churches? How many character educators would admit to needing the kind of character education *for their own children* that they enjoin the schools to impart? What special training and personal character development will these educators need, and who will decide? How exactly will the schools and colleges identify and recruit "moral mentors" to teach the young (Damon, 1988)? Do we run the risk of establishing a moral-character elite whereby only a privileged group possesses virtue and is alone qualified to foster it? Or is everyone a character educator regardless of personal or professional inclination or training?

Furthermore, from the perspective of someone who has taught teachers for 30 years, I have found few educators who have had academic preparation in communications theory and technique, moral psychology and philosophy, epistemology, literature, applied ethics, sociobiology and evolutionary psychology, family dynamics, religious studies, or history—disciplines, I contend, that must ground any kind of effective virtue training in the schools. Shaping character in both the formal and informal curriculum is a complex and demanding intellectual undertaking, requiring a lifetime of moral study that is broadly and profoundly interdisciplinary. Modeling character is even more challenging, I believe, calling for genuine "moral mentors" who first and foremost ought to exemplify in every action what they attempt to explicate (Damon, 1988). If educators are to teach peace, they must themselves be peacemakers. If they are to teach children the virtues of respect and caring, they must first be respectful caregivers. If it is true, as the declinists contend, that "moral rot" is pervasive throughout America, then where will it be possible to find these exemplars of virtue? And if these exemplars are available to us, how exactly have *they* escaped the "rot"? And if they have, what do they know that the rest of us do not?

I believe that Warren A. Nord (1995) has effectively captured the central dilemma that faces educators who, in response to the "moral decline" in the larger society, understandably want to provide some kind of ameliorative character training for youth. It would be instructive for all of us to ponder the current problem as he states it, before we reach for the neo-classical solution:

> For better or worse, the moral character of students is shaped to a great extent by their families, by our culture, and by that predisposition to self-centeredness . . . that lies in the hearts of everyone. It would be naive to think that public education can solve the moral crisis in our culture. It falls well beyond the competence of schools to eliminate the violence and drugs, the narcissism and psychopathology, of children raised in dysfunctional families and a corrupt culture. (p. 350)

THE CLASSICAL WORLDVIEW, DEMOCRACY, AND THE VIRTUES

All of the authors I have discussed above agree essentially with Plato and Aristotle that the world is an ordered cosmos with a prior purpose and design. Reason is the only way to penetrate the structure and meaning of the universe. Insight into the "true nature of things" is intellectually and spiritually liberating. We are required to live a harmonious, moral life, and in order to move toward a specific *telos* (our ultimate purpose), we need to live a virtuous life. And the virtues enable us to achieve our unique *telos*. We can only discover our *telos* as part of an ordered community. What troubles my students about this worldview, though, is that, while attractive and secure in many ways, it is so fundamentally discordant with the postmodern reality they and their own students inhabit. Yet the character educators refuse to acknowledge the basic incompatability between the two perspectives on reality and the difficulty teachers will face in trying to reconcile them.

In fact, as I pointed out earlier in the previous chapter, this classical worldview is often in conflict with itself, because there are elements in Aristotle's thought that are clearly antithetical to Plato's, although in some vital respects their views are complementary. Today, however, the Western mind is predominantly nonfoundational, nonessentialist, secular, and skeptical, in a sense more Nietzschean than Platonic, thanks to the intellectual legacies of the Renaissance, Protestant Reformation, and Enlightenment (Van Doren, 1991). Many character educators, though, tend to come across as rigid Platonists, morally dogmatic, and openly disdainful of modern ways of knowing. Bennett (1992), Allan Bloom (1987), and Kilpatrick (1992), for example, often engage in prolonged harangues against postmodern epistemologies. Bennett and Kilpatrick deride the use of "moral reasoning," "ethical dilemma," and "moral education" approaches in the classroom because these activities lack "objective criteria for deciding right and wrong" (Kilpatrick, 1992, p. 94). Kilpatrick believes, with Plato, that discourse about morality should be reserved for men over the age of 30, because in children the Socratic method "develops a taste for arguments rather than a taste for truth. . . . It is more important for young people to learn a love of virtue than to argue about it" (p. 89).

Neo-classical writing styles frequently reflect a moral authoritarianism, a ministerial quality, that my students find disturbing: Collins (1990) preaches; Allan Bloom (1987) orates, admonishes, and pontificates; Kilpatrick (1992) ridicules and hyperbolizes; Bennett (1988) lectures; and Wynne and Ryan (1993) cajole, accuse, and exhort. In contrast, most of my students are postmodern in temperament, eschewing any belief in a universal metaphysical or moral archetype. These students question otherworldly views of reality, preferring to remain persistently grounded in the here-and-now. For them, reality is socially constructed. Truth is always of the "small-*t*" variety and continually revisable. And morality is contextually shaped and up for grabs.

Students know—sometimes from painful experience—that there will always be competing conceptions of what is true and good in a secular pluralist democracy, and the best way to resolve philosophical, religious, and political differences in a diverse world is through mutually respectful, open-ended dialogue, characterized always by an honest epistemological skepticism. This is the spirit in which many of them teach their own classes and the way I try to teach as well, albeit, admittedly, with mixed success. It rankles my students that so few character educators tend to express any doubts about their own convictions and that fewer still speak to the need to stimulate open-minded, mutually respectful conversations in the classroom about what actually constitutes truth and morality.

Lickona (1991) does speak of "class meetings" where students learn to talk with one another in order to resolve their differences. But even here, in a chapter sandwiched between two other chapters on "moral discipline" and "teaching values through the curriculum," the intent is clear: "The class meeting is a practical tool for setting up rules and maintaining good discipline" (p. 159). Thus the "class meeting" becomes a pretext—a propaedeutic—for preparing students to receive the "right" moral messages from the adults who alone know them. What are these "right" moral messages? Lickona hints at their authoritative content (and source) with the dedication that introduces his *Educating for Character* (1991): "for God."

In the mimetic sense, it is Aristotle's teaching on the *virtues* that influences most contemporary writing on character education and also provides the source of much controversy in my classes. Every writer I have examined in the previous chapter assumes that the key to a happy, productive life is to live a life of virtue, in the Aristotelian sense. Thus, for Bennett, the reader can find the secret of a happy life in his *The Book of Virtues* (1993), a "treasury of great moral stories" culled from the history and literature of the Western heritage. For Wynne and Ryan (1993) and for Honig (1987), the key is a virtue-rich school "ethos." For Kilpatrick (1992) and Allan Bloom (1987), the critical determinants are the virtues found in the "great books." Aristotle (1976) thinks of a virtue as a "state of character that brings into good condition the thing of which it is the excellence and makes the work of that thing to be done well" (p. 91). For Aristotle, virtues are traits that help a person to be good and to do excellent work. Virtue is a habitual disposition to act well, and it is learned primarily through imitation, practice, and habituation.

Significantly, for Aristotle, though, habituation and example are never sufficient, as they appear to be for the character educators. In order to direct the habits toward the good and not the bad, and to avoid both excess and deficiency in moral living, Aristotle teaches that we need to appeal to *reason* to locate an individual's particular *telos* as well as the universal *logos* (an ultimate rational power). Mimesis is not always enough. While the character educators talk often of "habituation" and of fostering a "disposition" toward virtuous conduct, they speak far less frequently of the function of *critical reason* in living a virtuous life and in discovering a universal *logos* and a *telos*.

Moreover, Aristotle's conception of the virtues makes no sense to moderns unless there is an agreed-upon human nature, conceived teleologically, which defines the content of the virtues and describes the kind of flourishing to which the virtues lead (Audi, 1995). Absent a *telos* or a divine plan to which virtue is connected and by which it is ultimately justified, the character educators are left with a conception of virtue that is either highly subjective or located in the authority of some group larger than the individual. Thus, in so many of their writings, the character educators end up creating sundry "bags of virtues," many of which are noble and desirable, but some of which also seem arbitrary, contradictory, and occasionally heavy-handed and authoritarian.

For example, in Lickona (1991), Wynne and Ryan (1993), and Bennett (1993), certain virtues remain constant, particularly "diligence," "self-discipline," "respect," and "responsibility." But some character educators offer such lengthy "lists" of virtues that it is impossible to determine which, if any, should take priority. One character educator, in a relatively short volume, mentions at least 100 virtues students need to develop in order to "become the right sort" of people (Pincoffs, 1986). My students are left to ask: "Why these virtues?" "Who says so?" "Who are the right sort of people?"

As I pointed out earlier, for Aristotle, living virtuously requires living according to a rational principle, a *logos*, without which human beings would be purposeless. But what happens when there is no common *logos* or *telos* for students to consult when it is necessary to justify the virtues to others or to resolve conflicts among them? For example, Bennett's list of 10 virtues in *The Book of Virtues* (1993) is problematic: What is a student to do when, in a morally anomalous situation, the virtue of honesty might be in conflict with the virtue of compassion, or when courage might be incompatible with expressions of loyalty, or faith, or respect for tradition? The stark truth in contemporary America is that, in many ways, the Aristotelian conception of virtue is antiquarian, because it relies on a view of human nature that is obsolete (there is no definitive proof that each individual has a *telos* or possesses an essential human nature) and because in a secular pluralist society there is as yet no universal, or uncontested, *logos* for what virtues ought to be cultivated in the schools.

According to Alasdair MacIntyre (1984), "incommensurability" (no common basis or standard for making comparisons or reaching consensus) is the unwritten moral norm in America: "There is no rational way of securing moral agreement in our culture" (p. 6). Thus those character educators who claim to know with certainty that *their* virtues (often justified as "timeless truths," "core morality," or "traditional Western values") are the ones all reasonable parents would want their children to be taught simply do not understand the full implications of MacIntyre's incommensurability thesis.

In America today, all things moral are controvertible, and what seems "reasonably" certain to some is bound to be debatable to others. This is the price all of us must pay for living in a pluralist democracy rather than in a theocracy, with its absolute answers to difficult and ambiguous moral questions. For example, notwithstanding all the fine sense that Kilpatrick (1992) makes in his book about how sex and drug education has gone awry in this country's schools, nevertheless, his "good list[s] of moral content"—"the Ten Commandments and the Seven Corporal Works of Mercy" (p. 119)—will never be morally canonical for everyone, nor should they be. The agony and the ecstasy of living in a pluralistic America is that people will always disagree about what constitutes the "good life" and about the specific virtues needed to get there.

In this respect, the work of one particular liberal educator raises disquieting questions regarding the classical worldview, virtue, and the modern school in a pluralist, democratic society (Nash, 1988). Gerald Grant (1985), unlike the character educators I have analyzed above, is less interested in the possibility that objective virtues exist than he is in generating a just political order through the development of "core democratic virtues." Like the character educators, Grant (1985) also talks of an "ethos," as a "configuration of attitudes, values, and beliefs that members of a community share" (p. 133).

In a comprehensive study, Grant, an educational anthropologist, found that in schools with a "strong, positive ethos," leaders "clearly enunciated a character ideal" (p. 134). The teachers and administrators in these schools were involved in cultivating a wide range of virtues, including honesty and courage; and they stood proudly *in loco parentis*. Like good parents, the teachers and staff exercised a "caring watchfulness, concerned with all aspects of a child's development" (p. 134). What these schools had in common, according to Grant, was a perfect convergence between the needs and standards of the community and the needs and standards of the schools. Parents, community leaders, educators, and students voluntarily joined together in a "mutual orientation toward valued intellectual and moral virtues" (p. 134). Grant's schools were places where intellectual and moral virtues were seen as inseparable, where a rigorous academic education was balanced by a "harmonious development of character" (p. 138).

Grant's study raises disturbing questions for character educators regarding the tenuous intersection of virtue and the public good in most educational settings, which he himself acknowledges toward the end of his analysis. There are actually very few places in a pluralistic America where the intellectual and moral virtues of the public schools *and* their communities are inseparable (for two exceptions, see Noblit & Dempsey [1996]). Thus, how will it be possible to create schools that shape certain kinds of virtues in places where there is little agreement about ends between the communities and the schools, or even between the students and their teachers? In fact, as Grant (1985) points out, most schools today settle for a kind of weakly normed ethos characterized by a system of rules and procedures that reflect at best a "thin" moral consensus among the constituencies. A contemporary public school is less a community of shared virtues than it is a loosely organized bureaucracy that prevents any of the "disparate elements" within the school from gaining an edge on the others.

David Tyack and Elizabeth Hansot (1982) have argued that, in the last few decades, society's Protestant–Republican consensus that once provided the powerful character ideal for the schools has dissolved as a result of multiple internal and external system strains. In the absence of a shared moral consensus, they contend, the various constituencies within a school are less interested in learning how to live their lives by a worthy set of ideals than they are in knowing how to maximize benefits for themselves. According to Tyack and Hansot, a society that tends to elevate the principles of self-interest, diversity, and relativism above all others must give up any hope of monolithic character development in its schools and settle instead for a "fair" system that mainly insures due-process rights to various aggrieved constituencies. This is why in most American schools and colleges the emphasis is on laws, rules, procedures, individual and group rights, and entitlements, and less on becoming "good" human beings. The loss of a genuine consensus about a universal *public* morality beyond individual and group interests means the schools and colleges will always find it difficult to instill those virtues that reflect commitment to a public good.

It is in full awareness of America's strong dedication to an open, democratic, pluralistic society that Grant argues, rightly I believe, for the "teaching" of such "liberal" democratic virtues as decency, fairness, openness, honesty, respect for truth, recognition of merit and excellence, altruism, service to others, and recognition for personal effort and hard work. Grant calls for an "initiation" of children into these beliefs in such a way that the virtues are seen as "provisional," capable of being reevaluated at any time. However, in my opinion, although I agree with Grant that we need to identify and teach these "liberal" virtues (and others), I do not believe he understands the full postmodern implications of such character training.

How, for example, is it possible to avoid classroom "indoctrination" when he talks about "initiating" his liberal virtues? And is there something inherently contradictory about "indoctrinating" "liberal virtues"? Also, how can a student who is challenged continually to question any virtue at any time still subscribe with conviction and passion to some "salient, core beliefs" that shore up a democratic way of life? Grant simply declares the existence of these "salient, core beliefs," while leaving them virtually undemonstrated. What are these "core beliefs," where do they come from, and are they mainly procedural (democratic), or substantive (classical), or both? The character educators, for the most part, assume the existence of a "moral *logos*," a universal moral core. Thus, their virtues are frequently more conservative than "liberal." They look mainly to the past—the classical heritage—for guidance rather than to a more unstable, democratic future. Many of them return wistfully to the "great books," the classical texts, to find the moral precedents, the "core beliefs," for instilling the virtues. Where exactly does Grant go in order to locate his "salient, core beliefs"? What if there is actually no "place" to go, no "mono-moral" view from "somewhere," that people can agree on in a secular pluralist society (Nagel, 1986)?

The dilemma for Grant (and for all liberal democrats as well), I suggest, is similar to the dilemma facing the character educators: From very different perspectives, they both fail to appreciate fully the fundamental tensions that exist between the inculcation of Aristotelian virtues and the democratic ideal. As I have attempted to show above, talk about virtue, at least in the Aristotelian sense, assumes that excellences are traditional, definite, in place, and grounded in a universal *logos*. And yet talk about democracy entails a kind of relativizing of the virtues in the sense that they are now seen as tentative, experimental, and open-ended. Does it make any sense, for example, for liberals to elevate the basic freedoms above public debate when everything in a democracy is ostensibly up for grabs, including even those sacrosanct basic freedoms?

What never gets resolved by character educators is how they can reconcile their fixed lists of conservative "core" virtues with their commitment to foster "citizenship" virtues—those dispositions, by my definition, that should help us engage in an ongoing, peaceable, public debate contesting the competing visions of a just and free society. Without these "democratic dispositions," how will we ever achieve a functional consensus on any social problem that cuts across the political, cultural, and racial differences that currently divide us? This, for me, is the primary function of what I am calling the "democratic dispositions," and these virtues are fundamentally different from the types of virtues that excite Bennett, Kilpatrick, and Wynne and Ryan, as I will try to show in Chapter 9.

Two corollary questions, therefore, emerge from this dilemma, and it is time for character educators to address them directly: Does it make sense to foster any kinds of virtues in the schools at all in the absence of a belief in an ultimate public good, a *logos*? And how do we deal with the immobilizing contradictions that exist between our nation's dedication to the democratic ideal and to the local development of smaller communities of virtue, whose existence appears inevitable given the particular philosophical/political/religious leanings of so many character educators? Or to word it in a slightly different way: Is it realistic to talk of virtue in massive, pluralistic societies without people splitting off into self-contained "communities of virtue" with a distinctive political, ethnic, racial, or religious bias? I hope to deal directly with these kinds of questions in the following chapter on the "communitarian initiative."

BOOKS OF VIRTUE, PEDAGOGY, AND POSTMODERNISM

I frequently hear some version of the following whenever I discuss with my students *how to teach* the virtues in educational settings:

> We find much that is valuable in these readings, but we have no idea how to actually go about *teaching* character in the classroom. Obviously, these writers have never had to face a room of hyperactive middle-schoolers, or hormonal high-schoolers, or "know-it-all" college sophomores. Not only are these kids easily distracted and skeptical, but they are also juvenile lawyers who know their rights, and most are convinced that they have a right to choose their own morality, to determine what's good and bad. Nobody's going to tell them how to live *their* lives. In this sense, at least, Allan Bloom is right. Kids *are* relativists, and they're always asking: "Who says so?" "Why?" "Can you prove it?"

> So many of these writers are against using relativistic stuff like values clarification, applied ethical analysis, decision making, and conflict resolution with students, because they don't think there's any connection between moral reasoning and moral behavior, and because they think these techniques presuppose a position of value neutrality. They seem to be opposed to any cognitive problem-solving approach to teaching morality. We don't really care about their own ivory tower agendas regarding the evils of relativism and postmodernism. Isn't it good that we get kids thinking about what's right and wrong, in spite of the political correctness of the technique? Sometimes hands-on stuff is the best way to grab students' attention. Don't these writers know that critical thinking about values isn't all bad? Is it true that all these students will end up moral nihilists if we encourage them to think through ethical dilemmas on their own? This is doubtful!

> Too often, these writers just take for granted that if you dump a bunch of inspirational books on these kids, somehow they will end up with good characters. Or else they preach a gospel of academic rigor, rules, and making students toe the mark with clear-cut lines of authority separating them and teachers. Well, you and I know it just doesn't work this way. We respect Marva Collins, because at least she knows you need to get kids young and you need to mold them before they become jaded. She can indoctrinate her students

because she teaches in a private school and has a captive audience. To some extent, Bloom can do the same at the University of Chicago. But we can't. Everything we do, students and their parents see as imposing our values. Lately, we've even been accused of pushing a white, Eurocentric moral agenda on our minority students, whenever we talk about democratic values. We can't win for losing. So what are we to do?

And don't give us the cliché that modeling character is the best way to teach virtue. What a cop-out. Most students could care less about our modeling anything. They come to us with pretty rigid stereotypes about who we are, and only rarely can we change their minds. Sure we reach some kids, but not many. Besides, even if modeling is the way to go, it's damned hard work always being on your game, both in and out of the classroom. And even if I'm a perfect model, what happens when the teacher in the next room, or the professor in the next office, is a jerk? In this modeling business, who trumps whom? Can you give us any guarantees?

Sure, character education sounds great. But tell us how to do it. And be specific, please.

The truth is that most neo-classical thinkers are instructionally deficient, or disingenuously silent, on exactly *how to do it*, with Marva Collins (1990) being a notable exception. They are content mainly to argue the case for character education. Or they talk about modeling. Or they "list and dump" "books of virtue" on students. Or they resort to political exhortations about the need for educators to create a rigorous moral "ethos" in schools, one rich in "character, academics, and discipline" (Wynne & Ryan, 1993). The "books-of-virtues" educators are particularly irritating, I contend, because they not only take so much for granted regarding what books students should read, but they assume that teachers will automatically intuit how to teach the books in a morally compelling way.

Prescinding from the highly controversial question of *what* books should be included in the "virtue canon" (see Barber, 1992; H. Bloom, 1995; Bromwich, 1992; Gates, 1992; Graff, 1992; Martin, 1985), I wish to concentrate briefly here on the *pedagogical* and *political* difficulties that character educators pose for my students. My specific target is those writers who catalogue lists of "virtue" books and then run away from the responsibility to provide needed methodological assistance for teachers who try to use them. These writers belong to what I call the "moral contagion" school of character formation: the assumption that if readers are simply exposed to morality in an inspiring book, then they will "catch" it. The theory here is that virtues are communicable by (literary) contact alone. For example, Harold (*not* Allan) Bloom (1995), the Yale University literary critic, has written an encyclopedic, very persuasive work, in excess of 500 pages, about all the "great books" he believes college students should read. Ironically, though, he never utters a single word as to how these texts might be taught for maximum moral and intellectual effectiveness.

Although Allan Bloom (1987) talks about teaching the "classics" at the college level, I believe he also speaks for character educators at all levels who share similar "moral contagion" preconceptions about teaching (and reading) books of virtue: Bloom wants college teachers to assign the "classic texts" and then just "let students read them . . . letting [the texts] dictate what the questions are and the method of approaching them—not forcing them into categories we make up . . . but trying to read them as their authors wished them to be read" (p. 344).

Bennett (1993) agrees in principle with Allan Bloom. He says that the best way for adults to read these books preliminary to using them with youngsters is "in a quiet place, alone, away from distorting standards" (p. 13). For him, the simple act of reading *his* book, *The Book of Virtues* (1993), in this way will be enough to convince even the skeptical adult that it is indeed "a book of lessons and reminders . . . a compendium of great stories, poems, and essays from the stock of human history and literature. It embodies common and time-honored understandings of these virtues" (p. 13). Kilpatrick (1992) devotes almost 50 pages to an annotated list of "great books for children and teens" (p. 268). He claims that because "good books do their own work in their own way, it is not necessary or wise for adults to explain the moral in each story . . . adults should be careful not to treat books like doses of moral medicine" (p. 268). And Honig (1987) talks about the importance of reading literature that "broadens the moral perspective of the reader . . . great literature can create that sense of empathy, of shared values, of belonging to a civilization with a common history and common concerns" (p. 65). But nowhere in his book does Honig discuss strategies for getting students to read literature in this morally discerning manner. He merely assumes, with Allan Bloom (1987), that students should read the books "the way the authors intended them" (p. 344).

But does the "moral contagion" theory work? Is it possible for students to read books of virtue exactly "the way their authors intended," away from the "distorting standards" mentioned by Bennett? To some extent, "moral contagion" does work, I think, but not in the instructor-proof way the character educators would have us believe. In reality, what gets taught via this approach is primarily what the *teacher* puts into the text, rather than what the *author* puts into it. That is, whoever assigns the "classic" texts in the first place has already predecided what virtues and lessons they would like students to take away from a reading. Thus "categories" are inevitable, because character educators such as Bennett, Wynne and Ryan, and Kilpatrick have already "forced" their books into predetermined moral classifications. All the reader has to do to confirm this observation is to read any one of Bennett's several introductions to the primary source material in his *The Book of Virtues* (1993). There is no doubt where he stands regarding what "virtues" are desirable and what "vices" are repugnant.

In my estimation, no teacher ever reads or specifies a "classic" in a moral vacuum, *de novo*. Contra Allan Bloom, no book is simply a collection of "questions" awaiting an "immaculate reception" on the part of readers, or reflecting an "immaculate perception" on the part of those educators who choose and assign it. All of Bennett's (1993) 10 virtues, for example, and the vast majority of the readings he has chosen to illustrate these virtues, are irrefragably conservative, calculated to reinforce a sociopolitical (and moral) status quo. Please note that I am not intending here to be critical of these or any other neo-classical readings *because* they are conservative. What I am contesting is Bennett's and Allan Bloom's glib assumption that they are able to assign texts consciously devoid of their own political or philosophical pre-texts.

In this respect, Benjamin Barber (1992) has made a convincing case that Allan Bloom himself (now deceased)—once a student of the renowned, ultra-conservative neo-classicist Leo Strauss, a University of Chicago political philosopher—spent his entire career as a teacher and writer advancing Straussian political principles, all of which were politically conservative. And every one of which profoundly shaped Bloom's thinking about what and how the great books should be taught. Included among these conservative principles, according to Barber, were an animus against modernity and a bias toward ancient political ideals, as well as a preference for moral excellence and individual liberty over equality and social justice. "To Straussians, great books are great, not as popular guides to a philosophical life for the unphilosophical masses, but as secret codes . . . to be read by the prudent conservators of values" (pp. 167–168).

If the truth be told (and I wonder why these writers are not more politically forthright), most writing in the character-education genre smacks of ultra-conservative special pleading. These authors' political views and cross-references are virtually identical. As "prudent conservators of values," they decry a relaxing of moral standards; a proliferation of elective courses in the schools and colleges; an overemphasis on post-modernist, revisionist, and neo-Marxist studies, which are generally critical of American culture; the trend toward moral relativism in the social sciences; a loss of respect for authority; preoccupation with self-esteem, personal decision making, and cultural diversity in the schools; and a demeaning of such traditional values as patriotism, discipline, intellectual rigor, and respect for law.

For Kilpatrick (1992) and Allan Bloom (1987), any departure from "traditional education" is demonstrably evil, because it is calculated to overthrow the moral status quo. Both writers, for example, see Friedrich Nietzsche's fingerprints all over the "decay" of Western culture and democracy. In their view, Nietzsche is to blame for iniquities as far-ranging as Western relativism, nihilism, fascism, Nazism, anti-Semitism, radical feminism, rock music, values clarification, self-esteem education, and even the rejection of such principles as sacrifice, service, duty, obligation, and responsibility (A. Bloom, 1987; Kilpatrick, 1992). By implication, anyone who may be a supporter of self-esteem and values clarification in the schools is, to these writers, a Nietzschean, and ergo a relativist, even a fascist (R. J. Nash, 1996). The irony where Nietzsche (1887/1989) is concerned, of course, is that he actually spent his whole career trying to *reverse* the nihilism he believed would follow the fall of traditional religion and metaphysics. Neither a relativist nor a fascist, Nietzsche sought instead to direct human efforts to the attainment of a "higher humanity" that would enrich rather than diminish the moral life.

What, then, is the upshot of the "moral contagion" theory for the teaching of "books of virtue"? I wish to make two brief points here, both of which I will discuss further in the concluding chapter. First, essentially, I am in agreement with William Damon (1988), who criticizes the character educators for being so intransigently opposed to moral reasoning and reflection, that is, for stressing the acquisition of moral *habit* over the cultivation of critical moral *reflection*. Damon says, "Habit without reflection is adaptive only in a totalitarian climate" (p. 145), and I concur. It is unlikely that students will develop a commitment to democracy, and acquire the desirable virtues associated with it and necessary to sustain it, only by reading inspiring books of virtue. A passive reading of books of virtue (and, in the end, this is precisely what the neo-classical educators intend) teaches students the lesson that the compliant virtues are the desirable ones: submissiveness, deference to authority and tradition, obedience, and acquiescence. Again, here is Damon: "If we want to train passive subjects of a totalitarian state, we should be careful to provide children only with relationships in which they are mindless recipients of indoctrination" (p. 146).

Rarely do character educators speak of activities that prepare children to engage in the turbulent, give-and-take realities of postmodern, democratic life. These "hands-on" activities—negotiating, mediating, being comfortable with competing conceptions of right and wrong, dealing respectfully and constructively with different points of view, settling disputes and resolving conflicts peacefully and collectively, arriving at decisions fairly, making informed choices, knowing how to compromise, learning how to argue, challenge, inspire, and persuade effectively— form the basis of the "democratic dispositions" that I will discuss in the final chapters. I remain skeptical whenever neo-classical thinkers assume that an acquiescent reading of virtue texts, no matter how inspiring, is the best way to form the robust "democratic character" required of future citizens.

Second, I believe that character development must involve training young people to become discerning textual "hermeneutes" who know how to interpret and translate a variety of "texts" into present-day moral idioms, social situations, and meaning systems. No amount of mere exposure to books of virtues, rote reading, modeling, a rule-driven school ethos, or indoctrination is likely to produce an autonomous individual equipped to discern, interpret, and manage moral dilemmas effectively. Students need to understand that they do not simply read books. They also interpret them, and, in some sense, they interrogate the authors as well. Readers always bring a series of questions to every text, and frequently these questions collide with the questions the text asks. Students need instruction and practice in how to confront the ideological presuppositions and values contained in every text. Richard Rorty (noted in Graff [1992]), a postmodern philosopher, criticizes what he calls Allan Bloom's "just-read-the-books" theory with the challenge that interpreters must "give authors a run for their money" (p. 73). A hermeneute's obligation, therefore, is to show respect for a text by engaging and confronting it, by asking questions of it, as well as by trying to understand its unique vocabulary on its own terms. In the last two chapters, I intend to return to the role of hermeneutics in reading texts and the function of the "moral conversation" in promoting the postmodern virtues, as an alternative initiative in preparing youth for citizenship in a secular pluralist society.

Finally, underlying many of the observations my students offered in the opening paragraphs of this section is the concern that maybe the virtues are simply unteachable. While he does not agree, one researcher (Leming, 1993) has arrived, nevertheless, at some intriguing, somewhat troubling conclusions, following a major review of the research on the effectiveness of character education in the public schools:

1. Didactic methods alone have no effect whatever on character.
2. There is no proof that knowing what is good conduces students to do what is good. Thus, Socrates appears wrong about the cultivation of virtue, and Aristotle is closer to the truth.
3. Character develops best "within a social web or environment" (p. 66), when the school *and* community "ethos" is mutually reinforcing, consistent, clear, and supportive, but communities with this "social web" are hard to find in America today.
4. Dramatic transformations of character as a result of formal education are rare to nonexistent.
5. Most character-education programs have taken place in elementary schools. This is "puzzling" given the reports of "moral decline" among high school and college youth that neo-classical writers find so disturbing.
6. Huge variations in classroom climates, teacher personalities, and pedagogies make it very difficult to generalize about how teachers can promote good behavior.
7. "Not one research study has attempted to assess whether reading [morally inspiring] literature has the expected effect on character" (p. 69).

At the graduate school level, the findings of two researchers on the effectiveness of character education are also highly suggestive. Edmund D. Pellegrino and David C. Thomasma (1993) concluded from their research on medical students that moral character rarely gets changed by courses in ethics. They contend that while a medical faculty can never be a moral substitute for the home, church, or community, what a faculty can teach, at least in theory, is "what it is to be a good physician qua physician, and to practice and value the virtues requisite for good medicine" (p. 176). For the authors, the power of a faculty member to shape behavior for good or evil can be great or negligible, depending on the extent to which the student is responsive and ready, and on whether the medical instructor is willing both to model and discuss openly and frequently virtues such as fidelity, compassion, justice, fortitude, temperance, integrity, and self-effacement. But even when all these prior conditions exist, for Pellegrino and Thomasma, there are no guarantees that the virtues can be "taught and caught." To some extent, the authors remain skeptics on teaching moral character, even while they argue for it.

These findings on the effectiveness of character education suggest that, at the very least, we must proceed with caution and humility whenever we attempt to teach the virtues. Sometimes, to a degree, we will be successful in doing moral education. Much of the time we will not. As a parent, educator, and citizen, I strongly believe character counts, but I also know character formation is incredibly complex. In this respect, I am convinced John Dewey (1916) had it right almost a century ago:

> Moral education is practically hopeless when we set up the development of character as a supreme end, and at the same time treat the acquiring of knowledge and the development of understanding, which of necessity occupy the chief part of school time, as having nothing to do with character. On such a basis, moral education is inevitably reduced to some kind of catechetical instruction ... lessons "about morals" that signify as a matter of course what other people think about virtues and duties. (p. 101)

CONCLUSION

The character educators are correct to focus our attention on the need for teachers at all levels to think seriously and deeply about virtue. But as their program now stands, the final shape of the project is far from decided. An ultimately strong and serviceable character education cannot be separated from what Dewey calls the more formal acquisition of knowledge in schools, and neither can it be reduced to mere "catechetical instruction," to "what other people think about virtues and duties." The confounding complexity of character education will require us to consider the merits and weaknesses of other "initiatives" before we can satisfactorily settle the issue of whether the virtues are teachable, and, if so, which ones, and for what purposes. In the next chapter, I look at what I call the "communitarian initiative" in teaching the virtues.

CHAPTER 4

The Communitarian Initiative: Sectarian, Postliberal, and Civic-Liberal Virtues

What marks such a [constitutive] community is not merely a spirit of benevolence, or the prevalence of communitarian values, or even certain "shared final ends" alone, but a common vocabulary of discourse and a background of implicit practices and understandings.

—Michael Sandel, Liberalism and the Limits of Justice, *1982*

Families and communities are the ground-level generators and preservers of values and ethical systems. No society can remain vital or even survive without a reasonable base of shared values. . . . They are generated chiefly in the family, schools, church, and other intimate settings in which people deal with one another face to face.

—John Gardner, Building Community, *1991*

The central preoccupation of both ancient and medieval communities was . . . how may [people] together realize the true human good? The central preoccupation of modern [people] is . . . : how may we prevent [people] from interfering with each other as each of us goes about our own concerns? The classical view begins with the community of the polis *. . . ; the modern view begins with the concept of a collection of individuals.*

—Alasdair MacIntyre, After Virtue, *1984*

A community is a group of people who are socially interdependent, who participate together in discussion and decision making, and who share certain practices that both define the community and are nurtured by it. Such a community is not quickly formed. It almost always has a history . . . defined in part by its past and its memory of the past.

—Robert N. Bellah, Richard Madsen, William M. Sullivan, Ann Swinler, and Steven M. Tipton, Habits of the Heart: Individualism and Commitment in American Life, *1985*

In many ways, the character educators and the communitarians have much in common: Both hold that human beings have little or no purpose outside of a community, and therefore it is always as part of an ordered community that a person seeks the good (although character educators are not as likely as some communitarians to be absolutely dismissive of the doctrine of individual rights). Both believe that there is an essential correspondence between the character of a citizen and the welfare of the community. Both hold that it is the quality of an individual's life—excellence of character, not self-interestedness—that is pivotal in achieving human happiness. Both agree that education at its best can lead to the emancipation of individuals from the hegemony of their passions. Both understand that there can be no genuine public dialogue around democratic principles such as fairness, equality, and justice unless people are striving to live their lives in accordance with such virtues as self-denial, moderation, civility, and self-restraint. And both stress the retrieval of certain desirable moral characteristics from the great traditions of the Western intellectual, religious, and political heritage.

In general terms, however, character educators and communitarians differ—sometimes only to a minor degree—in the following areas: Communitarians are less neo-classical in their thinking about virtue, democracy, and education. Communitarians speak only infrequently about "moral decline." Communitarians—even some sectarians—are more concerned with civic issues and the duties of citizenship, including the notions of a public consensus and a public good. Their discourse highlights such concepts as tradition, shared values, mediating institutions, *polis* (democratic city-state), civic virtue, common practices, and communities of memory. Postliberal and civic-liberal communitarians rarely assume the existence of a *telos* or *logos,* although sectarian communitarians often speak of transcendence. Communitarians are highly critical of liberal conceptions of individualism and a rights-based ethic. And communitarians, by and large, are less concerned with a "great-books" approach to pedagogy or with creating a particular kind of "ethos" in the schools that is grounded in rigorous academics and stern discipline. In fact, while they are greatly interested in formal schooling as a medium for teaching the virtues, communitarians are equally interested in other educating institutions, such as the family, government, and the churches, as loci for virtue cultivation.

What clearly differentiates communitarian from neo-classical approaches to culture, politics, the family, and education is *their sharply focused critique of liberal excess*—especially excessive forms of individualism, "rights talk," and secularism and pluralism. For communitarians, the recognition that individuals are social beings who are "embedded" and "embodied" in their communities is central. It is the community, not the individual, that is the ultimate source of virtue and value. Communitarians argue that "human life will go better if communitarian, collective, and public values guide and construct our lives" (Frazer, in Honderich, Ed., 1995, p. 143).

In summary, communitarians seem to be saying that if individuals are only what they choose to be, if they can detach themselves from social and historical roles at will, if they can ignore their embeddedness in those communities from which they derive their identity, and if there is no common bond or commitment to give life direction and purpose, then society is little more than a collection of strangers, bereft of profound human connection, each person pursuing private interests with no restraints or sense of connection to others (Nash & Griffin, 1987).

THE HUNGER FOR COMMUNITY

As a modern political philosophy, communitarianism derives from the work of Plato in the *Republic* and from Hegel (1821/1977), who developed the idea of the spirit, or *Geist*. Against the Enlightenment claim that the self-willing individual is the center of the universe, Hegel argued that the individual is actually a "social subjectivity," a "collective subject," a product of a "complex social inheritance" that is continually evolving. Thus, for Hegel, no individual exists independently of other individuals, and, in fact, individual identity is the result of a dialectical interplay between and among several individuals.

Robert Nisbet (1982, 1983), a social historian of community, has written that since medieval times there has been a long history of the erosion of community in the West. In the Middle Ages, the "patriarchal family, kin, the village community, walled town, guild, and monastery" (1982, p. 52) were the units that provided people with primary relationships and personal identity. But when the nation state began its rise, it "consolidated its sovereign power" over traditional communities, resulting in the dissolution of intermediate groups. Capitalism, in its continuing quest for expanding national and international markets (Fukuyama, 1992), further destroyed the relationships of "kinship and locality," although, surprisingly, a country like Japan has been able to prosper economically while preserving families and neighborhoods (Nisbet, 1982). Democracy, ironically, increased the state's control over its citizens through its centralized political power, thereby weakening traditional venues of citizen participation—the town, neighborhood, and local community. In the last 50 years, we have seen the creation of public housing, shopping malls, condominiums, and high-rise retirement "villages," and, in the process, traditional communities disappear.

In the nineteenth century, Alexis de Tocqueville (1848/1988), following in Hegel's (1821/1977) footsteps, understood the isolation from community to which Americans were especially prone because of their immersion in private economic pursuits. These endeavors pulled citizens away from participation in civic organizations in which they might play a role in shaping public life through debate and public initiative. For Tocqueville, community life was the major bulwark against the condition he feared most: being easy prey to a political despotism. With considerable prescience, he saw that the centralized state, operating under the myth of participatory democracy and a "worship of equality," could easily become a tyrant. For Tocqueville, the tragic aftermath of huge democratic states, with their centralized political and bureaucratic power, is that eventually the people turn to the state as compensation for the loss of community (Nisbet, 1982).

Today, where do people go to satisfy what Bellah and colleagues (1985) call their "hunger" for community? Contemporary communitarians mourn the fact that most Americans do not see themselves as belonging to a bona fide community (Elshtain, 1995; Glendon, 1991; Kaus, 1992; Wilson, 1995b). Americans are not interdependent, do not participate politically, and do not share a common history or value system. Instead, the majority of Americans settle for membership in ersatz recreational or "lifestyle" communities, where people share only superficial features of their private lives: appearance, consumption, and leisure activities. Neither do most Americans generally see themselves as participating with one another in lively political discussion leading to genuine decision making in such a way as to relate their lives in concrete ways in the commonweal (Dionne, 1991). As one example, the restriction of town-meeting forums throughout the country to narrower and narrower (and more technical) economic agendas has seriously reduced active citizen involvement in the everyday affairs of government. People are left, as isolated individuals, to engage in vapid, private exchanges of e-mail via their personal computers; to carry on anonymous, Web-site computer conversations with strangers; and to tune in to an endless array of radio and television talk shows that provide the illusion of vigorous social and political discourse in a public forum but that leave the status quo of local, regional, and national government totally intact (Elshtain, 1995).

In the long run, though, according to today's communitarians, high-tech-communications solutions to the loss of community—like lifestyle enclaves—are actually a shallow and fragile substitute for genuine community. Americans are experiencing increasing anxiety and uncertainty about achieving more important and enduring relationships. The hunger for community runs deep throughout the entire country, cutting across economic, racial, and class lines. Therapists and pastoral counselors are aware of these fears and are encouraging their clients to get involved with church groups, support groups, and service groups as a way to "reconnect" with others (Wuthnow, 1993). Traditional needs to relate in certain ways—familial, religious, civic—persist stubbornly in a pluralistic and mobile United States, as does the search for common moral understandings. It is the moral content of community that best fulfills the human need for objective standards of right and wrong—for a sense that not everything moral is up in the air all the time, that perhaps common understandings about right and wrong can lead to moral consensus. Communitarians believe that to satisfy the hunger for community by joining one unstable group after another will lead only to dissatisfaction and despair (Etzioni, 1993); or, in Nisbet's (1982) ominous words, only to "the kind of community that Rousseau . . . promised: the total political community in which a general will, a collective political consciousness, becomes the haven for those tormented by the misery of being alone" (p. 54).

THREE TYPES OF COMMUNITARIANISM

Although all the thinkers I cite below may not agree with my designations, I believe communitarian authors today generally represent three strands, what I will call sectarian, postliberal, and civic-liberal communitarianism. For the most part, although the latter two designations have been around for awhile, the political and educational meanings I attach to them are my own.

I find *sectarian communitarians* to be the most conservative group. Stanley Hauerwas, a noted sectarian communitarian, succinctly summarizes this position: "[Sectarian communitarianism] challenges liberal intellectual and political presuppositions by providing an account of the power and truthfulness of Christian convictions" (1991, p. 15). I believe the *postliberal communitarians* are the most militant group in the sense that they believe the basic language of liberalism (rights, liberty, individualism, rationality, progress) erodes the strong sense of solidarity, shared history, and communal ties and duties that any society needs in order to survive. Many postliberal communitarians are highly aggressive in their absolute repudiation of liberal ideals. In my research, I found that C. A. Bowers (1987) was the first educational philosopher to refer to a "post-liberal" theory of education. And *civic-liberal communitarians* are the most moderate group, because they strive to bridge the gap between a radical liberalism based on individual liberty, rights, and equality, and a radical conservatism rooted in tradition, patriotism, duty, and merit. As far as I can tell, Mickey Kaus (1992) coined the term *civic liberalism*, and, along with other like-minded civic-liberal communitarians (Elshtain, 1995), he wants to revitalize civil society by stressing the importance of "mediating" institutions. Civic-liberal communitarians remain deeply committed to the liberal project, but they insist that families, communities, voluntarism, networks, and workplace ties are necessary to finish the work of liberal modernity (Elshtain, 1995).

In this chapter, I will briefly introduce the key elements of each strand of communitarianism by highlighting one highly visible, somewhat controversial, proxy figure, in order to capture the most dramatic flavor of each perspective. I will then present sectarian, postliberal, and civic-liberal communitarian perspectives on education and the virtues. I will withhold specific criticisms of each strand of communitarianism until the next chapter.

Sectarian Communitarianism

It is essential to note, at the outset, that the vast majority of those I am calling "sectarian communitarians" are religious, and they identify with one or another of the many denominations of the Christian faith. Thus, in this section and in the sections to follow on sectarian education, I will emphasize the *Christian* perspective on sectarian communitarianism. (Sectarians, of course, come in all stripes, and, as I will try to show in Chapter 7, the liberationists are political sectarians who talk, sometimes in apocalyptic, quasi-religious tones, about building "communities of resistance" and "solidarity.")

Stanley Hauerwas, a Christian theologian at Duke University, is perhaps the premier sectarian communitarian in the United States today (Nash, 1988). The author of more than a dozen influential books on community and virtue, Hauerwas is an excellent, though highly polemical, representative of this particular strand of communitarianism. I will touch on some of his more important points in what follows. Hauerwas's uncompromising attack on liberal society is based on his belief that people need a "shared [religious] story" to bind their lives together into community. But a liberal society seeks only a shared system of rules to ensure equity among individuals, for whom society is no more than an arena in which to pursue their private interests. This system of rules must be universalizable in order to be publicly acceptable. What gets omitted are the historical particulars of each person's narrative. The "first-person singular" is excluded in the sense that religious particulars are left out of the public realm in the name of fairness. Individualism is rampant, it is true, but only in private. Virtue in the public realm, therefore, is always "subordinated to the lowest-common denominator set of rules that can be affirmed by all citizens, whatever their virtues or vices" (Hauerwas, 1981, p. 130).

Hauerwas opts for the Christian "story" as the best context within which to cultivate a virtuous life. For him, liberal societies remove from the public arena precisely those subjects about which persons care most deeply, be they religious or otherwise. For example, for Hauerwas (1991), abortion is an issue that cannot be adjudicated solely in the procedural realm of legal argument. The Christian concern over abortion can only be understood against the background of such peculiarly Christian virtues as faith, hope, love, and redemption.

Hauerwas (1981) maintains that in a liberal society the language of Christian virtue is in flagrant opposition to the language of autonomy: Christian virtue will always be at odds with any account of morality that makes autonomy the goal of moral behavior. For the Christian, "autonomous freedom can only mean slavery to the self and the self's desires" (p. 131). It is the Christian belief that genuine freedom comes only when one learns to be dependent, that is, when the person becomes perfectly obedient to "one who wills us as his own and who wills the final good of all" (p. 131). Training in Christian virtues is risky, for Hauerwas, because it separates Christians from the larger society and from the socialization necessary to being a modern, autonomous self. To be trained to resist the state requires an alternative story and an alternative community in which the self can find a home. Hauerwas's "community of virtue" is strictly sectarian, and the youngster receives constant training in the Christian story and in the concomitant Christian virtues—hope, love, patience, faith. The Christian story "offers training in the hope and patience necessary to live amid the diversity of the world while trusting that its very plurality reflects the richness of God's creating and redeeming purposes" (p. 128).

Hauerwas, like many sectarian communitarians, unleashes a blistering attack on secular society and liberal democracy. The subtitle of one of his books (1988), *War and Survival in a Liberal Society,* typifies his perspective. He takes to a religious extreme what he and other sectarians believe to be the core truths of communitarianism: The teaching of virtue can best occur only when a community has an agreed-upon religious history and story; when there is a transcendent purpose to its existence; when people are aware of the "embedded" religious quality of their lives; when they are obedient to a religious community's rules; when they share common values, traditions, and revelations; and when they are in agreement that there is no "ultimate" salvation outside the religious community.

Educationally, Hauerwas believes that children and adults will have to give up a certain amount of freedom in order to belong to a nurturing, bonded community. And the cultivation of virtue is best taught in smaller, face-to-face, highly homogeneous communities where consensus is possible and where a shared religious vision shapes character. The virtues are always "narrative-dependent," and to be virtuous requires constant training: developing skills via prolonged exposure to the masters of Christian life who help persons to live "The Story" as their own and who then transform society through Christian love. Thus, for Hauerwas, and for other sectarians, education is meant to capture the hearts and souls of students as well as their minds.

Postliberal Communitarianism

Alasdair MacIntyre's *After Virtue* (1984), perhaps the leading communitarian account of virtue published in the last 20 years, is a work that hovers over any discussion of virtue today (Nash, 1988). The thread of MacIntyre's central argument is that contemporary ethical dilemmas in America will always resist satisfactory resolution, because there seems to be no rational way of ever reaching moral agreement. Thus moral debates rage on interminably, leading to "culture wars" and to "emotivism," the doctrine that all moral judgments are nothing but individual expressions of preference and that there can never be a valid rational justification for any claim that objective moral standards exist.

MacIntyre traces the roots of emotivism back to the eighteenth-century French, English, Scottish, and German Enlightenment and the separation of "morality" as a particular sphere of conduct from theological, legal, and aesthetic realms. At this time, the Enlightenment project became the discovery of an independent rational justification of morality. MacIntyre believes that the project ultimately failed because the liberation of individuals from a "theistic, teleological, and hierarchical" moral order left people bereft of any shared, public, moral rationale. And religion, philosophy, the social sciences, and politics have since been unable to provide the foundation for moral discourse and action because the liberal emphasis on moral autonomy has led inescapably to moral anomie (a lack of consensus concerning social norms and values).

In a choice between Nietzsche (who disposes of the Enlightenment project to discover rational foundations for an objective morality and replaces it with a "transvaluation" of all values rooted in a heroic act of the will) and Aristotle, MacIntyre turns to the classical worldview for moral guidance, as typified by the ideal of virtues in Homeric, Athenian, and medieval societies. Although there are substantial differences, the pre-suppositions about virtue that all three ideals share are similar to those that I discussed in the previous chapter in the section on the classical worldview. For MacIntyre, the "unitary core concept" of all the disparate virtues includes standards of excellence, an awareness of the embedded quality of all human life (each person is implicated in a human narrative with a past, present, and future), obedience to rules, and achievement of goods. Thus truthfulness, justice, and courage are key virtues because without them the "corrupting power" of institutions would be over-whelming. People would experience communities as Hobbesian jungles in which each individual would competitively pursue a narrow and selfish conception of the good life. For MacIntyre, this last assertion de-scribes the present condition of the modern liberal state.

MacIntyre reiterates the basic assumption all postliberals share: The modern liberal state, with its emphasis on tolerance and pluralism, is politically and culturally corrupt, because it makes moral commensura-bility an impossible ideal. In other words, according to MacIntyre, in spite of all the efforts over the years by existentialists, analytic philosophers, social scientists, and social philosophers, there is still no rationally defen-sible statement of liberal individualism. And because there is no agreed-upon conception of the good outside the self in a secular pluralist society, moral solipsism becomes a way of life in modern liberal societies. In an effort to reestablish some meaning in a society where he believes every single political tradition has now been exhausted, MacIntyre (1984) ar-gues that we must begin to move into a "postliberal epoch" in order to construct "local forms of community within which civility and the intel-lectual and moral life" can be sustained (p. 263). The virtues he lauds, in addition to the aforementioned classical virtues, are amiability, practical intelligence, self-knowledge, and constancy, because these, plus the clas-sical virtues, will help people to survive the "coming ages of barbarism and darkness" (p. 263).

Like most prophetic, postliberal communitarians, MacIntyre tends to be a philosophical conservative. He is relentlessly critical of liberal politi-cal ideals, because they lack a compelling and purposive "narrative" and because they are grounded in a doctrine of rights and opposed to tradi-tion. He looks to Aristotelian conceptions of the virtues in emphasizing the role of "excellences," "practices," the "good of a whole human life," and the importance of "ongoing social traditions." He is profoundly criti-cal of the turn toward tolerance, emotivism, and incommensurability in pluralistic democracies. Finally, unlike the sectarian communitarians, he is steadfastly secular and non-utopian in his account of the virtues.

Civic-Liberal Communitarianism

Jean Bethke Elshtain is perhaps the leading civic-liberal communitarian in America, along with Mary Ann Glendon (1991), whose work I will refer to in the next section. Elshtain's book, *Democracy on Trial* (1995), is an accurate rendering of civic-liberal political principles, as well as what she calls the "democratic dispositions." Elshtain is also a lucid commentator on civic-liberal education, and I will discuss her views on this topic in a later section. I believe Elshtain represents well the civic-liberal voice in communitarian thinking. In her latest book (1995), the "civic" voice is clearly that of Alexis de Tocqueville (1848/1988) and the "liberal" voice is unmistakably that of John Stuart Mill (1859/1982) and Isaiah Berlin (1992).

As a moderate, yet spirited, civic-liberal communitarian, Elshtain (1995) emphasizes the following themes: She is unalterably committed to a democratic, civil society, a "world of groups, associations, and ties that bind" (p. 2). She stresses the importance of "mediating institutions," such as families, churches, neighborhood groups, trade unions, self-help movements, and volunteer assistance groups, as a way to fill the "civic spaces" that exist between the individual and the state. She is opposed to rights when they become synonymous with entitlements but supportive of them when they function as "immunities" to protect people from "overweening" governmental power. She is critical of democracy whenever it becomes a mere "plebiscitary majoritarianism" (majority rule through the "electronic town hall" and impersonal polls), but she defends the idea of a "democratic polity" sustained by vigorous debate and informed, deliberative judgment. And she calls for clear distinctions between the public and private, the personal and political, in a democracy.

Briefly, Elshtain's (1995) argument is that American democracy is "faltering," showing signs of exhaustion, cynicism, and despair. Democracy is "on trial." Generally, people continue to vote, albeit in smaller numbers during national elections, and most show respect for the nation's laws and the Constitution. But in place of the democratic dispositions necessary to sustain and vitalize a democracy, Elshtain believes there is a widespread alienation and skepticism among the American people. For Elshtain, this erosion of democratic virtues is not the equivalent of the character educators' precipitous moral decline, but, rather, it signals something that, to her, is far more insidious—a refusal to get involved in everyday politics. Meanwhile, the "danse macabre" at the professional political level continues: Liberals try to "tame the logic of the market even as they celebrate . . . laissez-faire in cultural and sexual life," while conservatives opt for "constraints . . . in the cultural and sexual sphere but embrace a nearly unconstrained market" (pp. 2–3).

Most tragically, though, and echoing Tocqueville, Elshtain (1995) believes that Americans have largely lost faith in their "civic spaces," those mediating forms of community and public association (e.g., families, churches, schools, neighborhood organizations) that are at once a refuge from the bureaucratization and anonymity of large-scale public life and the source of those virtues (e.g., trust, neighborliness, fairness) necessary to undergird and sustain a robust political life. According to Elshtain, Americans experience their "democratic individuality" as a kind of radical autonomy that repudiates "all ties of reciprocal obligation and mutual interdependence" (p. 12). On the left, "wants" (lifestyle preferences) become "rights." On the right, an "untrammeled" economic market becomes a right, but the state is enjoined to legislate against unconventional lifestyles that the right views as "perversions" or self-indulgences.

Both the right and the left, therefore, rely on the state to define human needs, to solve problems, and to take the place of those local, particularistic groups and movements that were once the source of people's "concrete moral obligations" (Elshtain, 1995, p. 19). What is needed as an antidote to the growing cynicism and surrender of moral autonomy, according to Elshtain, speaking in the tradition of Mill and Berlin, is a "new social covenant" (p. 30). This is a covenant born out of a "politics of authentic democratic possibilities," where people practice the virtue of civility in their public conversations, while they struggle collectively to achieve a majoritarian consensus on the most troubling social issues of the day (p. 62).

COMMUNITARIAN EDUCATION

In this section, I will attempt to summarize the dominant communitarian *educational* themes. This will be a more difficult task than in the previous chapters on the character-education initiative, for three reasons. First, with a few notable exceptions (Knight, 1995), communitarian thinkers are less likely to be professional educators or university educationists. Thus they usually write as social philosophers, political philosophers, moral philosophers, theologians, sociologists, and, in one case, as a legal scholar, leaving the reader mainly to infer the educational ramifications of their accounts. Second, communitarian thinkers conceive of education very broadly, as occurring in a number of "mediating" social institutions in addition to the school. Thus, for them, in theory, society as a whole is educative, and other institutions in addition to schools are "educating" institutions in their own right. Third, while communitarian writers *across* the three strands do take similar positions on several educational issues, they also differ in some fundamental ways. Consequently, in the sections that follow, I will identify sectarian, postliberal, and civic-liberal educational differences.

Communitarian Educational Goals

In educational terms, communitarians are generally conservative, even though politically many are utopian and some are even populists. While contemporary communitarians would take issue with many of Edmund Burke's (1790/1960) conservative political principles, I believe they would support his concern for cultural tradition; his affection for the accumulated wisdom of human history; his respect for civil discourse; his mistrust of liberal individualism, with its encouragement of "untrammeled" personal liberty and reliance on majoritarian democracy; and his belief that only in "little platoons" (small, intimate, face-to-face communities) can people "proceed towards a love to our country, and to mankind" (p. 44). Also, while I believe that most communitarians today would reject Burke's rigid view of social order, with its penchant for elite, hierarchical, and paternalistic forms of leadership (Gutek, 1988), they would nevertheless agree with Burke that the school and university should build upon familial and religious communal traditions rather than challenge and reject them. Thus, for communitarians, the major goal of schools and universities ought to be to foster those virtues in youth that will sustain and strengthen local communities—the training ground for membership in the larger "platoons" that will call for young people's loyalties throughout the course of their lifetimes.

SECTARIAN EDUCATIONAL GOALS. Arthur F. Holmes (1975), a sectarian (Christian) communitarian, asserts that the goal of Christian higher education is to create "a community of Christians whose intellectual and social and cultural life is influenced by Christian values" (p. 77). For Holmes, an ordered community of rules and procedures is the best way to express an "inner community of interest and purpose" (p. 79). Because a Christian community is built on a foundation of love, and because it is a structure of "shared values and purposes," the Christian college must likewise be a community—not a local church, social club, service agency, or vocational training school, but a community of faith and learning, a place where "God is always honored in and through studies" (p. 84).

According to Holmes, the Christian college fosters three types of virtues: spiritual, moral, and intellectual, with the spiritual virtues defining most dramatically what characterizes the unique mission of a Christian college. The spiritual virtues are faith, hope, love, purposefulness, expectation, and humility, and they denote an "unreserved commitment" to God, a faith in the gospel, and a sense of piety and devotion (p. 102). The moral virtues are love, fairness, courage, integrity, and justice. And the intellectual virtues, in the tradition of Aristotle, are breadth of understanding, openness to new ideas, intellectual honesty, grace and eloquence in communication, and wisdom. Holmes adds other virtues to his list, including conscientiousness, helpfulness, self-discipline, persistence, involvement in community, and self-knowledge. The ultimate goal of the virtues is to help students "glorify God," seek His "saving grace," and approach the world with a sense of "justice, peace and love" (p. 102).

At the elementary and secondary levels of schooling, sectarian communitarians usually represent two perspectives, conservative and moderate. Notwithstanding their particular ideological perspective, however, most sectarians realize, today, that the public schools must never indoctrinate a particular religious position in a secular pluralist America protected by the First Amendment's establishment clause. All sectarians are in agreement, though, that what the clause forbids is the "imposition of religious belief by the state, *not* statements of religious belief in the course of public dialogue" (Carter, 1993, p. 112), or, by extension, in the transmission of knowledge in the public schools. Thus sectarian communitarians as diverse in their views as the very moderate Stephen L. Carter, the very conservative Stanley Hauerwas and John H. Westerhoff (1992), and the quasi-accommodationists Barbara B. Gaddy, T. William Hall, and Robert J. Marzano (1996) all argue that the goal of sectarian education in the public schools must be to "de-neuter" the "value-free" curriculum. Two possible solutions are to put the world's various religious traditions into a mutually respectful classroom dialogue, at least on the secondary level, or to withdraw students from the mainstream public schools and allow families, through a system of state-subsidized vouchers, to choose sectarian schools that explicitly teach (indoctrinate) the religious values and doctrines of their particular community.

No matter their solutions, however, most sectarians see themselves in some fashion as "resident aliens" in a far-reaching, liberal educational system. Sectarian communitarians resent such liberal educational ideals as "noninterference" and "toleration," as well as "neutrality" and "individual liberty" (Jung, 1992), because they think these liberal virtues are, ultimately, deceptions. These "procedural virtues" actually encourage an intolerance of more conventional religious teachings, while favoring a modernist "gospel" of secularism, pluralism, and cultural assimilation.

Ironically, sectarian communitarians are in agreement with the postmodern observation that no epistemology is ever impartial: Liberal epistemology ends up showing a bias against overt acts of religious witness in the public schools in respect of the principle of religious neutrality. As one example, Bates (1993) has shown in his account of the *Mozert* v. *Hawkins* case in Church Hill, Tennessee, that the very concept of liberal neutrality is destructive of sectarian communitarian beliefs. For his part, Hauerwas (1991) believes that the main goal of sectarian education ought to be to witness: "Because the story we tell of God is the story of the life and death of Jesus of Nazareth, then the only way to know that story is through witness" (p. 149). For Hauerwas, this Christian duty to witness in all places, including the public schools, requires "telling a counter story" to what he believes is the ubiquitous liberal myth that no religious witness is permissible in the name of tolerance.

POSTLIBERAL EDUCATIONAL GOALS.   In higher education, the communitarian Alasdair MacIntyre (1990) calls for the establishment of a "postliberal" university whose major goal would be to foster "constrained disagreements" by putting "rival versions of moral enquiry" into confrontation with one another (p. 234). MacIntyre is reacting to what he believes is the "poverty of shared morality" in a liberal society, resulting in the "increasing disarray" of the American university. According to MacIntyre, disciplines are "resourceless" in providing professionals, and nonprofessionals, with the moral justifications they need to solve complex ethical dilemmas. Because the liberal university has had a long history of "unenforced and unconstrained agreements," it finds itself in a grievously endangered state: It has effectively abolished the religious and moral standards necessary for reaching any kind of ethical agreement in the secular professions and in society at large.

Thus, in an age of irreversible moral incommensurability, there are only two goals left for the American university, according to MacIntyre: One goal is to initiate students into the great moral conflicts of the ages from a neutral vantage point *outside* a particular point of view (this is actually a goal that the postmodern literary theorist Gerald Graff [1992] recommends when he advocates "teaching the conflicts"). The other goal is to challenge rival moral views from *inside* a particular point of view (this is a goal that Hauerwas [1981] advances). The first goal is one that liberal universities claim to realize very effectively, but, in practice, they do not, because, according to MacIntyre, their alleged "neutrality" is a myth. The second goal is most emphatically illiberal, because it logically requires the establishment of a "set of rival universities" along the lines of the (Thomist) University of Paris in 1272. This latter goal, laments Mac-

Intyre, is often ridiculed and dismissed because it appears too "utopian" and closed-minded to liberal critics. Nevertheless, it remains MacIntyre's favorite choice.

C. A. Bowers (1987), a postliberal philosopher of education, argues that the goal of education at all levels of schooling should be the "restoration of community." In a very comprehensive and balanced critique of many types of liberalism (represented by John Dewey, Paulo Freire, Carl Rogers, and B. F. Skinner), Bowers asserts that education's most pressing task is to "de-center" the individual without weakening the individual's power to make a difference in the world. Bowers takes his goal for postliberal schooling to the most "radical" extreme in a concluding chapter: He advocates a "bioregional" vision for education, wherein students learn how to live a more "communal lifestyle" in harmony with the quotidian rhythms of the seasons and the "biotic community." For Bowers, there is always a dialectical relationship between the individual and community—the community representing the "what" of human existence, and the individual standing for the "what could or ought to be" (p. 77). The function of the school, according to Bowers, must be to help students understand the power of cultural embeddedness and tradition, as well as to point out the real possibilities of overcoming the more suffocating conditions of that embeddedness and tradition.

CIVIC-LIBERAL EDUCATIONAL GOALS. Two civic-liberal proponents of democracy, Elshtain (1995) and Glendon (1991), agree that education's goal ought not to be simply the transmission of a set of procedures or a constitution, but the engendering of "a [democratic] ethos, a spirit, a way of responding, and a way of conducting oneself" (Elshtain, 1995, p. 80). In behalf of a democratic education, America's schools and universities must begin to instill "some measure of commonality across differences," because "education is about opening the world up, not imprisoning us in terms of race, gender, or ethnicity" (p. 86). Both Elshtain and Glendon reserve their harshest criticisms for those multiculturalists who preach a "politics of difference." For Elshtain (1995), left- and right-wing ideologues stifle the public conversation with their "conformity, uniformity, and stultifying dogmas" (p. 88). She opts instead for an education at all levels that teaches young people that "none of us is stuck inside our own skins; our identities and our ideas are not reducible to our membership in a race, an ethnic group, or a sex" (p. 85). Elshtain's "democratic virtues" include honor, friendship, fidelity, and fairness, and these dispositions are "ruptured," she believes, whenever a "politics of difference" rushes in to take their place.

Glendon (1991) is a civic liberal who talks less about schools and more about alternative educational venues. For her, the best civic liberal education takes place "around the kitchen table, in the neighborhood, the workplace, in religious groups, and in various other communities of memory and mutual aid" (p. 174). The purpose of this type of "communitarian" education, according to Glendon, is to "help citizens to live decently together" by recalling each community's particular "stories" and, in so doing, "reaffirming the importance of relationships, obligations, and the long-term consequences of present acts and decisions" (p. 174). Glendon believes that women, as mothers and teachers, have done the most to "nourish a sense of connectedness between individuals," because they exhibit the virtues of "care, relationship, nurture, and contextuality" (p. 174).

In her own profession of law, Glendon calls on law school professors to be less adversarial and more concerned with teaching the value of dialogue, finding common ground, achieving mutual understanding while disagreeing, and encouraging open exchange. In support of her goals for professional legal education, she quotes Abraham Lincoln's exhortation to lawyers to become "peacemakers": "Discourage litigation. Persuade your neighbors to compromise whenever you can. As a peacemaker, the lawyer has a superior opportunity of being a good man. There will still be business enough" (p. 185).

Finally, Richard Pratte (1988)—although not technically a communitarian, but more of a progressive "civic republican"—advances many civic-liberal educational themes. For him, the central goal of education is to assert a "civic imperative": "We have now to adopt a moral compact composed of the principle of human dignity and mutual respect, the ethic of obligation, and civic moral virtues" (p. 182). Pratte contends that educators must be advocates for the importance of democracy, active citizenship, and community service. Not as antiliberal in his views as other communitarians, Pratte urges, in addition to cultivating a disposition toward community service and civic activism, that the schools should also cultivate such liberal virtues as impartiality, nonarbitrariness, and objectivity (p. 182). Pratte's cardinal civic virtues match the ones advocated by each of the communitarian educators, but especially by the civic liberals. They include friendship, trust, mutual respect, concern, caring, and tolerance for others.

The Communitarian School and College

Communitarian schools and colleges seek to become replications of the face-to-face communities they presume to represent. An important function of these institutions is to unite individuals with the wisdom and ethos of their originating and current communities, and to encourage in youth a sense of belonging and fidelity to those local traditions and narratives that the school ought to be celebrating. To achieve this purpose, the schools and colleges, as in Emile Durkheim's grand vision, ought to provide youth with the "symbolic" foundation of moral community in modern life (Wuthnow, 1993). This entails, among other things, that schools and colleges pay closer attention to the symbolism of ancestry, folklore, collective ritual, and traditional texts in the formation and maintenance of communities, so that the community and the sacred become one in students' minds.

Communitarian schools and colleges are also places that should provide a systematic critique of the philosophy of liberal individualism—America's dominant ideology—with special emphasis on the poverty of a rights-based ethic. In Glendon's (1991) words: "The exaggerated absoluteness of our American rights rhetoric is closely bound up with its other distinctive traits—a near silence concerning responsibility, and a tendency to envision the rights-bearer as a lone autonomous individual" (p. 45). In the estimation of communitarians, schools and colleges should be sites for deconstructing the dominant rhetoric of rights in order to demonstrate how such language precludes relationships and responsibility, and makes the fulfillment of such democratic virtues as consensus, accommodation, and a willingness to find common ground virtually impossible.

Finally, communitarian schools and colleges should be incubators for promoting the civic and democratic virtues, the sources of "competence, character, and citizenship in American society" (Glendon & Blankenhorn, 1995). James Q. Wilson (1995a), a highly respected communitarian, has written that in classical times, the purpose of politics in the community was to foster virtue. In modern times, it is to balance the "demands of public order and personal liberty," of rights and the virtues (p. 18). For Wilson and other civic liberals, the schools and colleges should become the official training grounds for showing students how to exercise a freedom that presumes a "natural moral order," the sine qua non for constructing a stable and orderly democratic life.

THE SECTARIAN SCHOOL AND COLLEGE. Regarding higher education, sectarians talk frequently about the "crisis of secularization" and the problem of defining what, if anything, makes any institution "distinctively" sectarian. The conservative communitarian Richard John Neuhaus (1996) has identified several characteristics of a Christian college that, for him, best define the kind of place Christian higher education should be: It should have a clear identity and purpose grounded in Christian truth.

It should be affiliated with a particular denomination for immediate religious recognition. Faculty should be supportive, not dismissive, of its central mission. Academic freedom and ultimate truth should be joined, in the sense that academic liberty ought to encourage the pursuit of ultimate religious truth. Christian higher education should examine the "whys" and the "what fors" of reality in addition to the "whats" and the "hows." And Christian colleges must become "communities of conviction," however variously expressed.

The more moderate sectarian George M. Marsden (1994) admits that it is impossible today to reach a Christian consensus either in public or parochial colleges, mainly because the mandate of pluralism in Western culture is too strong and because so many insurmountable differences exist among the various Christian denominations. Somewhat reminiscent of MacIntyre, Marsden therefore recommends two alternative roles for sectarian and secular colleges: They could become locations for a genuine "pragmatic" pluralism on all campuses, and this would include moral, philosophical, and religious pluralism in addition to the more popular ethnic and racial kind. According to Marsden, this pluralism does not imply that Christians should become relativists, but it does require that colleges welcome Mormans, Unificationists, Falwell fundamentalists, and Harvey Cox (a Harvard Divinity School professor and author of *The Secular City* [1965]) liberals to the pluralistic conversation, along with the postmodernists, the agnostics, and the atheists, in the spirit of mutual respect for a wide variety of religious opinions (Marsden & Longfield, 1992).

Marsden, however, is a realist who understands that such pluralism is unlikely. Hence he prefers the second option: Distinctly Christian colleges ought to go their own way, and, if they are effective, they will become exemplary intellectual and moral communities, even though they will not always be admired by the larger society. The truth, for Marsden, is that sectarians will invariably remain an "unpopular sect" in pluralist America, as skeptical secularists will continue to level charges of "fundamentalism" and "dogmatism" at those Christians who attempt to exemplify publicly what they believe most deeply.

Hauerwas and Westerhoff, the editors of a volume on elementary and secondary Christian education, *Schooling Christians: "Holy Experiments" in American Education* (1992), believe all their contributing authors would agree that the Christian school should be a place where children are able to strengthen those religious convictions by which they will live the rest of their lives. The editors maintain that liberalism has reached its "moral limits" in America, with the virtue of tolerance and the principles of noninterference and neutrality overwhelming all other virtues and principles. Consequently, sectarian schools must "stand outside" the social order and "expose" whatever is contrary to "gospel practices." The place of a sectarian school in America, therefore, is to witness to an alternative to the "hegemony" of liberal social life. The editors and contributors, like most other sectarian communitarians, have given up on the possibility that the public schools will ever stand for anything that is religiously or morally distinctive.

THE POSTLIBERAL SCHOOL AND COLLEGE. Willimon and Naylor (1995) believe that the American college should move beyond modeling the ideal of *individual* excellence: It is now time to teach students how to live in a *community.* For them, a community is a "partnership of people committed to the care and nurturing of each other's mind, body, heart, and soul through participatory means" (p. 145). Hence students ought to become models of "social excellence," understanding how they are in need of each other as well as how they can give and receive the acceptance and encouragement that community life offers. According to the authors, the postliberal college should be a place that embodies a community's most cherished ideals—cooperation, harmony, and love—in contrast to the standards most universities have perfected—"competition, hierarchy, busyness, and isolation" (p. 145).

At the public school level, Andrew Oldenquist (1986), an educational philosopher, believes that the schools should be places that provide students opportunities to learn how to live in "smallish moral communities." It is in these "nesting" communities, Oldenquist maintains, that teachers and students can best learn to respect social morality, a work ethic, a sense of usefulness, and responsibility to others. Oldenquist, like most postliberals, thinks that it is unrealistic to speak of community in a global sense. He prefers to talk about communities as "tribes" that provide their members with a social morality and purpose. For Oldenquist, there is a "moral core" that constitutes the minimum requirement for peaceable social living: honesty, fairness, and respect for people's bodies, ideas, and property. The correlative virtues are courage, diligence, self-respect, and respect for the democratic process. The ultimate question that teachers must ask, according to Oldenquist, is this: What are a child's chances to grow up to live well and happily without courage, without honesty, without a sense of fairness, without respect for the rights of others?

THE CIVIC-LIBERAL SCHOOL AND COLLEGE. For such civic-liberal communitarians as Benjamin R. Barber (1992) and Robert Coles (1993), the college ought to be a site for community service, where students can practice firsthand how to live in a democracy, be an active citizen, and struggle with the responsibilities of freedom. For Barber, to be a democratic citizen requires more than being simply a "rights bearer" or accepting responsibilities only to one's family and job. To be a citizen also obligates a person to become a civic activist who gives something back to the community. Mandatory community service, according to Barber, is one way for a youngster to fulfill the obligation to be a full-fledged citizen.

Barber goes so far as to say that American colleges are actually among the best places to satisfy youth's "longing for community," because it is this "longing" that is the source of the desire to do service. In Barber's words: "When sited in a learning environment, the service idea promotes an understanding of how self and community, private interest and public good, are necessarily linked" (p. 249). Robert Coles (1993) goes one step further. To him, service is a moral obligation, because it is "a function not only of what we do but of who we are" (p. xxvi). In story after story, Coles demonstrates how his Harvard students are able to answer the question "How should I be living my life?" through the various service commitments they make to others in a variety of neighborhood settings off campus.

In a chapter entitled "The Communitarian School," Amitai Etzioni (1993) advances the public school as a place for "character formation." Unlike most character educators, however, Etzioni advocates a year of national service as an excellent "character builder" for all high school students. Reminiscent of Barber's and Coles's proposals for higher education, Etzioni calls for a program of high school service that is useful to the community, encompassing such possibilities as environmental improvement, tutoring, and helping the infirm elderly. For Etzioni, national service is a "grand sociological mixer" that puts students in contact with people from different racial, class, and regional backgrounds, with the purpose of developing shared values and bonds. Etzioni maintains that community service encourages the cultivation of such virtues as hard work, productivity, responsibility, civility, and cooperation—virtues that will effectively prepare high school students to be productive democratic citizens and to go on to college or into the military or workplace with enhanced maturity and skills.

The Communitarian Curriculum

Generally, the communitarian curriculum is a culturally conservative one, with the possible exception of its emphasis on public service. It includes most of the traditional subjects embodied in the liberal arts and in America's cultural heritage, but, most important, the communitarian curriculum organizes these subjects in such a way as to encourage students' loyalty to the values of their local and national communities. To this end, the communitarian curriculum is rich in literature, history, and religion— content that is a particularly strong reinforcer of the sense of community, tradition, transcendence, and civic responsibility that all young people will need to develop in order to become excellent human beings and good democratic citizens. The communitarian curriculum also includes subject matter that is critical of the principle of liberal individualism whenever it intentionally or unintentionally threatens to trump the value of communal identity.

The Sectarian Curriculum.   Arthur F. Holmes (1975) maintains that because a Christian college ought to be a near-perfect communal embodiment of Christian values, its curriculum should be organized in such a way as to help young people relate everything intellectual to their religious faith. For Holmes, the liberal arts—especially literature, history, philosophy, theology, and psychology—are best equipped to get students to "glorify God in all [their] creatureliness" (p. 23). According to Holmes, the question to which a sound, sectarian curriculum responds is not "What can [the student] do with it [education]?" but "What can it do to [the student]?" Thus a sectarian curriculum eschews narrow career content. In its place, it encourages "not only self-understanding, but also an understanding of other people and of social institutions and processes" (p. 35), with the purpose of helping students "become more fully human in the image of God" (p. 36).

At the elementary and secondary levels of *public* schooling, Robert L. Simonds, President of the National Association of Christian Educators and Citizens for Excellence in Education (1994), sums up what he believes a sound secular curriculum should include in order to solidify the public schools' "traditional ties with parents and the public" (p. 14). Among the subjects he mentions are: the Ten Commandments; "reading, writing, science, geography, English, grammar, composition, mathematics, patriotism, democracy, and American culture" (p. 14); and creation science. He is equally clear on what he thinks the public school curriculum should omit: multicultural education, sex education, and New Age religious practices. Simonds is particularly upset with educational scholars such as Theodore Sizer and John Goodlad, because their "agenda" is "atheism, socialism, and an anti-democratic world globalism" (p. 15). For Simonds, any public school curriculum that teaches "children to empty themselves of their own values [transmitted from parents, church, and culture] and accept a set of suggested values [atheist/socialist]" (p. 15) only serves to separate children from their communities.

THE POSTLIBERAL CURRICULUM. For Willimon and Naylor (1995), the postliberal curriculum in higher education demands nothing less than a "counterrevolution." Specific to the detail, Willimon and Naylor assert that every undergraduate student should be required to take 20 required academic courses, 21 elective courses, and 8 physical education courses (p. 129). Included in the required courses would be a semester-long seminar on "The Search for Meaning" that would "integrate the spiritual, intellectual, emotional, and physiological dimensions of life" (p. 130). Additionally, all students would study English composition, mathematics, a foreign language, literature, history, philosophy and religion, basic science, social science, fine arts, and physical education. Such a curriculum, according to Willimon and Naylor, sends two messages: Faculty are willing to accept the moral responsibility for the character formation of their students and begin requiring a set course of study complete with rigorous intellectual expectations; and students understand that "there is no intellectual life that is not lived in community," the fundamental setting for any person's "search for meaning" (p. 143).

While he does not identify specific academic courses, C. A. Bowers (1987) does suggest that elementary and secondary curricula should attempt to "restore community." To this end, he recommends the following: Curricula should expose students to a sense of their "collective history," which will necessitate a knowledge of their community's traditions and memories. Curricula should help students to develop "communicative competence," in order that they might learn how language has shaped them as particular social-cultural beings—that is, how they both use and are used by language. Curricula should assist students in "rethinking the liberal paradigm" (p. 142). Curricula should give students the opportunity to learn the "oral traditions" and the "Western literate tradition" (p. 169), as well as encourage them to "retell their [own] stories," so they might locate themselves in particular "communities of memory" (p. 150). And curricula should help students to "live in harmony with the rhythms and resources of the natural environment" (p. 172).

THE CIVIC-LIBERAL CURRICULUM. Without designating particular courses, except for one—"a mandatory civic education course"—Barber (1992) believes a good college curriculum "folds notions of community, democracy, and citizenship into pedagogy" (p. 254). He believes that a curriculum should be grounded in the following "civic" principles: Civic education must be experiential; show the link between rights and responsibilities; prohibit discriminatory and abusive/addictive behavior; teach respect for diversity, pluralism, and equal rights; and provide community service (pp. 254–256). Although this type of civic education course is currently being offered at Barber's Rutgers University, it is experimental and voluntary. But its early success demonstrates to him that college can, indeed, "educate the young to the obligations of the democratic citizen" (p. 261).

Diane Ravitch (1984), an educational historian and a civic liberal, believes that all children need an understanding of their culture's traditions, including art, literature, philosophy, law, architecture, language, government, economics, and social life. These subject matters establish for students a context of living a human life in a particular time and place, and give them resources on which they can draw for the rest of their lives. Ravitch would organize a public school curriculum in such a way as to show that justice, autonomy, and community are realizable ideals only in a society where the spirit of social continuity is dominant. For her, citizenship in America is rooted in a moral tradition, beginning in the ancient paideia and extending to the contemporary ideal of a more humane and just commonwealth.

Communitarian Instructional Methods

Communitarian educators see themselves as agents of transmission. What they transmit is mainly a communal sense of the self that students can then incorporate into their moral characters. Instructionally, communitarian educators themselves try to model the communitarian virtues by being paragons of stability in a society racked by continual change, moral relativism, the deterioration and virtual disappearance of local, constitutive communities, and loss of personal identity. *Inter alia*, communitarian educators lead face-to-face, seminar conversations; work with small learning groups; establish traditions, ceremonies, and rituals that give students a sense of place; provide on-site, experiential opportunities for service learnings and civic practices; and allow for personal and group expressions of religious devotion.

SECTARIAN INSTRUCTIONAL METHODS. Although Mark R. Schwehn (1993) does not explicitly identify himself as a sectarian communitarian (he does call himself a Christian who values community), he nevertheless reveals that he resigned a tenured position at the University of Chicago in order to teach at Valparaiso ("vale of paradise") University, a church-related institution (p. viii). He did this, he says, because Valparaiso keeps certain questions alive for him about the relationship between religious faith and the pursuit of truth that are "at the center of [his] understanding of the meaning of academic life" (p. viii). For Schwehn, classrooms are communities where students learn the "disciplines and the virtues" that are fundamental to communal life elsewhere (p. 34). These "disciplines and virtues" include such spiritual dispositions as "humility, faith, self-sacrifice, and charity," and they are indispensable to the type of "spirited inquiry" that universities, both secular and religious, should foster (p. 34). Thus, when Schwehn teaches, he tries to profess the Christian virtues by being a personification of those virtues—by putting the "best construction" on everything, in the name of charity and humility, always looking for the good in what an author or student proposes, and never ridiculing or diminishing the worth of another's insight.

Also, Schwehn believes that teaching should be the primary activity that a college values, rated over publication, collegiality, research, consultation, and advising (p. 58). And colleges must interpret and appraise these other activities, as important as they are in their own right, in light of how effectively they function as *teaching* devices. Schwehn wants college professors to think of their students as friends, in the Aristotelian sense, who engage in conversation together as the "highest expression of a kind of love" (p. 62). Ultimately, for Schwehn, these Christian virtues are social and relational, and therefore they are able to "sustain community" because of their historically religious nature (p. 84). (I will return to Schwehn's work in the last chapter.)

For John H. Westerhoff (1992), teachers in a "parochial" school should be "intentional" about every aspect of Christian life in and out of the classroom. Each day, for him, would begin with prayer and celebration of the Eucharist. Teachers would organize the school year around the church calendar, celebrating only church holidays. In the classroom, teachers would reward cooperation and other Christian virtues, and they would attempt to live a simple life of compassion and service, praying in public frequently. There would be ample opportunity each day in the classroom for work, service, and play, and the study of the arts especially would encourage students to intuit and feel as well as to think. There would be no groupings based on age and ability. Teachers would value equally both verbal and nonverbal communication, as students live out their Christian stories in a variety of formal and informal ways. The key for the teacher, according to Westerhoff, is to be a role model whose life is exemplarily Christian, whose major task is to teach young people how "to be Christian in an alien world" (p. 281). In other words, Christian schools exist to make Christians, and, instructionally, a teacher is a "Christian-maker."

POSTLIBERAL INSTRUCTIONAL METHODS.   Willimon and Naylor (1995) quote Stanley Hauerwas on college teaching: "Having been given the privilege to spend most of our lives reading books is a reminder that our task as teachers is to ensure the wisdom of our civilization by instilling in our students a passion for the examined life" (p. 119). In the spirit of Hauerwas and the need to live an examined life, the authors urge that professors, first of all, be provocateurs of meaning in students' lives. To this end, professors need to develop relationships with their students, need to teach core courses, and need to interact with students in the classroom, sometimes as colleagues and sometimes as mentors. According to Willimon and Naylor, all professors are ipso facto moral educators, and hence they should always take responsibility for being moral examples. Professors should continually raise ethical questions, no matter the academic discipline or topic being discussed. They should do much more team-teaching, in order to hone their "undeveloped" pedagogical skills, and should downplay the use of computer technology in favor of residential college seminars, lectures, discussions, and small-group research projects. For the authors, too much student "research" has become merely "a quick trip to the computer" to search for databases. Willimon and Naylor believe that only in "small learning communities" where faculty and students share values and common aims will students be most likely to cultivate the communitarian virtues of integrity, cooperation, trust, and human empathy (p. 147).

C. A. Bowers (1987) believes that teachers ought to interact with students according to a "bioregional" approach to communitarian education. His teachers would get out in the world of nature with their students, and teach the principles of self-sufficiency and ecological balance by practicing them directly. They would grow and prepare food, share planning activities with students, use fewer energy-intense technologies, and encourage the use of oral traditions of communication (p. 160). In addition to this experiential, Deweyian orientation to teaching a bioregional ethic, teachers would also help students learn about their literary past, particularly the heritage accumulated in the Western literate tradition. Teachers thus would be storytellers, story eliciters, and book-discussion leaders, all with the aim of helping students to resolve their "deepest existential questions" (p. 169). The root metaphor of bioregional education, for Bowers, is the "interdependency of all life forms," and this is the ideal teachers should strive to realize in all they do with students (p. 163).

CIVIC-LIBERAL INSTRUCTIONAL METHODS. Jean Bethke Elshtain (1995) quotes the political philosopher Michael Oakeshott on the value of conversation in the university:

> A conversation [should be] an endless unrehearsed intellectual adventure in which, in imagination, we enter into a variety of modes of understanding

the world and ourselves and are not disconcerted by the differences or dismayed by the inconclusiveness of it all. (p. 84)

Thus, for Elshtain, the college teacher is foremost a conversation leader who, despite fundamental ideological, class, and ethnic differences with students, still engages them in the classroom as political equals. Notwithstanding their many differences, according to Elshtain, she and her students still inhabit the "same world together," and because they both presumably value the "democratic habits," then they must be willing to engage in mutually respectful, rough-and-tumble debate and dialogue on highly controversial issues. For Elshtain, professors and students must be open to the possibility of forging "at least provisional agreements" on the issues that separate them.

She dislikes the "new multiculturalism" because it promotes "incommensurability," it "serves interests and ends imposed by militant groups" (p. 81), and it ruptures any sense of democratic community. As a professor, Elshtain presumes that neither she nor her students are "stuck inside our own skins," and so she teaches in such a way as to "open the world up" instead of "imprisoning [students] in terms of race, gender, or ethnicity" (p. 86). She wants her students to know that "decency, honor, friendship, fidelity, and fairness" (p. 88) are the moral stuff of democracy and that democracy is the one thing "worth fighting for in a world of paradox, ambiguity, and irony" (p. 89).

For Amitai Etzioni (1993), the teacher is primarily a moral educator whose task is to form civic character. His fundamental pedagogical principle is that "experiences are more effective teachers than lectures" (p. 103). Thus teachers should take pride in constructing classroom environments that exemplify the best virtues of communitarian living: Educators must stress that the school is "a set of experiences," and these experiences should be nonconfrontational, orderly, supportive, respectful, and fair. According to Etzioni, activities such as the classic one generated by Jane Elliott in 1968 to divide her third-grade class into two groups by eye color teach the immorality of racial discrimination far better than any lecture or sermon. He believes that the most effective instructional methods for communitarian teachers grow out of the bonds they create with their students. Thus teachers must spend a lot of out-of-class time with young people in order to make contacts that are "more encompassing, extensive, and value rich" (p. 108).

CONCLUSION

In the next chapter, I will touch critically upon some issues in the communitarian initiative that students frequently raise in my classes. While I fundamentally agree with the communitarians' general assertion that it is mainly in our primary groups that we shape our moral identities, I am also aware that individuals do, in fact, belong to a number of affiliative groups during the course of a lifetime, many of which are in continuous and serious moral conflict. Some are voluntary, some involuntary; some require more internal ideological agreement than others; and some stress inclusivity rather than exclusivity. Essentially, I support David A. Hollinger's (1995) observation that, in a "postethnic America," instead of asking "What identifies the *we*?" and "How can *I* belong?" we should ask "How can I *widen* the circle of the we?" and "How can I change the *power structure* within the circle?" and "How can I build 'life-projects' *outside of*, rather than through, particular communities?" (p. 106).

At their margins, I contend, the sectarian and postliberal communitarian perspectives encourage a morality of conformity, a provincialism that binds individuals to ideologically restrictive groups. This is in direct contrast to the "moral cosmopolitanism" I believe pluralistic democracies will require of its citizens in the future. For example, one of my hopes is that civic-liberal communitarians can help citizens to reconcile the demands of their local communities with the needs of emerging global communities. I take seriously Jeremy Waldron's assertion that "We owe a debt to the world and to the global community and civilization, as well as whatever we owe to any particular region, country, nation, or tribe" (quoted in Hollinger, 1995, p. 108).

CHAPTER 5

Imparting the Communitarian Virtues: A Morality of Conformity

[Communitarians] rhapsodize about neighborhoods, churches, school boards, and so forth; but they never provide sufficient detail about the institutions they favor to allow us to compare the advantages and disadvantages of illiberal community with the vices and virtues of the liberal societies we know.
—Stephen Holmes, The Anatomy of Antiliberalism, *1993*

How much more satisfying the life in an "organic community" than the life of alienation in a modern state! The ideal of the hive is seductive and fuels all communitarian ideologies. But the bee-like creatures of our hive-like world are not in fact kind to each other; each is indifferent to the others except insofar as the others are parts of the whole. . . . The ideal of the state as hive cannot be made real: it is amazing that communitarians have expected otherwise.
—Judith Jarvis Thomson, The Realm of Rights, *1990*

A morality of conformity has a good face and a bad face. Among its benefits, a morality of conformity correctly reminds us that virtues are always intimately bound up with the group—shaped, transmitted, and reinforced in a community, sustained and nurtured by personal associations. Without communal connections, morality would lack context, history, common goals, and group validation or censure. Among its liabilities, a morality of conformity creates dependency, suppresses autonomy, and, in its worst forms, encourages an unswerving "groupthink." It becomes a morality of pseudo-connection, a morality of the hive. The ultimate losers can sometimes be personal liberty and an overriding concern for rights, and social justice, beyond the local group. Thus a morality of conformity can frequently become a vindication for ideological uniformity and bigotry.

At this juncture, even though I risk breaking up the flow of the more formal narrative that precedes this section, I will recount a personal experience I had in teaching the communitarian initiative that raises compelling questions about the weaknesses of communitarianism. Several years ago, in a moral-education course, I circulated an article consisting of an "exchange of views" between someone who identified himself as an "individualist" and someone who called himself a "communitarian." I deliberately deleted the authors' names, as well as other identifying characteristics, for reasons I will mention shortly. When we discussed this "exchange of views" in class, every single student agreed that the "communitarian" had convincingly "won" the "debate." In fact, for most, it was no contest. But when I asked if the communitarian had convinced anyone to "convert" to his way of thinking about virtue, not one student responded positively. In fact, every student in the class initially identified with the individualist's view on education and morality, even though the majority regretfully acknowledged that liberal individualism was a fundamentally indefensible moral position. Predictably, this outcome occurs every time I decide to distribute the article in my classes.

Eventually, when I confess to students that *I* am the author of the communitarian piece (Griffin & Nash, 1990) and that I kept my authorial identity a secret from them so as to provoke a more candid conversation about the two points of view, nobody undergoes any startling change of mind. A few even attack me for my "duplicity." But, as if to confirm MacIntyre's allegation that, in an incommensurable age, we are all liberal individualists, most of my students remain resolute liberal individualists to the very end, even while they find the communitarian perspective— especially the civic-liberal strand—to be the more morally compelling one. I think one of the reasons why students generally like the ideas in my article but nevertheless decide to maintain a healthy skepticism regarding its pertinence to their own situations is that they see through the exaggerations and blindspots in my defense of communitarianism.

I originally wrote the article for a couple of reasons. I wanted to provide a lively intellectual counterpoint to my colleague's libertarian ideas. And, at the time, I was struggling with some philosophical questions of my own. By way of trying to be scrupulously fair to the communitarian view, and perhaps being a little too eager to find the truth in this perspective for my own life, I made three basic mistakes when writing the piece. (1) I overestimated the extent to which I thought religion could bind a nation together in a way that most closely approximates a community, and I underestimated the dangers of complacency, self-righteousness, and undue political influence whenever *sectarians* deliberately extend themselves into the public square. (2) Because I did not truly "live inside" the *postliberal* hermeneutic, I downplayed the antiliberal darkside of this initiative, with its deep-seated suspicion of such democratic principles as individual liberty, self-governance, and tolerance of difference. (3) Because I was very sympathetic to the citizenship piece of the *civic-liberal* initiative, I tended to mitigate the sentimentality and middle-class nostalgia of its faith in the ameliorative role of so-called "mediating" institutions and traditional mores. I also chose to ignore the distortions in this initiative's unremitting criticism of a rights-based moral language.

At the present time, however, I intend to take a more critical look at the communitarian initiative from a virtue perspective. The guiding questions for me are the following:

- Is the communitarian vision a viable one for a democracy?
- What special virtues do communitarians wish to impart in the nation's schools and colleges?
- In what senses is the communitarian initiative helpful/harmful to the character-building mission they would carry out in our nation's educational institutions?

SECTARIAN COMMUNITARIANISM

I find that few of my older students have remained lifelong members of their childhood churches. And, increasingly, a number of younger students arrive in my classes having had no prior formal religious experience at all. Wade Clark Roof (1993) found in his extensive research on the spirituality of baby boomers that the vast majority of his respondents thought of themselves as "spiritual individualists" rather than religious believers. He discovered that, if they had any religious predilections at all, boomers tended to express their faith in language that was private, subjective, flexible, elastic, nonauthoritative and nonauthoritarian, highly relativistic, diverse, self-fulfilling, transient, and nonaffiliative (Roof uses all of these terms to describe boomer faith several times throughout his study).

Roof's research accurately mirrors my own experience with students whenever we discuss religion and morality, and explains, for me, why so many of them frequently recoil from what they consider to be the authoritarian moral pronouncements of the sectarians we study. I often hear from students the familiar complaints that sectarian education is bad because it breeds the vices of bigotry, divisiveness, and intolerance; that it presupposes an absolute truth that then gets imposed on people; and that, in the end, it is totally dysfunctional, because it is powerless to settle moral disputes and resolve doubts in a secular setting with so many competing perceptions regarding right and wrong. As liberal individualists and as postmoderns, my students see little place in today's world for a sectarian approach to community building because, for them, "religious tolerance" is an oxymoron, as even a cursory glance at twentieth-century history will confirm. And so, in place of institutionalized religion, many opt instead for a "personal spirituality" to guide them.

Constitutionally, America is not a Judeo-Christian country. However, from its earliest years, as Bellah and colleagues (1985) have shown, the United States had religious meaning to the colonists. In fact, a pattern of religious establishment existed in America's colonies throughout their history. Over time, the sheer diversity of religious groups, the presence of dissenters, deists, and rationalists in the colonies, and the overall impact of Enlightenment thought on American liberalism finally resulted in the disestablishment of religion and its ultimate consignment to the private sphere of life. Religion did not stop being concerned about moral order or community, of course, but now it began to emphasize self-control and voluntary association (Bellah et al., 1985). Americans, in general, became more autonomous in their practice of religion, more privately spiritual, more skeptical of religious leaders speaking *ex cathedra* and making dogmatic declarations on matters as wide-ranging as politics, sex, and economics.

From the sectarians' point of view, of course, such independence is a false ideal: It delivers not autonomy but loneliness and vulnerability, and separates people from their communities forever. In fact, Steven M. Tipton (1982) has shown that a "personal mysticism" often lacks an effective social discipline, makes too many compromises with the world, and is frequently indistinguishable from the therapeutic quest for self-esteem. But from my students' perspective, a little loneliness and metaphysical uncertainty are not too high a price to pay in the process of winning their independence from "dogmatic" religious authorities. As one student recently declared in class:

> My self-esteem is much better now that I'm living my life as an exile from the Catholicism of my parents. It's true I miss our tight little Sunday-morning community after mass and the Saturday-evening socials, but now I'm my own person, and I make up my own mind about morality. Those church folks would absolutely "freak" if they knew I've been living with my boyfriend, we use birth control, and we haven't been to mass since high school.

What this student utterly fails to understand, I think, is that it is most unlikely many Catholics today would "freak" over her living arrangements—nor would the majority of people from any other mainline religion, for that matter. In my estimation, the problem of the mainline churches is not that they are too doctrinal or authoritarian but that they have become far too secular. In fact, one could make a case that it makes no sense at all to look to the mainline churches, or even to smaller evangelical ones, to restore a sense of community and virtue to American private *or* public life. Most churches, including even the smaller nondenominational types, are in the throes of great self-doubt about their true mission (Weaver & Appleby, 1995; Wuthnow, 1988). And, to a great extent, sectarian schools and colleges are in the same situation as well (Marsden, 1994; Noll, 1994). American mainline churches everywhere are in a bind: On the whole, they are anti-ecumenical, beset on all sides by evangelicals who themselves are caught up in various types of internecine strife, facing scores of dropouts, and delicately allied with the secular society, which wants religion confined to the private sphere (Bellah et al., 1985; Marty, 1985).

When sectarian religious educators such as Stanley Hauerwas (1991), John H. Westerhoff (1992), and Arthur F. Holmes (1975) talk about removing themselves from the secular arena and carrying out their "holy experiments" to "make Christians," in isolation from the larger American society, then, I believe, they are actually playing into the hands of a secular America that experiences them as atavistic, somewhat irrational, but certainly tolerable if they will only stay in their place. What is becoming increasingly apparent, however, is that sectarians advance neither the common good nor their own interests very well. Too often they align themselves with the view of politics as a contest of warring ideologies around special-interest topics such as abortion (e.g., the Christian Coalition), or else they confine their influence to their own rapidly diminishing communities, motivated mainly by a rudimentary need to survive and provide intragroup comfort.

Actually, the question of the interplay of smaller religious communities, the schools and colleges, and the larger society is extremely complex. How, in a pluralist society, can unique sectarian communities nurture and transmit their virtues? How can the churches and the schools and colleges carry on normative conversations with the larger society? On the one hand, if Christian educational communities such as Hauerwas's (1991) and Arthur Holmes's (1975) are serious about transmitting only the sectarian virtues, then they somehow have to separate themselves from the dominant secular culture. On the other hand, these sectarian communities cannot be irretrievably rigid and severed from the dominant society either. A certain amount of freedom and engagement with the outside world is essential because, as Plato and Aristotle never tired of reminding their followers, virtue can never be fulfilled in isolation. Virtue is essentially a social undertaking. This is why sectarians such as Schwehn (1993) and, to some extent, Westerhoff (1992) talk about the need to initiate stimulating, *pluralistic* religious dialogues in the schools and colleges.

In my estimation, the Christian churches are able to make their most important virtue contributions by consistently and openly living their beliefs, and by challenging those trends in the society that are notoriously anti-Christian in outlook; for example, runaway consumerism, excessive corporate profiteering, racial bigotry, sexual exploitation, and, yes, the media's and higher education's trivialization of religious belief. The self-described populist and communitarian Christopher Lasch (1995) reminds us that the "heart and soul" of religious faith is not to console believers but to confront evil. In fact, there are at least a few communitarians who believe that the *schools and colleges* should also exhibit that same "heart and soul" and start to challenge similar kinds of secular abuses (Carter, 1993; Neuhaus, 1987).

The valid insight of the sectarians is that, today, public (and private) schools and colleges are caught between two conflicting missions, neither of which gets at the true "heart and soul" of education. Either the schools and colleges default on their obligation to teach Judeo-Christian virtues in favor of cultivating those academic and technical competencies calculated to get students into first-rate colleges, graduate schools, and careers—or they become social service agencies whose charge is to bolster students' self-esteem and liberate a number of minority groups from their "oppression." Rarely, in the view of the sectarians, do they hear schools and colleges express much interest in matters of religion, faith, character, or virtue—for them, issues that form the irreducible core of genuine community life. In the equally valid view of the secularists, however, the uncertainty is always how to raise these concerns in public without stepping over the sacrosanct line that separates church and state, home and school, and offending non-Christian believers, agnostics, and atheists.

Stephen L. Carter (1993), Christopher Lasch (1995), and Warren A. Nord (1995), moderate communitarians who also express strong religious convictions, warn that the line is often ephemeral. The problem, for them, is not always how to keep religious issues out of politics and public education, but how to subject political and educational life to religious criticism without losing sight of the inevitable tension that exists between the realms. In their view, sectarian insights and criticisms regarding the secular realm can revitalize—without invalidating—the traditions of the Enlightenment and Western democracy. The biblical view of the dignity of all human beings keeps alive an alternative perception of humanness that is fundamentally different from the one-dimensional idolatries of so many advanced capitalistic societies; that is, if human beings are created in the image of God, then they are not simply "capital" or "human resources." While each of these more moderate sectarians is correctly critical of right-wing religiosity, each still remains convinced that the religious perspective alone has the power to address so many levels of human need, including morality, community, wholeness, tradition, peace, faith, justice, hope, and love.

The sectarians have an important contribution to make to the fostering of virtue in our nation's schools and colleges. Christopher Lasch (1995) has pointed out that the function of religion in a secular-dominated society should be instructional: It should continually point out the disparity that so often exists in a secular pluralist society between public *professions* of faith and actual *observations* of faith in practice. In a way, Hauerwas (1991) is right. Religion ought to be at "war" with the larger culture, calling politicians, clergy, and the rest of us to task whenever we claim to be what we are not. Today, as in biblical times, religion more than ever needs to shake people out of their complacency and self-righteousness, and challenge their "self-esteem" whenever it is too easily, or conveniently, won. The key problem, though, and one that Hauerwas mostly evades, is to find the most effective *language* for shaking and challenging a democratic polity. Hauerwas would choose to enrage. He would do better to engage.

Biblically, religion was never meant to give people a set of definitive and comforting answers to the existential complexities of life. From Job in the Old Testament to Paul and Peter in the New, religious faith has always been a struggle to reconcile the devastating presence in the world of good and evil, wealth and poverty, authenticity and hypocrisy, kindness and cruelty. At the very least, religion must continue to force the perennial existential questions on the modern world that make us all very nervous and very insecure: Why do I exist? How can I live a morally authentic life? How do I deal with my human finitude? How can I live virtuously with others? What can I ever really know, or hope? These questions remind us that purposelessness, suffering, alienation, and death will continue "to hang over our pleasures and triumphs, calling them into question" (Lasch, 1995, p. 244). Or in William James's more dramatic language: "Back of everything is the great spectre of universal death, the all-encompassing blackness" (quoted in Lasch, p. 244). In America, where the cults of physical exercise, dieting, and psychological support groups have become the "new religions," people need to realize that there is no final, secular fortification against the obdurate fear of powerlessness, alienation, pain, and death.

But I believe the sectarians have an even more significant contribution to make as well—a *civic* one. Democracy is desperately in need of many of the more conservative sectarian virtues: self-sacrifice, humility, charity, faith, hope, love, patience, even a sense of redemption. But these need to be tempered with other kinds of dispositions. Americans everywhere have been shaken in recent years by the fragility of the social bond: racial, ethnic, and gender animosity; the "culture wars"; corporate greed with its massive downsizing and buy-outs; and the resultant ever-widening gap between the social classes, marked by a dramatic increase of "poverty amidst affluence." The sectarians need to be far more aware that a political system grounded exclusively in the principles of individualism, self-interest, and entitlement is not only inimical to the communitarian interests of Christians. Equally important, this political system has simply not been adequate to protect the rights of the most vulnerable groups in the United States, including an expanding segment of the disenfranchised middle class.

In a past era, another sectarian, the Protestant theologian Reinhold Niebuhr (1932, 1935, 1943), maintained that belief in God is not like feeling warm inside, nor is it an invitation to abandon the secular world. Niebuhr was put off by easy belief, angered by cost-free piety, and thoroughly mystified by a fortress mentality on the part of some Christians. His own lifelong task was to weld together the tragic sense of life *and* the pursuit of justice. For his entire career Niebuhr sought to combine the virtues of self-interest, social commitment, social justice, ultimate concern, and community affiliation in a way that recognized the finite character of life, but also attempted to transform the world (Fox, 1985).

What I find most powerful in Niebuhr's Christian vision is that, like postmodernists today, he recognized the *hermeneutical* element in human existence: There are no decisive answers to the problems of human finitude, only provisional solutions. All of our interpretations are conditioned by our historical contexts and hence, while useful, they are not absolute. We need "metanarratives" to make sense of our lives, even though we know them ultimately to be flawed social constructions. And life is best understood as a complex admixture of contingency, opacity, irony, and paradox (Diggins, 1994). I believe the sectarians could learn much from Niebuhr's sense of irony and paradox whenever they attempt to speak their truths to the nonsectarian world. Their insights into virtue and community would be far more salient and persuasive, I am convinced, if they also included a genuine hermeneutical element in their discourse.

Finally, I think the sectarian communitarians could benefit greatly from reading the work of a Catholic social theologian, the Jesuit John Courtney Murray (1960), who wrote the highly influential *We Hold These*

Truths: Catholic Reflections on the American Proposition. Inter alia, they would learn a great deal about *how* to communicate their "truths" to the society at large. Murray never once advocated that the church abandon the "naked public square" in order to live mainly with like-minded others who happen to share the same "religious story." Instead, Murray, the intellectual who drafted the "Declaration on Religious Freedom" for the Catholic Church's Second Vatican Council in 1965, claimed that the church must always be a vital part of the public conversation. But because America is a pluralist society, the public function of any church must never be to convert others to a particular theological point of view or to intrude itself in a doctrinaire way into the world of politics. Neither is it the function of government to resolve disputes among conflicting theological truths. Rather, for Murray, "the highest good of the civil multitude and the perfection of its civility" (pp. 74–75) is dialogue striving for consensus. And in a nonpartisan manner, the church must find its rightful and effective place in that civic dialogue. The best position, he thought, was for the church to share its traditional moral wisdom in a way that binds people together instead of tearing them apart (McBrien, 1987).

This may be very difficult, because many secularists believe the historical record on religion is all too clear: Sectarians throughout the world appear to have caused proportionately more evil than good, including censorship, censure, factioning, religious inquisitions, bigotry, terrorism, and wars. Louis P. Pojman (1995) catalogues some of these evils:

> The Medieval Crusades and Inquisition, the religious wars of the Reformation period, the present religious conflict in Northern Ireland between Roman Catholics and Protestants, the current devastation of the former Yugoslavia—where Christians and Muslims are killing each other, the Hindu–Muslim massacres in India, and the Ayatollah Khoumeni's order to kill author Salman Rushdie for writing his allegedly blasphemous book *Satanic Verses.* (pp. 246–247)

The difficult dilemma for sectarians today is to keep their religions from becoming dogmatic and intolerant without compromising their basic beliefs. In a cacophonous postmodern world of belief, unbelief, and disbelief, I would argue that sectarians and secularists need to agree on some fundamental moral "reference points" if each is to live peaceably and productively with the other. One beginning, of course, is for sectarians to demonstrate by their *witness* and not their *proselytism* that religion can be a force for good as well as evil. They might also show, in addition, how Western civilization has actually been living off the interest of Judeo-Christian religious capital for centuries, at least in trying to live up to its democratic ideals of human rights, social justice, and personal liberty. However, I do not believe a religious foundation is at all necessary to validate these democratic ideals. They are both worthy and defensible *in se* (in themselves).

Murray (1960) understood that exclusivist appeals to the Bible or to sectarian theology of one kind or another are the poorest ways to participate in public dialogue in a pluralist society. These types of pronouncements are counterproductive, Murray thought, because they fail to persuade people who do not share the same view of revelation, religious authority, or moral tradition. The correct role for any sectarian institution in America, according to Murray, is to generate greater clarity, coherence, and civility in the public conversation about controversial social issues by developing moral arguments that would be compelling even for non-Christians and atheists. And this should be done always in the spirit of "openness." In Murray's memorable words, "Civility dies with the death of dialogue. We are either locked together in argument or locked together in combat" (p. 14). My fear—shared by many students—whenever we discuss the sectarian communitarians in class is that sectarians would inadvertently "lock us together in combat," because of their open-and-shut approach to conversations about virtue and moral truth, and because so many, like Hauerwas (1981), opt to *separate* Christians from society rather than *incorporate* them.

POSTLIBERAL COMMUNITARIANISM

The postliberal communitarians, unlike the sectarians, speak less about religion and more about the excesses of liberalism, especially what they perceive to be liberalism's emphasis on individual rights and liberty, and its tendency to shatter traditional conceptions of community life by centering on the individual. The advantage of reading thinkers like C. A. Bowers (1987) and Alasdair MacIntyre (1984) is that they challenge students, many for the first time, to think seriously about the problem of virtue within a secular pluralist morality. These authors force us to ask whether the cardinal *liberal* virtues of tolerance, fairness, and openness are enough to satisfy people's deeper needs for meaning and belonging. And, by implication, they raise the question of whether the best that schools can do concerning the teaching of virtue is merely to help students to respect the freedom of others to construct their particular visions of the good life, and then to tolerate the certain amount of uneliminable chaos that is bound to result. For postliberals, this uneliminable chaos is the disastrous legacy of postmodernism's infatuation with relativism, nonfoundationalism, pluralism, and alterity (MacIntyre, 1984), concepts I examine in the last chapter.

The postliberal communitarians remind us that the recovery of virtue in the schools and colleges will not occur in any significant way until educators become highly sensitive to certain moral contradictions in the culture and to the apparent irreconcilability of these contradictions. The most difficult conflict, of course, is between a liberal state's commitment to autonomy, to welfare entitlements, and to a quest for universalizable moral rules, as opposed to a postliberal commitment to local communities with their familial and civic obligations and traditions. The contrast, as the postliberals see it, is between virtues shaped to deal with the specificity and traditions of local circumstances and those shaped to deal with overriding, community-free moral principles. The difficult question for my students therefore is whether it is ever possible to reconcile the virtues emanating from particular ethnic and family ties, religious heritages, and personal responsibility for behavior with virtues emanating from more abstract liberal rules about autonomy, fairness, and what is sometimes called free "consensual relationships" among adults.

My students are especially attentive to the *educational* implications of the postliberal moral vision. Postliberals are convinced that there can be no virtues worth imparting until citizens of a democracy have some recognition of a common good, one that transcends mere procedural safeguards such as due process, one that is rooted in enduring and vital reference points. They maintain there can be no virtue without a profound sense that my neighbor is my obligation and that communal life, along with the qualities it encourages, necessitates shared ideals and common dreams. And until the schools and colleges accept the challenge to transmit the heritage of the past with its enduring reference points, postliberals believe the search for worthwhile, teachable virtues is destined to be nothing more than an insipid pedagogical exercise—like reading "books of virtues," or doing values-clarification activities, or participating in character-building exercises without a common frame of moral reference or an interest in reaching moral consensus.

The postliberals continue to touch a highly responsive chord in my students when they raise additional sorts of educational questions: With all the emphasis on the principles of individual liberty, right to privacy, and freedom of choice in America today, how will teachers get young people to recognize their embeddedness in a particular community's narrative, traditions, symbols, rituals, languge, theology, and philosophy? How many of these youth will ever believe in anything worth fighting for, let alone dying for? Why is it that the younger generation is largely apolitical, anti-ideological, irreligious, and hedonistic? How many youth will hold even one uncompromising conviction about anything, beyond what they think is their absolute right to choose how to entertain themselves? Why is it that so few youth know, or even care, that the central American principles of self-determination and individual liberty have their origins in Judeo-Christian teachings? Where will young people go today, other than to the popular entertainment media, to form that set of core beliefs that ought to claim their devotion? And, finally, how can teachers help youth to stand for something, to speak truth to error because they are in possession of truths beyond the easy clichés of the day, when, in fact, youth (and some of their teachers) appear to believe in so very little and hope for even less?

The deeper we delve into the postliberal initiative, however, the greater the number of counterquestions my students raise in turn, especially as the postliberal repudiation of liberal individualism grows more and more intemperate. Then, in reaction, the students' questions flow:

- Are emotivism and incommensurability necessarily inevitable in a liberal democracy?
- Why do we need a *telos,* hierarchy, and tradition in order to arrive at a shared public moral rationale?
- Is it true that "unshakable foundations" are necessary for moral discourse and action?
- Why will moral autonomy and individual liberty inevitably lead to moral anomie?
- Is liberalism, in practice, always so narrow and selfish?
- Why are the virtues of tolerance, pluralism, and open-mindedness so corrupt?
- Is it, in fact, true that liberal individualism is philosophically indefensible?
- Are the postliberals right when they claim that there is no sense of community, no "narrative" to the liberal view?
- Why do postliberals consider "rights" to be such an unmitigated evil?
- Where would postliberals be without the right to question the value of the very liberal doctrine that guarantees them the right to question in the first place?

In my view, postliberals undercut the force and value of their communitarian initiative whenever they narrow their project to an attack on liberalism, as thinkers such as MacIntyre (1984) and, to some extent, Charles Taylor (1992) do. While these "antiliberals" tend to focus on liberal excess in their jeremiads, they end up caricaturing and demonizing all of liberalism. As a result, postliberals inaccurately depict liberal ideas. They also create a false dichotomy between community and individual liberty. And they misinterpret the function of rights in a democracy (Beauchamp & Childress, 1994). In a very balanced account (which I summarize in the next few paragraphs), Will Kymlicka (1995) argues that liberalism as a political philosophy is largely the creation of Enlightenment thinkers, such as John Locke, Immanuel Kant, and John Stuart Mill, and, in the postwar era, Isaiah Berlin, John Rawls, and Ronald Dworkin. What all of these thinkers agree on is the fundamental significance of the civil and political rights of individuals, especially in the areas of personal freedom—including freedom of conscience, speech, association, and occupation.

Basically, liberal individualists, the particular bane of postliberals such as MacIntyre (1984), contend that toleration is the only alternative to a state that would impose a particular religion on its citizens. Thus the separation of church and state is essential if people are to practice religious liberty. Liberals extend this principle to other spheres of life where citizens might have conflicting conceptions of what is good for them. The best the state can do, according to liberals, is to provide a "neutral" or "thin" framework for citizens to work out their own views of the good and then get out of the way, allowing individuals to pursue their goals as long as they avoid harming others. How else, argue liberals, can individuals coexist peaceably in a secular pluralist society with others who are probably different in philosophy, temperament, and lifestyle?

Furthermore, liberals argue that individual rights do not necessarily have to undermine membership in specific communities by competing with community rights. After all, rights have meaning only when they are understood, and supported, by smaller communities. Thus loyalty to the smaller group actually provides the best protection for individual rights. Neither does individual liberty have to destroy family and community life by privileging the freedom of individuals over the group. There is no reason, in principle, why individuals with the widest range of freedoms need to be alienated from smaller groups, including families. In fact, if the "hunger for community" that postliberals talk about is an accurate assessment of human need, then smaller "constitutive" (Sandel, 1982) communities will always find a way to survive.

Moreover, while shared commitments are certainly important, they do not always have to take the form of a strong solidarity or commonality. Why is it not possible for individuals to forge a common bond around some of the liberal principles, such as social justice, equality of opportunity, personal liberty, individual rights, self-restraint, and a mutual agreement to avoid harming others? (Ironically, the communitarian

Charles Taylor [1989] makes this same argument.) In a "postethnic" society, where people are more likely to be "moral cosmopolitans," lacking a unifying moral conception of the good life beyond these "thin" liberal principles, what else could realistically and noncoercively replace them (Hollinger, 1995)? And while MacIntyre argues that liberalism has no coherent conception of the good life—and thus ends up in moral incommensurability and subjectivism—as yet he has not come up with his own conception of the good that all people, including liberals, might embrace. In fact, MacIntyre (1984) sees only "barbarians" and "darkness" around him at this time, and so he is content to settle for "local forms of community" in order to sustain some degree of "civility, and the intellectual and moral life" (p. 263).

Contra MacIntyre, in spite of the recurring communitarian criticisms of liberal individualism through the years, I believe liberalism has proven to be remarkably durable, and resilient, since the Enlightenment. In Kymlicka's (1995) words:

> Dire warnings about liberalism's inability to contain the centrifugal tendencies of individual freedom can be found in every generation for the last three centuries, yet it appears that liberal societies have managed to endure while various forms of monarchy, theocracy, authoritarianism, and communism have come and gone. (p. 485)

For 300 years right up to the present, people throughout the world have increasingly opted for an open society rather than a closed, traditional one; for communities in which citizens can improve their beliefs and conventions through free discussion and collective effort; and for individual rights that provide protections against the arbitrary authority of the state and religious institutions, while promoting a sense of self-determination and individual safety during times of dissent and crisis (Beauchamp & Childress, 1994).

Jeffrey Stout (1988) diagnoses the postliberals as suffering from a case of "terminal wistfulness." Stephen Holmes (1993) claims they have ended up constructing a "community trap" that looks dangerously illiberal. Both thinkers remain skeptics on whether any kind of community can actually produce the kind of fraternity, solidarity, and harmony that postliberals promise for a postmodern world. Stephen Holmes (1993), in the excerpt that introduces this chapter, charges that while the postliberals tend to "rhapsodize" about neighborhoods, churches, and schools, they are notoriously deficient in providing helpful detail about how to create such "loving" communities. For example, he wonders: What sanctions will be necessary to sustain communities? What will be the proper role of the outsiders, the minorities, in communities governed by the majority? Will nonconformists be weeded out, or will they be allowed to become members of a disloyal opposition? Who in communities will defend civil liberties and individual rights?

C. A. Bowers's (1987) educational efforts to undertake the "restoration of community" around a "bioregional ethic" may be praiseworthy for some, but will he require this goal of everyone in the public schools? How will he handle the dissenters, be they students, teachers, or parents? What will Willimon and Naylor (1995) do to those students (and professors) who repudiate their "restructuring of higher education" into smaller "communities of learning" in order to pursue "meaning"? How will they handle those "apostates" for whom "meaning" is coessential with liberal individualist values? In spite of the dearth of concrete detail in the writings of most postliberals, though, the "hunger for community" appears as irrepressible as the "hunger for individual liberty" throughout the last 300 years and has lately begun to invade the writings of educators at all levels, as I have tried to show in the previous chapter.

I propose an educational alternative to the one-sided postliberal attack on liberal individualism: helping students to understand that there are at least six "senses" of individualism (Stout, 1988), three that we might consider "bad," and three "good." The bad senses are when individualism is excessively narcissistic, hedonistic, and utilitarian. All three have been used as an apology for selfishness and pleasure seeking, often at great cost to others as well as to the self. Utilitarian individualism is the individualism of the marketplace, the American university, politics, the entertainment world, professional sports, and to a large extent the everyday worlds of our students. It is bad when it is dangerously pragmatic—when utilitarians base moral decisions mainly on financial outcomes and cost-benefit calculations, as well as exclusive maximizing of self-interest. The good senses are when individualism is pluralistic and egalitarian; when it stresses self-transformation and the attainment of a personal excellence (the *arete* meaning of "virtue" in ancient Greece); and when it "de-centers" the individual in order to make the point that it is *together* that individuals stand or fall in the postmodern world, especially with respect to the protection of rights, liberty, and equality.

At the beginning of this chapter, I mentioned that I once wrote an essay supporting communitarianism. In that essay I came down on the side of what I called an "authentic-democratic-communitarian individualism." In spite of the essential irreconcilability of the three hyphenated adjectives, and my obvious desire to salvage something from each of the conflicting perspectives in order to reach a compromise, I still find this position personally attractive although very difficult to defend, either on liberal *or* communitarian grounds.

Historically and, I believe, laudably, education in America has provided many individuals with the utilitarian training necessary to attain the desirable middle-class lifestyles. And traditionally education has also been a noble means to form the democratic character that prizes individual liberty and rights. For a majority of citizens, schools have been quite effective in providing them with the occupational skills useful to the system and in forming this minimalist democratic character. But what this often crowds out, I am more than willing to acknowledge, is an education that goes beyond seeking private rewards and the advancement of individual liberty for privileged groups to one that promotes personal excellence *for all people* in the pursuit of the common good as the ultimate reward. However, I am simply unwilling to concur with the antiliberals that the principle of the common good must always override such democratic principles as fairness, individual liberty, and rights whenever these are in conflict. I am continually struck by the wisdom of history's lesson that while Americans have craved community, they fear dependence and tyranny more.

CIVIC-LIBERAL COMMUNITARIANISM

Mickey Kaus, author of *The End of Equality* (1992), represents the social egalitarian wing (I believe his book is mistitled) of the civic-liberal group of communitarians. He argues that liberals have historically tried to solve the problem of social inequality by advocating equality of income and wealth. He calls this approach to social equality "money liberalism," and his assessment of this strategy is that it has failed to reduce social inequalities. The reason, for Kaus, is that money equality is not the crucial variable in determining social equality. The key is to "change the attitudes and institutions that translate money differences, however large or small, into invidious social differences" (p. 20). Thus, for Kaus, civic liberalism tries to create a "noneconomic sphere of life"—a public community sphere—where people mingle with one another as citizens, equal in the sense that each has one vote and each has the right of equal access to the important social institutions—schools, libraries, parks, the military draft, museums, post offices, softball leagues, and so forth. The objective of civic liberalism is "to reduce the influence of money in politics, and to revive the public schools as a common experience" (p. 21) in order to enlarge the sphere of "egalitarian community life."

My students appreciate Kaus's distinctions between "money" and "civic" liberalism, and they enthusiastically support his wish to enlarge the civic sphere of community life where people from different social classes and ethnicities can mingle as political equals. They particularly approve of his desire to make the public schools the primary civic sphere. While some students are reluctant to accept his proposal that work should become the major qualification for government income assistance for families on welfare, most agree that somehow the middle class in America needs to assimilate the "underclass." Kaus is optimistic that, when the current welfare system ends, so too will middle-class resentment of the underclass with its attendant racial prejudice—because now the "ghetto poor" will have become a "working class." And refurbished public institutions like the draft, daycare centers, national service, a national health care system, and a genuinely democratized political process will place rich and poor Americans in frequent, face-to-face contact with each other.

While Kaus is a social utopian who pushes civic liberalism as far as it can go in trying to secure political equality for all people, Jean Bethke Elshtain (1995) and Mary Ann Glendon (1991) are far more moderate, and realistic, in their claims. Often, these two authors speak to educators in my classes in ways the other communitarians completely miss. My students are all too eager to agree with the authors, for example, that there is currently too much apathy regarding the democratic process among America's youth. Few of their own students know anything about America's classical political documents. Not many of their students ever bother to read a newspaper, watch a news broadcast on network television, or acquaint themselves with state and national political issues. Few have any intention of registering to vote, and many boast that their parents have not voted in years—so why should they? I remember a high school social studies teacher mentioning in my class that when one of her students disclosed in a discussion that she had watched "a little C-Span" with her parents the night before, not one student in her class knew what she meant. The teacher guessed, somewhat sheepishly—because she had never watched C-Span herself—that very few of her students' parents would know either.

Many of my students also share Elshtain's and Glendon's worry that those "mediating" institutions any democracy needs to survive are fast disappearing from people's lives. What, they ask, will be left to fill the "civic spaces" that exist between individuals and the state besides MTV, computer chat lines, shopping at Wal-Mart or "hanging out" at the local mall, or maybe a twice-yearly visit to the local church or synagogue? They wonder, along with Elshtain and Glendon, about where young people today will find worthy "virtue substitutes" for the fast-disappearing neighborhoods, churches, civic organizations, sandlot sports teams, groups like the CYO (Catholic Youth Organization), and even get-togethers around the kitchen table that were so prominent and supportive when they were growing up. Elshtain and Glendon have a way of whetting my students' appetites when it comes to communitarianism, and with minor quibbles, some of them even proclaim themselves to be "civic liberals," confessing with great relief that, now, they have finally found a nomenclature that fits their political inclinations.

But, of course, there are always the skeptics. Some wholeheartedly agree with the quote from Judith Jarvis Thomson (1990) at the beginning of this chapter that "the ideal of the state as hive cannot be made real" (p. 223). Some believe that Elshtain and Glendon are apolitical sentimentalists who overidealize the glories of the past and rely too much on so-called "mediating institutions" to provide a moral safety zone between individual and state interests. They fail to see, for example, how a local community can successfully stand up against the overweening power of the news media, multinational corporations, state departments of education, the Supreme Court, the federal government, the FDA, and the IRS. These institutions shape attitudes and set policies—not always beneficially—that eventually control everybody's life, membership in small, solidaristic groups notwithstanding. And students fear that mediating institutions, contrary to the authors' well-intended purposes, will actually end up domesticating and pacifying individuals who need less succor and therapy and more training in how to engage in vigorous political discourse in order to promote the goals of social equality and justice.

The skeptics are also very wary of the authors' blanket condemnation of a rights-based ethic in America and suspicious of their tendency to criticize and downplay those initiatives that come from the political left. They point out, for example, that the authors find much that is wrong with a politics of race, gender, and ethnicity but appear oblivious to the dangers of a local, provincial politics or of those intermediate institutions that may be racist or sexist in pursuing and protecting their own special interests. And they challenge the authors to justify their elitism whenever they denounce or patronize those working-class or poor people whose family arrangements do not fit the communitarian mode, or who spend their leisure time watching television or "hanging out" at malls rather than attending town meetings or doing community service, or who receive a third-rate education in the failing public schools and consequently do not go on to college.

Even though I grant the validity of the important caveats skeptical students raise, I happen to respect the civic-liberal agenda very much. In spite of its merits and continuing appeal, the principle of individual liberty is not enough to guarantee the good life to all of us. Civic liberals are right to challenge the axiom that it is only when individuals are left alone to pursue their own best interests that life will automatically improve for everyone. This premise is becoming less and less convincing as a moral argument for maintaining the liberal state. Furthermore, I appreciate the virtues civic liberals would impart in the schools and colleges as a powerful antidote to the three "bad senses" of liberal individualism I mentioned earlier: a capacity for hard work, connection, cooperation, public-spiritedness, civic activism, self-restraint, civility, mutually respectful dialogue and debate, a sense of moderation, equality of opportunity, social cohesion, and spiritual and moral sensitivity.

I do worry about one major problem, though, that rarely comes up in my course when we discuss communitarianism, even among the skeptics, and when it does they try to tiptoe around it—the unlimited accumulation of wealth in the United States and the political power that often accompanies it. So few civic liberals, and communitarians in general, are willing to mount a challenge against the growing economic inequality in this country, especially between the corporate classes and all the rest of us. Lasch (1995) says it well:

> A democratic society cannot allow unlimited accumulation. Social and civic equality presuppose at least a rough approximation of economic equality . . . a moral condemnation of great wealth must inform any defense of the free market. (p. 22)

And I would add that those civic liberals who identify themselves as social egalitarians need to back up their "moral condemnation" of unlimited wealth with potent political action—beyond mere armchair outrage and critique.

One civic liberal, Michael J. Sandel, has recently made a similar kind of argument in his long-awaited sequel to *Liberalism and the Limits of Justice* (1982). In his latest book, *Democracy's Discontent: America in Search of a Public Philosophy* (1996), Sandel argues that an "[un]fettered capitalism does nothing to repair the moral fabric of families, neighborhoods, or communities" (p. 315). Sandel makes the point that when 98% of the $826 billion increase in household incomes from 1979 to 1992 went to the top fifth of the population, Americans became more and more frustrated with politics and the civic life in general. Sandel blames Ronald Reagan for this state of affairs and criticizes him for being more of a "market conservative" than a "civic conservative" (p. 315). Of the four initiatives (including the postmodern) I cover in my classes, the liberationist initiative alone

manages to work up enough moral outrage to condemn obscene concen-
trations of wealth in the United States. Unfortunately, as I will show later,
the liberationists' moral wrath, at this stage of their work, alienates many
of my students, because it ends up mainly encouraging inveterate cultural criticism, social-class envy, and ideological self-righteousness.

In spite of my concerns regarding civic liberalism, however, I find it
very difficult to gainsay the importance of preparing young people to
be involved, active democratic citizens, able to participate effectively in
political discourse. I wholeheartedly applaud Glendon's (1991) insight
that youth need to know the *civic skills:* how to dialogue with each other,
how to compromise and find common ground with adversaries, how to
engage in open exchange—all with the purpose of becoming "peacemakers." I have had more than a few teachers and counselors in my courses
whose work in mediation and conflict resolution has actually changed
students' lives and transformed schools and communities in the process.
And I find Pratte's (1988) and Barber's (1992) emphasis on community
service and civic activism a wonderful way to integrate liberal learning,
experiential activities, and moral and citizenship education. What could
be a more effective approach in teaching young people how self and community, rights and responsibilities, and private interests and public goods
are tightly linked? I balk, however, at making community service a *mandatory* academic requirement for all youth, because the coercion of service
might just as easily produce undesirable as desirable social behavior.

An education in civic virtue realizes that all citizens in a democracy
must participate in governance and that full participation depends on the
virtues of moral awareness, prudential judgment, and reason. The way
that a free society solves its problems depends not only on its economic
and administrative resources but also on its political vision. The survival
of a free people depends on an informed, virtuous, and visionary citizenry. This rather platitudinous insight is no less true today than it was
when Thomas Jefferson made a similar observation in 1781. It is important to remember, however, that, even though Jefferson was a demo-
crat and a civic-liberal communitarian, he also hated every kind of absolutism, including the absolutism of any political order that might
arbitrarily restrict individual freedom. In a letter to James Madison of
January 1787, he boldly asserted: *Malo periculosam libertatem quam quietam
servitutem*—"I prefer freedom though fraught with dangers to servitude
with security" (quoted in Ulich, 1968, p. 257).

Democratic citizenship requires the sensitivity and sensibility to assess, weigh, and reach conclusions about public and private issues related
to the common good. Where but in the schools and colleges will students
learn these virtues? Further, a conception of the public good assumes the

existence of at least a roughly agreed-upon moral consensus in America. Where but in the schools and colleges will students come to grips with a common heritage and a common set of ideals? Further, there is a basic incompatibility between an unbridled free-market economy and a virtuous citizenry, as Lasch (1995) and Sandel (1996) have shown. Where but in the schools and colleges will students learn best how to balance these competing values?

I am well aware, as are many civic liberals, that the forging of a moral consensus should not be the exclusive function of the school or college but should occur in other mediating institutions, such as the home and church, as well. In theory, of course, educational institutions at all levels are far too entangled in the current *Kulturkampf* to take on such leadership alone. At the same time, I believe, it is mainly in the schools and colleges where changes in the moral climate of a society are channeled, however diffusely. It is over the course of their many years in educational institutions that youth acquire a vision of human nature and virtue. It is in the school and college, at the most rudimentary existential level, where people daily experience success and failure, the mystery of awe and terror, and where they initially attempt to resolve the tension between a life of private and public virtue.

In the end, though, what matters most to people in their everyday lives takes place not in the political arena but in the mediating structures of their own personal existence. It is on this point that the sectarians and the postliberals make their most cogent cases. As long as political systems in America continue down the path of moral delegitimation (Dionne, 1991), it will be education—as well as the church, family, and other smaller, civic structures—that holds the only real promise of binding together a nation, *and the world*, in a way that more nearly approximates *civitas* (a community that recognizes the rights of citizens).

CONCLUSION

Notwithstanding the above, however, Budziszewski (1995) makes the important point that "the polity is not a community in the simple sense, but a community of communities; not a hearth but a vestibule. That means that many stories contend" (p. 26). Budziszewski realizes, as do I, that in order to preserve the peace and to advance the public good, the various communities in this country, and in the international community as well, must try to reach a "strategic mutual accommodation" as a means to bring together the moral "stories" of contending communities. My fear, though, is that because neither the sectarians nor the postliberals appear interested in this kind of "accommodation," the search for common moral ground among the various communities seems doomed from the start. It is still my hope, nevertheless, that perhaps the civic liberals can someday overcome the deficiencies in their own brand of communitarianism enough to help the rest of us reach accord on those pivotal democratic virtues that cut across a variety of sectarian and secular "stories."

In the next chapter, I consider the liberationist political initiative in fostering a particular set of civic virtues—the "transformative" dispositions—and, by implication, the liberationist critique of neo-classical and communitarian conceptions of virtue and education.

CHAPTER 6

The Liberationist Initiative:
The Transformative Virtues

Education for liberation does not merely free students from blackboards just to offer them projectors. On the contrary, it is concerned, as a social praxis, with helping to free human beings from the oppression that strangles them in their objective realities.

— *Paulo Freire,* The Politics of Education: Culture, Power, and Liberation, *1985*

The transformative intellectual . . . is one who attempts to insert teaching and learning directly into the political sphere by arguing that schooling represents both a struggle for meaning and a struggle over power relations . . . one whose intellectual practices exhibit concern for the suffering and struggles of the disadvantaged and oppressed.

— *Peter McLaren,* Life in Schools: An Introduction to Critical Pedagogy in the Foundations of Education, *1994*

If all pedagogical practice is implicated in the production of stories, then it becomes imperative to raise the questions: Whose stories are being produced under what circumstances? What social relations do they legitimate? What histories do they exclude or include? How are they complicitous with legacies of patriarchy, colonialism, racism, and other forms of oppression?

— *Henry A. Giroux,* Disturbing Pleasures: Learning Popular Culture, *1994*

Feminist teachers, if they are to work to create a counter-hegemonic teaching, must be conscious of their own gendered, classed, and raced subjectivities as they confirm or challenge the lived experience of their students. This does not mean avoiding or denying conflict, but legitimating this polyphony of voices and making both our oppression and our power conscious in the discourse of the classroom.

— *Kathleen Weiler,* Women Teaching for Change: Gender, Class and Power, *1988*

In its most radical sense, critical pedagogy seeks to unoppress the oppressed and unite people in a shared language of critique, struggle, and hope to end various forms of human suffering. . . . Critical pedagogy incorporates a moral vision of human justice and decency as its common vision.

— *Barry Kanpol,* Critical Pedagogy: An Introduction, *1994*

What I am calling the "liberationist initiative" includes four main components: (1) It is a complex social analysis growing out of the interests of relatively powerless, oppressed groups—children, women, racial and ethnic minorities, among others. (2) It is a systematic critique of state power and authority and the ideologies sustaining them. (3) It is an analysis of particular kinds of oppression—silencing, denial, invalidation, indoctrination, and physical violence. (4) In its strictly educational form— *critical pedagogy* (my focus for this chapter)—it prescribes as the primary task of public schooling the identification of when individuals (and groups) are both oppressors and oppressed, as well as strategies for "liberating" individuals from these various oppressions—that is, ways to "undo the effects and eliminate the causes of oppression" (Berlak, 1994, p. 41). Critical pedagogues consider themselves to be "agents of liberation," and this is the reason I have entitled the chapter the "liberationist initiative." Liberationist virtues are "transformative" in the sense that the ultimate purpose of education ought to be to prepare people to transform the social order. Hence liberationist moral education emphasizes the shaping of a particular kind of moral character committed to social justice and equality, exhibiting "civic courage," and able to engage effectively in "emancipatory" struggle.

THE GROWING INFLUENCE OF CRITICAL PEDAGOGY

As I hope the excerpts at the beginning of this chapter make clear, what I am calling the "liberationist initiative" features a drastically different language and worldview from the preceding two initiatives—the neo-classical and the communitarian—although there are a few ironic overlaps in the three *moral* agendas that I will discuss later in this chapter. Liberationist language is born of moral outrage, and it is generally very technical, analytical, critical, political, and utopian. It is a language grounded more in the social sciences than in philosophy, and, lately, it has integrated considerable postmodern theory into its critique of established socio/political/economic/educational structures, especially drawing upon the work of political postmodernists such as Michel Foucault (1981), Jean-Francois Lyotard (1984), and Edward W. Said (1993). It is a complex academic language, redolent in its content of earlier forms of sociopolitical criticism in the traditions of Marxism, the Frankfort School of critical theory, the educational reconstructionism of a previous generation, and liberation theology, and its vocabulary is remarkably similar to that of all these movements.

Many of the terms contained in the above excerpts appear frequently in liberationist writing: *praxis, liberation, oppression/oppressed, transformative, struggle, power relations, social relations, patriarchy, colonialism, sexism/*

racism, hegemony/counter-hegemony, power, justice, and resistance. These words take on great moral significance for liberationists because they establish a framework for understanding, critiquing, and transforming what is often presented as a bankrupt, "predatory," immoral, capitalistic culture. For my purposes in this chapter, I intend to concentrate on the dominant liberationist initiative in education today, *critical pedagogy,* a mode of socioeducational analysis that continually recycles the above nomenclature, along with a particular ideology adopted by an expanding group of thinkers. These scholars include Michael W. Apple (1979), Stanley Aronowitz (1992), Paulo Freire (1973), Henry Giroux (1983), Jonathan Kozol (1991), and Peter McLaren (1994), among others. In order to keep the analysis sharply focused, I will not be dealing in these pages with those liberationists who are Enlightenment–Marxist in orientation (e.g., Eagleton, 1996), because these social critics, with a few notable exceptions (e.g., Bowles & Gintis, 1976; Shor, 1986), have failed to achieve the preeminence in educational circles today comparable to the more postmodern liberationists.

These postmodern liberationist writers (whose most influential works I have indicated by the dates in parentheses) continue to produce a large body of work in critical pedagogy, and their ranks are growing almost exponentially to include such people as Michelle Fine (1991), Barry Kanpol (1994), David E. Purpel (1989), Roger I. Simon (1992), H. Svi Shapiro (1990), and Kathleen Weiler (1988), among others. At this time, all these thinkers tend to concentrate their scholarship on the public schools, K–12. While there are a number of literary theorists, culture-studies scholars, and feminist critics (e.g., neo-Marxists, new historicists, postcolonial theorists, postmodern Foucauldians) in the American university who currently employ critical theory in their individual disciplines (usually the humanities), few of these academicians call themselves critical pedagogues or liberationists, and fewer still bother with developing radical, systemic critiques of higher education.

As yet these liberationists have not attempted to introduce critical pedagogy in any systematic or concerted way into higher education (one attempt is Warren, 1997; another is hooks, 1994), although, increasingly, some of these writers are beginning to describe how they actually use critical pedagogy in their own university teaching (Apple, 1993; Giroux, 1994; Herron, 1988). A notable exception is the *paterfamilias* of critical pedagogy, Paulo Freire (1994a), who published a long-awaited book on higher education that resulted from an extended dialogue he held at the National University of Mexico. Unfortunately, his observations, although informative, dealt mainly with the problems of higher education in Latin

America and Mexico, with few direct references to university education in the United States.

Finally, it is no exaggeration to state that the scholarship of critical pedagogues dominates many graduate programs in educational policy studies, as well as the educational offerings of entire publishing houses, including Bergin & Garvey, Routledge, and, to a lesser extent, the University of Minnesota Press and the State University of New York Press, with a number of other publishers rapidly expanding their titles in this area. And people like Stanley Aronowitz, Paulo Freire, Henry A. Giroux, and Peter McLaren exercise considerable power over who gets published and who does not, because they edit Critical Studies series for these publishers. Additionally, some of the leading educational journals in the foundations field are edited by scholars highly enamored of critical pedagogy. Consequently, articles written from this perspective tend to be published more often than other types, as even a brief sampling over the last few years of such journals as the *Harvard Educational Review, Educational Foundations*, and *Educational Theory* will substantiate.

LIBERATIONISTS' CONCEPTIONS OF THE VIRTUES

Unlike the neo-classicals and the communitarians, liberationists do not speak at all about ordered communities, excellence of character, a *telos* or a *logos*, the cardinal classical virtues or even civic virtue (some do talk of "civic courage," though), mediating institutions, transcendence, or the need to retrieve what is good from the great traditions of the Western intellectual, religious, and political heritage. In fact, liberationists exercise what postmoderns call a persistent "hermeneutics of suspicion" toward these ideals, most of which they find "classist," "oppressive," and "hegemonic." Liberationists continually attack an entrenched white patriarchy that, they claim, wields these ideals "hegemonically" to perpetuate an unjust socioeconomic system, thereby maintaining unyielding control over the fates of women, non-Western peoples, and the urban, racial, and ethnic underclass in the United States.

Liberationists do not frame their concerns about education, democracy, citizenship, and morality in the notions of public consensus or a public good, or even in shared values, as do the neo-classicals and communitarians. Instead, liberationists talk about establishing democratic "communities of resistance," contestation, and conflict, and creating a "new public sphere" that is a genuine "social and economic democracy," where resources are equally distributed and where gross inequalities of wealth and political power will finally be eliminated (Giroux, 1994). Giroux's "new public sphere" is a "set of practices, institutions, and values ... that provide a mediating space between the state and private existence. ... It promotes emancipatory processes through collective self-reflection and discourse" (p. 236). Unlike the communitarians' "mediating institutions," which serve mainly to protect individuals and small communities from the "overweening" power of the state, the liberationist "public sphere" provides a place for citizens to engage in critical public discussion in order to challenge and transform the power of ruling elites.

While all three initiatives are critical of liberal individualism, the liberationist critique differs substantially. Much less preoccupied than communitarians with the evils of a rights-based ethic and the excessive forms of individualism and annihilation of community life that often accompany an overemphasis on individual rights, liberationists nevertheless express more fundamental *political and economic* concerns about liberalism. They warn that a liberal approach to politics—and, by implication, to education—totally omits a class analysis and therefore tends to ignore underclass, working-class, and middle-class differences among people and the resultant misery brought on by class oppression and exploitation.

Liberationists also caution that only a profound social and economic analysis will explain the real origins of oppressive and exploitative practices—the structural injustices, or the inequalities, inevitably built into a capitalist society. The logic of a market economy stipulates that the distance between the "haves" and the "have-nots" in America will continue to grow, regardless of government efforts to curtail such growth. Liberalism as an explanatory political theory is deficient, according to the liberationists, because it virtually ignores the crippling constraints of a market system, along with the concomitant power and privilege of wealth that mutually reinforce an unjust social order (Weiler, 1988).

Liberationists are far more concerned with formal schooling than the communitarians, believing that the schools ought to be the primary launching sites for creating the "new public sphere." In fact, the liberationists make a distinction between education and schooling, because it is the schools that directly serve the interests of the state. Thus it is in the schools—as well as in those formal educational institutions directly or indirectly linked to the state through funding or certification—that the first stages of massive social upheaval must occur. It is in the schools where teachers must initially come to terms with their own, and their students', "ideological constraints" (how class, culture, gender, and race determine how they act); where they must make democracy possible (give oppressed groups, both inside and outside the school, a voice in shaping policies and controlling procedures); and where they need to link their critique of the schools to the need for a more global social transformation (Giroux, 1983).

Liberationists, by and large, see many of the moral virtues championed by neo-classicals and communitarians as being either passé or self-serving. For the liberationists, the "work ethic" is nothing more than a broken promise, given the monopoly of wealth in the United States by a very few individuals and groups. They point out that the internal logic of modern, supply-side capitalism virtually guarantees the existence of a growing class of "have-nots," people who are the inevitable human detritus of an economic system controlled by the wealthy and powerful. One tangible proof of this failure is the ever-increasing concentration of wealth in this country and the alarming diminution of a genuine middle class.

According to liberationists, the late-twentieth-century failure of corporate capitalism to advantage *all* classes has occurred because of the tragedy of workplace downsizing; the loss of millions of manufacturing jobs to the cheaper, exploited labor available in foreign countries; and the "de-skilling" of professionals due, in part, to bureacratization, standardization, mechanization, and prepackaged computer software. All of this has been accompanied by the rise to (inordinate) economic and cultural power of Robert Reich's (1992) "symbolic analysts," the communications and technological elites who form a new "knowledge class" in America. Moreover, for liberationists, "family values" have been appropriated by ultra-conservative forces in the society in order to prop up the capitalist ideals of achievement, competition, performance, hierarchy, tradition, and conditional love, and to create an outright "moral" disdain for alternatives to the traditional family arrangement (Purpel & Shapiro, 1995).

Furthermore, according to the liberationists, the "moral decline" postulated by the neo-classicals is nothing more than a political pretext for bolstering a corrupt political order. Liberationists, in contrast, urge students to "interrogate" the neo-classical moral canon to determine whose interests the canon best serves, what authors are excluded, and how the argument for moral decline actually reflects narrow class interests. The liberationists would argue that the neo-classical dismay about moral decline is motivated primarily by the fact that youth are "getting out of hand" and are no longer respectful or obedient or diligent when the state exerts control and tries to channel them into their appropriate educational and career slots. The real moral decline, in the eyes of the liberationists, is seen when capitalists are allowed to create greater and greater disparities of wealth and privilege in the culture, resulting in massive poverty and injustice, and when youth, women, and minorities are systematically silenced in their attempt to create "counter-hegemonic spheres of cultural resistance" (McLaren, 1995).

Finally, liberationists would charge that communitarian consternation about the dissolution of civic virtue is at worst a sham and at best a self-deception. Genuine "civic courage" does not merely urge students to adapt to existing configurations of power and privilege by stressing "nonoppositional" forms of citizenship training and obligatory community service. This "training for docility" is actually "civic cowardice" (Giroux, 1994), because it is designed to prepare young people pliantly to accept the logic of the market, to privatize their individual interests, and to continue overemphasizing competition and achievement as they strive to achieve the ever-elusive "good life" in an unjust social order.

According to liberationists, students will acquire a courageous civic virtue only when educators conceive of democracy, and the schools, as an opportunity for expanding economic and political power so that all groups, including the economically disenfranchised and the historically silenced, can engage in an ongoing struggle over the true meaning of democracy. For liberationists, questions about what democracy is, who controls it, who benefits from it, and how it can be exercised more radically, justly, and humanely must move to the center of school and public dialogue, where people can create alliances to address these crucial political issues.

A BRIEF REVIEW OF CRITICAL PEDAGOGY SOURCES

As I have tried somewhat sketchily to show above, liberationists are political ideologues who pride themselves on being social visionaries. With a very different set of background moral beliefs from those of neo-classicals and communitarians, liberationists present a sharply focused political critique of established institutional and social structures in the United States. Their critique of American life is grounded in Western Marxist philosophy and the Frankfurt School's analysis of culture (Adorno & Horkheimer, 1972; Giroux, 1983); in the educational reconstructionism of the 1960s and 1970s; in the civil/feminist/gay rights and radical student movements of the 1950s, 1960s, and 1970s; in the work of Paulo Freire (1973), the Brazilian educator, in the late 1950s and early 1960s; in the liberation theology that first emerged in Latin America during the 1960s and 1970s (Berryman, 1987); and in the postmodern turn, especially in the work of Michel Foucault (1981), toward knowledge and power, discourse, alterity (otherness), and difference in the last two decades (Aronowitz & Giroux, 1991). In the paragraphs that follow, I will briefly summarize each of these influences on critical pedagogy, as I understand them.

From *Marxism,* the liberationists borrow the concept of *reproduction.*

They argue that the main function of schooling has never been to equip all people equally with the intellectual and technical skills necessary to realize their fullest potentials and to pursue the good life in America. In contrast to this myth of equal success for all, the liberationists charge that the main purpose of schooling has always been to reproduce the dominant ideology of a society, along with the accompanying knowledge and skills required to reproduce the social division of labor. The schools, in brief, are hermetically bound up with the state and the economy, and, wittingly or unwittingly, they function as agencies of cultural reproduction and maintainers of the established hierarchical order.

The main function of reproduction theory in education, according to neo-Marxists, is to demonstrate that the schools' "hidden curriculum" is to provide students with the knowledge and skills they need to maintain a labor force stratified by class, race, and gender, as well as to distribute and legitimize a particular knowledge, value system, language, and style, all of which constitute the "dominant" culture. The upshot of cultural reproduction is to bolster the political power of the state by authenticating its economic and ideological ideals (Aronowitz & Giroux, 1985). Where liberationists depart from this strictly Marxist analysis of cultural reproduction, however, is in repudiating what they see to be a kind of determinism and despair in reproductive theory. Liberationists choose, instead, to emphasize "resistance," "hope," "human agency," and the power of women and other minorities to develop "counter-hegemonic" spheres of "contestation," both inside and outside the schools (Freire, 1985). Paulo Freire has even written a book called *Pedagogy of Hope: Reliving Pedagogy of the Oppressed* (1994b), in order to show how a combination of "rage and love" must coexist in any critical theory, because without this dialectic, hope is all but impossible.

From the *Frankfurt School of critical theory* in Germany, originating in the 1920s, liberationists appropriate the overall revision of Marxism. Following the ideas of Max Horkheimer, Theodor Adorno, Herbert Marcuse, and Jurgen Habermas (Geuss, 1981), liberationists attempt to give rigorous, empirical, and verifiable explanations of the causes of oppression. These explanations serve many purposes, among them to critique current critical theories; to provide a sharper self-understanding of how ideology and economic dependence cause oppression; to enable people, through a series of dialectical, theoretical insights, to "emancipate" themselves in order to improve their social conditions; and to construct "alternative epistemologies" to counter the dominant scientific, political, and educational knowledge systems of today.

Critical pedagogues use the insights of critical theory in the schools and colleges to attack the "positivist rationality" of educational leaders.

They continually stress the dialectical nature of social theory and the importance of creating complex educational epistemologies grounded in personal, historical, social, and private experiences. Much of their writing points out the possibilities of "emancipation" in students' "repressed cultures and struggles" and is geared to fashion new ways to analyze the hidden curriculum, in order to understand more profoundly how teachers and students become part of the system of cultural reproduction. Finally, liberationists attempt to develop a depth psychology that gives insights into how and why people allow their sensual and imaginative faculties to be denied in the schools and to help in reclaiming these faculties as lived (and valued) educational experiences in their own right (Giroux, 1983).

From the work of the *educational reconstructionists* (ca. 1920–1970), liberationists have developed a critical theory of citizenship. The original educational reconstructionists—George Counts, Harold Rugg, Willystine Goodsell, and Theodore Brameld (Dennis & Eaton, 1980)—saw the possibilities in the public schools for creating democratic citizens whose primary obligation would be to rectify social injustice in America. Liberationists today often speak of the need for teachers to become "transformative intellectuals," a concept whose meaning originated with the early reconstructionists. For the reconstructionists, the purpose of teaching was to transform the social order. This meant that teachers had to become social critics dedicated to helping students struggle against power and privilege in the wider society (Brameld, 1956, 1965).

The reconstructionists believed that democracy ensured everyone the right to participate as active citizens in the political, economic, and social spheres of decision making. Thus good citizens needed training, not just in the schools but also in labor unions, churches, and neighborhood organizations. Liberationists have appropriated this understanding of democracy and citizenship from the reconstructionists (Giroux, 1988), and now they think of the school as a sphere for struggle as well as a site for a social movement—or, in the words of the most well known of the reconstructionists, as an instrument for building "a new social order" (Counts, 1932).

The liberationists have also been deeply influenced by the various *human and civil rights movements* of the last 50 years. Philosophically, *civil* rights are those possessed by a citizen, and *human* rights are guaranteed by virtue of being human. The liberationists conflate the two senses of rights and, as a result of their direct and indirect personal experiences with the rights revolutions of the past 50 years, tend to see them as one and the same. Thus liberationists believe that women, blacks, gays, students, and children, for example, have both a civil *and* human right to be treated fairly. More important, in addition to the right to be free from unjust interference by the state, liberationists believe these groups also have equal political, social, and economic rights, such as the right to an adequate standard of living. This is a claim that necessitates a radical redistribution of economic and political resources to those groups that have suffered tangible historical oppression.

In their own lives, many liberationists were actively involved in the various resistance movements connected to the rights revolutions, for example, the Vietnam resistance, the women's movement, the black power movement, and the gay rights movement. And as Weiler (1988) notes, during the height of the rights movements, many liberationists experimented with educational reforms such as open classrooms, curricular innovations based on "women's ways of knowing," and consciousness-raising groups. Thus they developed a faith in education as a means for social transformation. In a powerful sense, then, critical pedagogy grew out of the struggles of the human and civil rights movements, and today a generation of young rights activists are attempting to translate the legacy of these movements into direct educational practices.

Liberation theology is rarely mentioned by liberationists (some exceptions are Freire [1985], McLaren [1995], and Purpel [1989]). Yet the influence of this inquiry on liberationist thinking is unmistakable. Liberation theologians, who first appeared in Latin America during the 1960s and 1970s, attempted to describe the Christian faith from the perspective of those peasants who struggled to overcome their oppression (Gutierrez, 1973). Liberation theologians challenged the established Catholic Church to be more critical of oppressive regimes and to change its own unjust social structures. According to Paul J. Wojda (1995), there are four major themes in liberation theology:

1. "Preferential option for the poor" (p. 768). This requires a solidarity with the victims of oppression and direct involvement in their struggles to be free.
2. A "unity of theory and practice" (p. 769), or, in Freire's term, a *praxis*. Because *"doing* is as important as *seeing* the truth" (p. 769), liberation theologians favor the applied ideas of political and social thinkers over the theoretical ones of philosophers, whose contributions they believe to be mainly interpretive.
3. A "critique of ideology" (p. 769). The critical task of liberation theology is to expose the oppressive ideologies of the dominant church and other social structures, and to construct oppositional, liberating ideologies.

4. Reading the Bible "from below" (p. 769), that is, by interpreting the Scriptural God as someone who forms an alliance with the poor and vulnerable.

In a recent book, Peter McLaren (1995) asserts that liberation theology has a great deal to offer critical pedagogy, because it is essentially an "exercise of hope and possibility" (p. 50). He particularly likes the "hermeneutical wager" in this theology that affirms God's preference for the poor, the oppressed, and the marginalized. He also approves of liberation theology's emphasis on class struggle, its rejection of patriarchy and dogma, and its support of a "contestatory ethical stance" (p. 51) in favor of freedom. Moreover, he sees in liberation theology a challenge to a "reactionary God often championed by the forces of the New Right" (p. 51). Finally, McLaren believes that liberation theology offers radical pedagogues a theory of hope that is neither "cheerily optimistic" nor self-righteously certain.

One of the major influences in the development of a pedagogical role for liberation theologians in Latin America has been *Paulo Freire* (1971), whose work with the poor in Brazil occurred in the late 1950s and early 1960s. Today, Freire is the *primus inter pares* (first among equals) in the critical pedagogy movement, and rarely do liberationists publish an article or book without several laudatory references to his seminal influence on their thinking. In fact, many of their books carry Freire's imprimatur in the form of a glowing foreword, introduction, or preface (e.g., Giroux, 1983; McLaren, 1995). McLaren places him in "the front ranks of that 'dying class' of educational revolutionaries who march behind the banner of liberation to fight for social justice and educational reform" (1995, p. 304). He lauds Freire's "theoretical refinement and his success at putting theory into practice" (p. 305).

In South America, Freire gave priests, nuns, and lay activists a pragmatic tool for teaching the gospel to illiterate adult peasants (Berryman, 1987). He developed a pedagogy that conceived of learners as active subjects rather than empty containers. Against educational convention, he treated his students as rational, political beings who could understand the complexities of freedom. And, in Gramsci's (1971) words, he thought of teachers as "organic intellectuals" who could organize a community to act in its own best political interests.

In teaching peasants how to read, Freire offered them words and images from their own adult worlds: their crops, tools, customs, families, and so forth. He asked them to draw implications from these words that revealed something about their troubled lives; for example, making ends meet or being treated unfairly by a landowner. By design, in addition to teaching them their first words, this "de-codification" of peasants' real-life situations raised their political consciousness (*conscientizacao*). Not only did peasants learn to read in just a few weeks by using Freire's method, but they became active in their own political development as a direct result of their critical consciousness. Freire's call to educators, more than four decades ago, to democratize education by concentrating on the marginalized and to treat them as subjects fully capable of their own liberation has, today, touched every aspect of liberationist thinking about education.

Finally, liberationist educators distinguish between two types of *post-modernism:* conservative and critical (Aronowitz & Giroux, 1991; Kanpol, 1994). In its conservative forms, postmodernism is mainly concerned with multiple interpretations and multiple ways of knowing. Conservative postmodernism delights in deconstructing language, challenging episte-mological absolutes, and de-centering the authors of texts. In Aronowitz and Giroux's words: Conservative postmodernism "raises important questions about how narratives get constructed, what they mean, how they regulate particular forms of moral and social experience, and how they presuppose and embody particular epistemological and political views of the world" (pp. 80–81). But generally critical pedagogues remain wary regarding the emancipatory benefits of conservative postmodern-ism because of its tendency to engage in endless language games—in clever interpretations and deconstructions of conflicting epistemologies, but absent a clear political project.

In its more critical forms, however, postmodernism not only gives liberationists a complex understanding of the relationships of culture, power, and knowledge; it also contributes to the creation of a "public philosophy and a revitalized democratic public life" (Aronowitz & Giroux, 1991, p. 81). Critical postmodernism emphasizes the existence of dif-ference and otherness in all aspects of life, but it does not simply stop there. Too often, public schools acknowledge difference but then proceed to devalue—indeed, to suppress—racial, class, and gender differences, along with the variety of learning styles that accompany them (Kanpol, 1994, p. 33). In contrast, critical postmodernism links difference to democ-racy, and it pushes in the direction of an education in which critical dia-logue among differing voices and traditions is always a vital aspect of democratic discourse. Thus, for the liberationists, the postmodern project is actually a political project in which dialogue is the first stage in the creation of a critical democracy whose major objective is to eliminate society-wide suffering and domination.

LIBERATIONIST EDUCATION

As the previous sections suggest, liberationist education has tended to be stronger on critical theory and weaker on tangible pedagogical specifics. It is only recently that critical pedagogues have begun to write about hands-on curricular and instructional issues, and this in a very unsystematic, but highly suggestive, way. In this connection, I believe it is important to understand how liberationists (e.g., Freire, 1971; Kanpol, 1994; McLaren, 1995; Simon, 1992) use the term *pedagogy,* because their educational writing naturally stresses those aspects of the term they think most pivotal. For them, pedagogy is more than simply the art and science of teaching; it is both a *professional* and *political* word. Professionally, *pedagogy* refers to everything a teacher does in a classroom, including instruction, assessment, curricular content and design, and goal setting. Most professional writing about schooling concerns itself with this sense of pedagogy; for example, articles in the *Journal of Teacher Education* typify this emphasis. But pedagogy also includes an *ideological* element that represents (wittingly or unwittingly) the following:

- What the teacher believes about what constitutes worthwhile knowledge
- What students are capable of learning this knowledge
- The most effective ways to transmit this knowledge
- Who ought to have access to this knowledge
- Whose interests are being served when students possess this knowledge
- What knowledge ought to be restricted, by whom, and for what reasons
- The extent to which students can contribute to the construction and distribution of this knowledge
- How knowledge ought to be used, and in whose interests, once it has been chosen and disseminated

In this dual sense of pedagogy, then, liberationists insist that we must never engage in discourse about teaching and learning without first discussing politics. Thus liberationist writing about education tends to accentuate a social and political analysis of schooling, with far less attention given to the concrete particulars of day-to-day classroom practice. Therefore, in the sections that follow, at times I will be making educated guesses concerning liberationist schools/colleges, curricula, and instructional methods. For the most part, these concrete entities and practices do not yet exist in the real world. Moreover, because liberationists rarely write directly or extensively about the shaping of moral character, desirable virtues, or even ethical behavior, I will have to draw what I believe are warranted inferences in the moral area as well. Nonetheless I am convinced that behind the liberationist initiative is a commanding moral agenda—present as much in the omissions as in the commissions—that has much to contribute to the central concern of this book: character education.

Finally, in order for me to be as true as I possibly can to liberationists' educational ideas, I will try to articulate their major themes within the context of the technical discourse they employ, replete with some of their highly specialized vocabulary. Whenever possible, I will "unpack" ideas in my own language, in order to clarify some of their more recondite nomenclature. In the next chapter, I intend to comment critically on my students' difficulties with liberationist language. I will argue that the language per se makes a moral statement, with unintended implications for imparting the virtues and shaping a particular kind of moral character.

Liberationist Educational Goals

Liberationists think of educational goals in two ways. "Micro goals" are the stuff of conventional teaching. These represent the facts, the course content, and the more objective data of teaching. But Giroux (1988) claims micro goals never occur *de novo;* they always represent particular political interests. "Macro goals," the stuff of liberationist teaching, enable teachers and students to detect the political connections that exist between the so-called facts that teachers claim they transmit and the wider sociopolitical objectives that advance certain class interests and agendas. Micro and macro goals always exist in a dialectical relationship, and it is the macro goal of the liberationist educator to uncover how the declared micro goals of the schools and colleges actually reinforce the class interests of the wider society. Liberationists from Paulo Freire (1971) to Henry A. Giroux (1983) to Kathleen Weiler (1988) to Michael Apple (1993), each in their own ways, attempt to explain the relationships that cohere between micro and macro educational goals in the nation's public schools. Thus far, Jerry Herron (1988) is one of only a few critical pedagogues who is trying to do the same in higher education.

In what follows, I have found Peter McLaren's (1994) analysis of what he calls "major concepts in critical pedagogy" to be very helpful. I will paraphrase and reframe his concepts as a way of describing what I think are the macro educational goals of critical pedagogy:

- *Class.* Liberationist educators attempt to expose the impact that economic, social, and political relationships have on people's everyday lives in America. Liberationists hold that an important educational objective ought to be to teach students how an individual's or group's class and culture produce conditions of oppression and dependency in America, especially when these are linked with race, gender, age, and ethnicity factors.
- *Hegemony.* Hegemony is nonviolent domination by the class in power in the United States, and frequently those who are powerless give unwitting consent to their own oppression. Liberationist educators see as a significant goal the laying open of hegemonic practices, both in the culture and in the schools and colleges, by challenging the "domination myths" perpetuated by such social structures as the church, state, school, university, mass media, government, and family. Popular culture is often an arena where dominated groups are able to express their resistance to the dominant culture's control. Thus one objective of liberationist educators is to bring the content of popular culture into the classroom for analysis and to examine it for the "oppositional" voice it presents to the hegemonic culture (Giroux, 1994).
- *Ideology.* Liberationist educators attempt to help teachers and students become aware of how their ideologies—their unique ways of viewing, giving meaning to, and acting in the world—are actually "disguises" for power and privilege, or "recipes" for powerlessness and privation. One important educational goal, therefore, is to help students to understand how people in power use dominant ideologies to prop up unjust economic and political systems. A capitalist ideology, for example, can provide a rationale for an ideology of competitive grading in schools and colleges. This in turn encourages such practices as tracking, ability grouping, rewards and punishments, testing, and an approved academic regimen for getting into the "best" colleges. This, then, locks certain people into lower places in the socioeconomic system, while freeing a select few to accumulate greater wealth and influence.
- *Critical discourse.* A major educational goal for liberationists is to get students to understand how the knowledge that schools and colleges ratify as "important" actually reinforces the economic, political, and educational status quo. The *dominant* discourses of the ruling class, in Foucault's (1979) phrase, are "regimes of truth," and these "regimes" set the standards for talk about what is acceptable and unacceptable, moral and immoral, in all the major social institutions. For liberationists, the goal of critical discourse in education is to identify just who it is that speaks with special pedagogical authority in America; why schools and colleges choose particular curricula, teaching methodolo-

gies, and disciplinary procedures; and why they designate some behaviors as virtuous and others as vicious.

- *Cultural capital.* Another goal for liberationist educators is to respect the cultural capital that all students bring with them to schools and colleges. Cultural capital represents the sum total of a student's culture, including values, dispositions, skills, discursive patterns, and styles of dress and behavior (McLaren, 1994). Too often, schools and colleges depreciate the cultural capital of minorities, and this results in poor job prospects and dismal lifestyles for those already economically disadvantaged. It is therefore important for liberationist educators to demonstrate clearly to students the links between social class, cultural capital, educational achievement, and economic success, so that they understand that educational success and failure are always class-related rather than the result of moral superiority or deficiency.

The Liberationist School/College

In the liberationist conception, schools and colleges are places with great potential for both good and evil. Henry A. Giroux (1983, 1988, 1994) has done much to advance an image of schools as possible sites of "resistance," as "democratic public spheres" devoted to the struggle for a truly democratic society. Liberationists readily acknowledge, however, that schools and colleges spend far more time in adapting students to *what is* than in preparing them to shape *what ought to be*. Liberationists emphasize instead the dual role that schools and colleges play: On the one hand, educational institutions function simultaneously as sites of indoctrination, domestication, and social-class preservation. On the other hand, they possess an untapped potential to promote individual empowerment and social justice. Thus, for analysts like Giroux and McLaren, schools and colleges are not simply the mechanical, reproductive forces that Marxists portray them to be, wherein administrators, teachers, and students docilely act out the master script written by the dominant class interests. Instead, schools and colleges can also function as active sites for personal and group liberation, depending on the will and training of critical thinkers in these insitutions.

Giroux (1988) imagines schools as places where teachers and students ground everything they do in the work of constructing a more genuinely democratic society. Thus schools would be locations that would "nourish civic literacy, citizen participation, and moral courage" (p. 32). While it is true that schools and colleges are ideological terrains wherein the dominant culture produces its "hegemonic certainties," it is also true, particularly for Giroux (1983) and Roger I. Simon (1992), that they can be other kinds of places as well. They can be locations where people who represent dominant and subordinate interests come into open conflict, in a mutually agreed-upon exchange, in order to identify and contest the ideologies and practices that too often separate students from students, teachers from teachers, and students from teachers. In this sense, schools and colleges become centers of "critical insurgency," "spaces of the possible," where nobody's authority is simply taken for granted, where "debate" continually rages, and where "insurgents" always feel that their concerns about social identity, justice, and self-empowerment are genuine possibilities for everyone.

Finally, liberationists such as Giroux (1983) have been quick to note that schools and colleges alone will never transform the larger public sphere unless they link with other sites that are also democratic public spheres. According to Giroux, liberationist teachers will have "to establish organic connnections with those excluded majorities who inhabit the neighborhoods, towns, and cities in which schools are located" (p. 237). This connection would serve the important purpose of getting working-class people, minorities, and women actively involved in the formulation and implementation of school policies and practices. For the liberationist, there are several spheres of struggle, the school being just one. And the commitment to end class, racial, and gender oppression must eventuate in action in all spheres, as teachers "act not simply as teachers but also as citizens" (p. 239).

The Liberationist Curriculum

Michael W. Apple's (1979) voice has been an early, influential one on liberationist curriculum theory. For him, a curriculum is a "relational" entity, because it is always integrally related to cultural, political, and economic institutions. And just as these social institutions are unequal by race, gender, and class, so too does the school curriculum reproduce these inequalities. One of the more pernicious functions of what Apple and other liberationist educators call the "hidden curriculum" is precisely this reproduction of inequality: Students emerge from schools and colleges with differential amounts of power and potential, according to their membership in a particular race, gender, or social class. Upon graduation, some will go into the military, some into dead-end retail and fast-disappearing manufacturing jobs, some into the trades, some into chronic unemployment, and some onto higher education. Only a few, however, will be "slotted" to enter the ranks of the "cream of the crop," and those who do will attend the elite colleges, virtually assuring them lifelong economic and social success (Katchadourian & Boli, 1994).

Liberationist educators ask the following types of questions (Beyer & Apple, 1988) about curriculum:

- What should count as "official knowledge"?
- Who actually controls the selection and distribution of this official knowledge?
- Who "owns" the knowledge and why? Why are most curricula developed and implemented in a top-down, hierarchical manner?
- In what ways is the control of knowledge connected to inequalities in the larger society?
- How does the knowledge maintain these inequalities?
- How can students and teachers repossess this knowledge?
- Can there truly be a "democratic" curriculum?
- How can teachers make this knowledge more accessible to everyone?
- In what ways can students' "stories" become a central element in this "official knowledge"?
- How does the way teachers teach this knowledge reflect their moral concerns about social justice, equality, and oppression?
- Why is the dominant language of curriculum theory today the language of efficiency, standards, competence, cost-effectiveness, computer technology, and basic knowledge?
- What alternative curricular languages are missing?

For the liberationist educator, these sorts of questions ought to inform the construction, content, and implementation of curricula at all levels of schooling.

Although liberationist educators have yet to offer many concrete curricular proposals for the public schools and colleges, a few have discussed in print what they are doing by way of curricular experimentation in their own college classes. These activities provide some indication of what a liberationist curriculum might look like in the future, although most liberationists are emphatic about wanting to avoid imposing a particular curriculum on anyone. Giroux (1994) advocates bringing popular culture into the classroom in order to provide an alternative to the official discipline-based public school curriculum. He wants teachers to use popular films, books, journals, videos, music, photography, and so forth in their classes, because this is the knowledge that actually shapes young people's values and identities. Teachers who enlarge their curricula to include these familiar cultural items are far more likely to get students to express their deepest desires, struggles, hopes, fears, and need for solidarity than top-down, teacher-imposed subject matter. In one of his own courses, "Post-

colonialism, Race, and Critical Pedagogy," Giroux (1994) included a unit
on popular culture in order to get students to be "self-reflective" and to
"rethink" the ways that power works through "diverse regimes of repre-
sentation, institutional structures, and the larger spaces of social power"
(p. 140).

In the university, Jerry Herron (1988), an English professor, presents
a list of "things a [liberationist] professor might do" (pp. 137–138) as a
way of restructuring a course curriculum. Among his suggestions are
the following:

- Invite students to write an "academic autobiography" wherein
  they candidly talk about why they hate and/or love their college
  education.
- Read a professional paper written by the professor to students,
  watch their faces, do not tell them who wrote it, get them to give
  critical feedback, and then reevaluate the necessity for making the
  trip out of state to present the paper at a conference.
- Give students a copy of the college catalogue's mission statement
  and try honestly to defend it—see if they believe it.
- "Watch TV as if it mattered as much as John Milton" (p. 138).
- Hide lecture notes every semester. Do not use them.
- Appear at local organizations and service clubs to explain why a
  particular discipline or course is useful; have students do the same
  with their majors.
- Ask students to compose a list of what they would rather be doing
  than sitting in a class, and then request that they read their lists
  publicly; do the same yourself.
- Demand that all writing be done in intelligible, jargon-free English
  that a student's parents would understand.
- Make a list of personal adversaries at the college and share the list
  with students, along with detailed rationales for each name on the
  list; ask for critical feedback.
- Teach a completely different way every third or fourth class; see if
  anyone notices.

Herron hopes that his "curriculum" will encourage students to experience firsthand the political "conflicts and confrontations" that should ani-
mate academic life but rarely do.

Kathleen Weiler (1988) observed a number of feminist teachers in
their classrooms who were trying to "build a more just society" (p. 113)
by teaching a hidden curriculum of "critique and possibility." Based on
these observations, Weiler believes that the most effective teachers try to

sensitize students to the "ideological messages" they receive regarding gender and race. They shatter stereotypes, define themselves and their students as "gendered subjects," model competence and authority, constantly raise feminist issues in a classroom by linking specific subject matter to sexist and racist practices, "interrogate" sexist textbooks, are caring and nurturing instead of competitive and intimidating, and engage students in respectful but challenging dialogue about women's oppression. Weiler believes that the feminist hidden curriculum of confronting sexist assumptions and accepted definitions of gender is the most effective way of building "counter-hegemony" in classrooms throughout the United States.

Liberationist Instructional Methods

Aronowitz and Giroux (1985) think of the liberationist teacher as a "transformative intellectual," someone who resists the "technocratic rationality" of educational managers, social science experts, and "clerks" (pp. 26–27). For Aronowitz and Giroux, there are no technological solutions to the explosive political and social problems confronting students and teachers in the United States today. In fact, technocratic rationality is itself the source of so much that is wrong in education today, because it seeks mechanical, system-preserving answers to intractable political and economic problems. Liberationist teachers, in contrast, are "reflective practitioners" who are always ready to raise the probing political questions about what, how, and why they teach, and they encourage their students and the larger community to do the same. Transformative intellectuals demand more influence over the ideological and economic conditions of their work, not to perpetuate dominant power relations and hegemonic values but to challenge and transform them. Thus liberationist teachers at all levels of education are continually struggling, challenging, questioning, advocating, arguing, critiquing, pointing out the relationships between knowledge and power, engaging, discoursing, forming alliances, showing how the personal, political, and pedagogical are intimately related, and, above all, liberating.

Furthermore, as creators of a new and enlarged "public sphere," transformative intellectuals must be ever-ready to join with other social groups who are likewise engaged in "emancipatory struggle." They need to look for ways to connect with activists in the community who are working for equity, peace, labor rights, consumer rights, and racial and sexual equality. Transformative intellectuals are continually reading, sharing their work with others both inside and outside the school and college, producing a variety of pedagogical materials, and publishing their ideas for wider audiences.

As yet, there are no liberationist primers on actual instructional methodologies, unless one takes into account Paulo Freire's many writings (e.g., 1971, 1985, 1994b) on how to teach literacy to adult peasants in a manner that empowers them both politically and intellectually. Once again, though, liberationist educators are adamant about not stipulating for others the "correct" pedagogy, because they believe transformative intellectuals need to find their own way in the classroom in overcoming oppression, alienation, and subordination. Nevertheless, some liberationist writers have lately given their readers glimpses of instructional approaches they have used in their own teaching.

Ironically, as liberationists themselves point out, their teaching, in these examples, has clear structure, form, and direction, in spite of critical pedagogy's antistructural, democratic, and postmodern spirit. Kanpol (1994), for example, presents a step-by-step "unit plan" for a course on "Similarities Within Differences Through Multiculturalism." He specifies length, goals, objectives, course requirements, readings, materials, discussion questions, and suggested activities for each day of each week. He claims that on the surface a curriculum should meet state guidelines, but beneath the surface liberationist teachers must be critical, political, and democratic. Kanpol continually asks himself: "Is what I am teaching counterhegemonic?" (p. 155). He thinks of himself as a "visionary" and a "social architect," to the extent he has been both critical and transformational in his teaching.

Giroux (1994), in a chapter on the "cultural studies classroom," describes how he uses writing "as a pedagogical practice to challenge certain dominant assumptions about the meaning of schooling, the discourse of authority, and [his own role] within the politics of [being] a university teacher" (p. 133). In a course titled "Postcolonialism, Race, and Critical Pedagogy," Giroux assigns a series of reading and writing activities that he calls "border pedagogy." He wants his students to write about their own experiences in a critical way. He begins the class by raising a series of political questions about the role of knowledge and about his own authority in the class, all the while inviting students to challenge him and to take control of their own learning. Like Kanpol, Giroux establishes clear goals for the course, and he frequently breaks up the class into small groups in order to produce collaborative writing. There are four major writing assignments, including formal analytical writing on the readings, where students must also take personal positions on their topics; teaching an assigned reading to the class, accompanied by a personal, written exegesis; and developing a collaborative "position paper" based on applying a specific, personal learning about race and pedagogy. The final writing project of the semester is a combination of analysis and self-reflection about each student's engagement with the course.

In his teaching, Giroux encourages students to learn from one another. He occasionally presents brief lectures to get them started. He tries to "de-center" the power in the classroom by encouraging students to "deconstruct" his authority by analyzing the "hidden agendas" in his own pedagogy. And he frequently crosses disciplinary "borders" in his analyses. All told, he models a "restless critical pedagogy" that both he and his students can "rewrite, reaffirm, and struggle over" (p. 140).

Other firsthand examples of instructional techniques in the liberationist literature include a personal account of Michael W. Apple's (1993) work with a particular group of people, "the Friday Seminar," that has been meeting at his university for 20 years. This group consists of doctoral students, visiting scholars, and activists, and its purpose is to exhibit an "ethic of caring and connectedness" and also "challenge the existing politics of official knowledge" (p. 152). His experiences with group building, democratic procedures, and institutional and cultural critique parallel Giroux's and Kanpol's, although, admittedly, Apple works with a very different, more sophisticated type of group.

And in an anthology of critical pedagogy, Rebecca A. Martusewicz and William M. Reynolds (1994) include a number of actual classroom examples, at all levels, of liberationist teaching. These include cross-cultural methods, "antiracist pedagogy," and feminist teaching. What all of these instructional pieces have in common is that each of the teachers is trying to function as a "transformative intellectual," as someone who recognizes that schools and colleges reflect the gender, racial, and class conflicts in the larger society, and as someone who neither avoids nor denies conflict but legitimates the "polyphony of voices" in the discourse of the classroom by encouraging these voices, no matter how outrageous, to find the fullest expression.

CONCLUSION

In the next chapter, I examine critically some key liberationist themes, especially as these relate to the imparting of what I call the "transformative dispositions." I do this from a dual perspective: my own and my students'. As best I can, I try to express my views, and theirs, in a language I hope is honest, yet fair. In a nutshell, I argue that, to its credit, the liberationist initiative has effectively shown how the traditional idea of value-neutral knowledge in schools and colleges is often an ideologically loaded cover for class privilege, capitalistic values, and imperialistic dispositions toward the rest of the world. I also argue, however, that the liberationist critique of Western bourgeois society, capitalism, and hegemonic schools has become formulaic and hyperapocalyptic. And, for many students, liberationist language, because it is so ideologically rigid, pretentious, and humorless, has functioned mainly to subvert its own important moral insights regarding the "hidden," "hegemonic" nature of schooling. It does this, I submit, by "privileging" a morality of habitual contestation over a morality of reconciliation in America's schools and colleges.

CHAPTER 7

The Liberationist Virtues:
A Morality of Contestation

The fact that Marxist influence so endures in the American academic left—to the point where you can find an Althusserian or two—is a proof of the power of nostalgia. . . . Marxism is dead; that part of history is over, [but] its carcass will continue to make sounds and smells, as fluids drain and pockets of gas expand.
　　　　—*Robert Hughes,* Culture of Complaint: The Fraying of America, *1993*

[How to get an academic essay published]: The first sentence should feature hegemony; *the second,* itinerary; *the third,* foregrounding; *the fourth,* privilege *used as a verb. . . . There should be plenty of* de- *or* dis- *prefixes, beginning with* deconstruction *and* dismantling, *and as many* -ize *suffixes, such as* problematize, valorize, contextualize, totalize. *A good way to begin your* discourse *(you must always call it that) is . . . to call into question some* binary opposition . . . male *and* female, nature *and* culture, center *and* periphery.
　　　　—*David Lehman,* Signs of the Times: Deconstruction and the Fall
of Paul de Man, *1992*

A morality of contestation is inherently hazardous, because its virtues and vices are so readily transmuted. As a virtue, contestation rightfully opens up for questioning and argument those "authoritative" moral, educational, political, and economic pronouncements a state intends to be indisputable. As a vice, a morality of contestation as a *terminus ad quem* (the end toward which all else leads) can become ideologically contentious, creating an ethos of strife, political controversy, and truculence in a democracy, resulting in sustained division and fractiousness among the people.

My unit on the liberationist initiative is always the most controversial in any moral-education course I teach and usually elicits the strongest reactions, both pro and con, from every single student in the class. Nobody in my classes ever remains neutral on the topic of critical pedagogy and character education. What follows is an imaginary dialogue among four students that occurs in a small group, as my unit on liberationist character education begins to heat up late one semester. I believe the "manufactured" exchange I have created below accurately represents the variety of views that customarily surface whenever we study the critical pedagogues. I will comment later on many of the issues the students raise.

AN IMAGINARY DIALOGUE

A: I can't for the life of me understand what liberationist pedagogy has to do with moral education. These writers never actually talk about morality or ethics, the way the neo-classicals and communitarians do. It seems to me their main agenda is a political one. If anything, they'd probably dismiss most of the virtues we've looked at so far in the course as being "hegemonic." Why do you suppose the professor assigned these authors anyway? What is his "hidden moral agenda"?

B: I disagree! I think their whole attack on Western culture, particularly American capitalism, is a *moral* critique. Sure, these authors are political, but aren't they being "political" in the neo-classical sense of *polis* that we studied earlier: Don't they want people in this country, *all* the people, to be actively engaged in their own governance, to take responsibility for their civic destiny, to create a more just society? In fact, isn't the practice of citizenship a virtue for Aristotle? I know, like all the ancients, he was a racist and a sexist, at least from our perspective today, but he did believe that Athenians had a right, indeed a moral obligation, as citizens to control their own lives. These liberationist authors want the schools to teach children what true democracy is all about, and it begins with what Giroux calls "civic courage," the capacity to seize the *polis* from those in power who use it to advance their own self-interests. Also, in my opinion, I don't think the professor is trying to put anything over on us. He's very clear when he asks us to read *all* the course authors with the same questions in mind: Whose character education do you like the most? Why? Whose do you like the least? Why? What difference will your answers to these questions make in your own professional and personal life, if any? I don't think he's pushing a special agenda, because we're reading about three very different orientations. Do you really think he favors one over another? Of course, the liberationists would probably charge him with practicing hegemony in his supposed neutrality. They would say that by taking such an "even-handed" approach, he's just another academic liberal who does nothing to contest the inequalities in our present system. In fact, by remaining neutral, which, of course, is impossible, he actually shores up a corrupt economic and political system.

C: What bothers me about liberationists is that their politics are so radical, so one-sided. They make me feel like *I'm* the enemy, because I've worked hard and I'm fairly successful. I'm on the top rung of the pay scale in my school system, it's true, but I'm proud of it. I deserve it; my yearly ratings show I'm a damned good teacher. I don't see myself as somebody from the privileged class who's trying to keep people in their places. Like Marva Collins [1990], I teach *all* my children, minority *and* majority, that through honest effort and achievement they can be successful. My students always have the strongest self-esteem when they go up to the middle school at the end of the year. My colleagues tell me that my students are usually the most self-confident and the best behaved. I must be doing something right, even though I belong to what these writers call the "dominant" culture. I just don't see how critical pedagogy is going to help my kids become "good" human beings. As far as I can tell, it's just going to get them angry, and then they'll become discipline problems in school and at home. And guess what? Their parents will probably vote down another bond issue, and this time with good reason, I should add.

D: As a person of color, I'm with these writers all the way. Even though I'd like to read more *black* liberationists, and women too, I still think they've put their finger on how stacked the system is against people like me. I taught for a while as a sub in Boston, and it's tragic how rotten those schools are. In the high school where I taught, predominantly black and Latino, about 10% of the seniors went onto four-year colleges my last year there. I don't know how many of these kids survived in college, but I'll bet not many did. The high schools in Boston, in any big city, are rigged to fail students, because the "powers that be" don't think they'll ever amount to anything, and after a while, the kids tend to agree with them. I'm not even sure the authorities have a conspiracy about this sort of thing; it's just in the air they breathe and the water they drink. Isn't this what the liberationists mean by "hegemony"?

A: I still don't understand how a *political* agenda can be a *moral* agenda. I'm sorry about those kids in Boston who will never realize their dreams, but, instead of trying to turn them into little revolutionaries, why don't liberationists start doing some character education? What's wrong with the "work ethic" anyway? "Civic courage" sounds to me like a euphemism for overthrowing the system. Don't get me wrong; I like the liberationist analysis of our social system, and I agree that, at times, capitalism does seem to reward the selfish and the greedy, and penalize the generous and the unambitious. Also, I don't always blame those who are "down on their luck" for their situations, you know. One of my students has a father who's been out of work at the granite mill for over two years because it is downsizing, and in spite of his efforts, he can't find a job anywhere. It's not his fault he can't do anything else; he doesn't have a high school diploma, and he's started to drink heavily. He's devastated over losing his job, and he's stressed about the bleak employment prospects ahead. He's feeling hopelessly defeated. The family is on welfare, the mother is homebound with breast cancer, and some nights the father sleeps on the village green downtown, because he's too drunk to get home. Who's at fault here? The father? The system? The schools? The employer? Probably they all are, but it's just too easy to say that capitalism alone is the cause. Is it true that only the privileged benefit from a market economy? What's the father's responsibility to his family?

B: The trouble with the work ethic, as I understand it, is that it is a lie. It works mainly for those people who belong to a particular social class, who buy into the values of that class, and who have already made it in the system. But what has the work ethic done for the underclasses and all the other marginalized economic groups that will never, ever have a better life? No matter how hard these folks will work, they will never be able to overcome fully the prejudices against them. What do these liberationists call it—I know—their "cultural capital" will always disadvantage them, because the schools, and the society at large, depreciate their way of life. And this depreciation has a lot to do with moral education, because, in the schools, we push certain virtues at kids—sincerity, honesty, thrift, industriousness, obedience, politeness, productivity, ambitiousness, competitiveness—that are calculated to beef up the present economic system and our own social-class standing within it. The work ethic, you see, is actually a way for us to reward the kids who subscribe to our values and to punish those who don't. If this isn't a statement about moral education gone awry, I don't know what is.

C: There you go again, siding with these writers. What's wrong with the work ethic, anyway? You're putting the worst possible spin on it. Maybe it's a kind of moral education we ought to be teaching more often than we do. Don't you think that every person who lives in the "underclass" wants to become a member of the "overclass"? Why do you suppose immigrants come to this country in the first place? Why do some people from Mexico and Latin America, for example, risk imprisonment for coming here illegally? I'll tell you why. They want work, and dignity, and political freedom, and the ones who practice the work ethic the best will be successful here. Look at how successful immigrants from Korea, China, Taiwan, and Vietnam have been in our inner cities. They possess all those middle-class virtues you seem to dismiss so easily. Do you know that in my son's high school last year, a Vietnamese girl who has spoken English for only five years graduated as valedictorian of her class? She will attend Wellesley College in the fall on a full scholarship. That's Hillary Clinton's alma mater, you know. Neither she nor Hillary got to be valedictorians without hard work. Why can't that father who's out of a job go back to school to get retrained instead of feeling sorry for himself and hurting his family? What do you think the liberationists who work at the university would do if they were downsized? I'll bet they wouldn't be out sleeping on the village green. They'd find some way to make a buck. Didn't our professor say that Giroux was denied tenure at Boston University years ago? Now look at him. He didn't roll over and die.

D: This "cultural capital" business is pretty accurate, I'd say. It seems to me you're "blaming the victim" because the father was "downsized" by the granite company. I learned early on in my own schooling how to get my white public school teachers to relate to me by showing them the "stuff" I knew they valued. Even though I grew up in Roxbury, I learned how to talk like them, act like them, dress like them, and even think like them. Then, when I got to college I could be a lot more independent, because my "cultural capital" as an African American was a valued resource; and so, in the name of multiculturalism, I hustled my racial identity anywhere and everywhere to get what I needed. But you know what? The system turned me into a hypocrite, a schemer, so that I could be taken seriously. I still don't know who the hell I am today, even though I'm a lot better off financially than I was. You might say my "character education" was a lesson in how to play the system, how to trade in *cultural* capital, so that I could get the *economic* capital I needed. What's the virtue in that, pray tell?

A: I agree there's no virtue in becoming a fake, and I feel badly you thought you needed to do that to get ahead. But as much as I'm in sympathy with the basic message, I don't feel that critical pedagogy will necessarily help students, or teachers, to become more virtuous human beings. What moral message will students receive if teachers continually tell them that everything is reducible to politics and economics, and that people are always implicated in, how do the liberationists say it, "relations of power"? Liberationists "talk the talk" about "possibility," and "hope," and even *tikkun*, which, as I understand it, is a kind of healing and transforming spirit. But the underlying message of critical pedagogy is that "oppressed" groups are valorous; the system is rotten to the core; racial, gender, and class oppression is rampant; most teachers and administrators are "de-skilled," robotic system-conservers; and the real enemies are right-wing politicians, capitalists, and the Moral Majority. Given this "hero–villain" ideology, how is it possible for students and teachers to feel hopeful and healing rather than victimized, alienated, furious, and powerless? Won't liberationist "discourse" in the classroom, and in the teachers' room, become accusatory, polarizing, and harmful? What's to keep us all from becoming spies, looking for the good guys and the bad guys? On my son Tom's college campus, the pressure to be "politically correct" is so bad that his roommate reported to the residence hall director one day that Tom told him a so-called "sexist" joke at lunch. This was my son's best friend, and he turned Tom in to his p. c. supervisor for a trivial, boyish indiscretion! Where is the healing in this?

B: We are on such different sides of this issue, because I find the liberationists tremendously hopeful and not at all interested in the trivia of political correctness. I think they would consider political correctness to be a system-manufactured distraction rather than a genuine instance of "counter-hegemony." As I understand people like Giroux and Aronowitz, critical pedagogy is about bigger "fish to fry." It's all about systemic resistance, self-empowerment, and social transformation. Their "cardinal virtue," to use our professor's phrase, is *social justice,* and they have great faith in the ability of ordinary classroom teachers to be "transformative intellectuals," people who can empower students and others to resist the dehumanizing pressures of the dominant culture. I hear these thinkers continually reminding us teachers that our work is, first and foremost, *moral* work and that our moral project must be to unite with those students with the poorest economic and political cachet, so that together we can stop the exploitation and injustice. Do you honestly believe that the neo-classicals and the communitarians hold teachers in such high regard or that they are more hopeful about social change than the liberationists? The neo-classicals are hung up on "moral decline," and the communitarians are hung up on nostalgia. Where exactly do *we* fit into their character-education plans? We've got a lot to learn about "transformative discourse," all right, but I'm willing to take the risk. What kind of discourse do we have now in the schools? In my school, I can tell you for sure that we don't talk about "liberation," "hope," or "possibility" in the lunchroom or in the classroom.

C: I admit you make some good points, and I am pleased that these scholars think so highly of teachers. In my experience, too many teacher educators talk down to us, patronize us, and the readings they assign are so simplistic and impractical. But, in my opinion, these thinkers have gone to the other extreme. This has certainly been the toughest group of readings I have ever waded through in a course. I can barely understand what these liberationist authors are saying. In fact, although I don't think they intentionally mean to, they make me feel dumb. Do you understand their language? Why can't they write in plain English? My husband, who works at IBM, claims that if you can't say something simply, then you don't know what you're talking about. At his office, the manager sends back poorly written reports stamped KISS: "Keep It Simple, Stupid."

These liberationist writers would never make it in the real world of corpo-rations, or in the public schools, where memos have to be succinct, under-standable, and practical.

D: I'm really tired of all the whining about how hard it is to read these folks. They've got something important to say; they think we're intelligent enough to understand it; they're not talking down to us. Why can't we meet them half-way? Nothing can be tougher than programming my VCR, but yet I take the time to read the incredibly dense instructions, because I want to record the Knicks' game. Maybe we don't really want to hear what the liberationists are telling us, because the message would challenge our comfortable way of life. The schools and the colleges, the media and the government, "dumb down" so much stuff that, in spite of what I said earlier, I'm beginning to think there's a conspiracy to keep us all stupid so that we don't know how to challenge the logic of the system. What's happening in this country—in our corporations, in education, and in the media and politics—is complex, and it requires complex language to explain it. I love Giroux's notion of "emancipatory" or "directive" knowledge. Emancipatory knowledge helps us to understand how power and privilege distort all social relationships. As a black man, I'm here to tell you that if we're ever going to get beyond all the mutually self-destructive crap when we talk about race relations in this country, we need to know what's going on economically, politically, and socially in the larger system that feeds the racial antagonisms. Who ultimately bene-fits? I just don't know how you can describe this stuff in a dumbed-down way and really get at the heart of the matter.

A: Oh, oh, it looks as if the professor wants to get us back to the big group. I've enjoyed the conversation, but I want you to know I'm still not convinced that these writers are character educators. By the way, has any-one been taking notes? Somebody's got to report what we said to the big group, and I'm not volunteering.

In my teaching, I frequently hear three interrelated themes from stu-dents about critical pedagogy, and I have attempted to address them in the imaginary conversation above: *politics/democracy, virtue,* and *language.* I will elaborate on these themes in the following paragraphs, with addi-tional critical commentary where appropriate.

LIBERATIONIST POLITICS/DEMOCRACY AND THE TRANSFORMATIVE VIRTUES

For liberationists, politics, democracy, and virtue are inseparable. Libera-tionists think of democracy both as a "site" for struggle and as a series of "social practices" (politics) wherein competing ideologies engage in perpetual combat (Freire, 1985; Giroux, 1988; Kanpol, 1994; McLaren, 1994). More than legal rules, administrative procedures, voting, defending the free-market economy, or constitutionally defining the limits of individual rights and liberties, democracy, for liberationists, is really about politics—contestation, conflict, and resistance. Democracy happens when oppressed citizens come together to demand their political, economic, and social equality. This conception of democracy requires a particular kind of citizen; someone who is willing and able to engage in what liberationists call "emancipatory discourse and practice." Citizenship, in the liberationist view, is actually an ongoing public dialogue of "critique and possibility," whose objective is to create alliances among all disenfranchised peoples in order to "criticize, constrain, and overthrow" state power and capitalistic monopoly in America (Giroux, 1988, p. 11). In this scheme, the function of democratic schooling therefore is to produce citizens who have the knowledge and skills to critique and transform the social order.

Many of my students, upon first reading the liberationists, are rightfully excited about their vision of politics, democracy, citizenship, and teaching. I have tried to capture some of this enthusiasm in the preceding imaginary dialogue in the persons of *B* and *D*. Interestingly, though, few students, even the most ardent liberationist supporters, think of critical pedagogy as moral education or character training. They tend to agree with *A* that the liberationist initiative is mainly political, not moral. In fact, I once had a student who tried to make the case in a research paper that liberationists are actually advocates of an "antivirtue" ideology. She argued that, like Nietzsche in *On the Genealogy of Morals* (1887/1989), the liberationists actually think of virtue as a mask for a "will to power." Or, in Foucauldian (1981) language, objective morality is a "fiction," invented by the powerful to celebrate their own internal goodness and to reinforce certain virtues calculated to strengthen the present capitalist "regimes of power."

In truth, liberationists seldom talk in any explicit or extensive way about morality, virtue, or moral character, although some do speak the language of "political ethics," as in "Authority, Ethics, and the Politics of Schooling," the title of a chapter in a popular Giroux (1988) text. In preparation for writing this chapter, I reviewed dozens of publications on critical pedagogy, and I found not one reference to *morality* in their indices, nor a single one to *character* or *virtue*. One obvious reason for this void, I think, is that liberationists view the "religious right" (some neoclassicals and the sectarian communitarians) in this country as coopting moral-character language in order to push a very conservative political agenda, and they simply refuse to use the same language associated with this reactionary group. Another obvious reason is the wish to avoid sounding prescriptive or moralistic while encouraging various oppressed groups to make their own moral senses of the world. It is my contention, however, that liberationist ideology is, in fact, rooted in a particular set of virtues, and although these virtues are admirable, even defensible in some cases, as currently conceived I think they are deeply flawed. As the liberationists present these virtues, they are divisive, full of revolutionary fervor, and a serious obstacle to the kind of slow, deliberative, collective decision making I believe to be necessary in a secular pluralist democracy.

I cannot recall a single instance in the liberationist literature when students are asked to consider seriously either the morality of critical pedagogy's educational methods or those virtues they will have to cultivate in order to become "transformative intellectuals." Without systematic ethical training, how will it be possible for liberationist educational leaders to avoid the loss of their humanity in "liberating" others? The likelihood is great, I contend, that without sustained moral reflection students trained as critical pedagogues will leave their graduate education believing that they alone have overcome their political retrogression and that the rest of the world is incorrigibly racist, sexist, and capitalistic. A single-minded obsession with the mission of delivering the "oppressed" from the "oppressor" can only blind students to the reality that most normal people steadfastly resist the arrogance of "liberators" and feel patronized and insulted when they get treated as hapless dupes. Although there is much to support in liberationist conceptions of democracy and education, I worry about how the excessive political zeal of liberationists so often undermines the cogency of their keen social analysis with my working-class students. More important, though, I regret that the powerful moral insights in liberationist writing frequently get lost in the "us-against-them" rhetoric.

There is moral indignation in the liberationist initiative that is noticeably absent in the neo-classical and communitarian initiatives, and, at times, I believe this outrage is inspiring and accurately felt. For example, it is impossible not to be deeply moved by Paulo Freire's (1971, 1985, 1994b) writings describing the oppression of Latin American peasants by an entrenched ruling class intent on keeping them illiterate, poor, dependent, and powerless. I have even had some students moved to tears when we discuss Freire's extraordinary success in helping poor people learn to read (what he calls the practice of "transformative literacy") and, as a result, seize control of their own lives in Brazil and in other Latin American countries. In his fieldwork and in his writing, Freire is an exemplary model of such transformative virtues as empathy, hope, possibility, absolute respect for the peasant as a thinking, feeling person, and authenticity in dialogue; he is visionary, prophetic, reflective, activistic, utopian, humanistic, political, and realistic. Unfortunately, however, not all liberationists are Paulo Freire, and his virtues, when pushed to extremes in their hands, threaten, at times, to become vices. An old medieval saying about virtue fits perfectly here: *"Corruptio optimi pessima"* ("The perversion of the highest virtues can lead to the worst vices" [My translation]) (Pieper, 1992, p. 35).

Like Freire, liberationists think of morality as a "preferential concern for the suffering and struggles of the disadvantaged and oppressed" (Giroux, 1988, p. 175). But unlike him, their virtues are predominantly the *virtues of contestation:* struggle, conflict, resistance, and counter-hegemony. They think of themselves as being "under siege" (Aronowitz & Giroux, 1985). They rail against patriarchy, colonialism, racism, sexism, and capitalism. They speak of such "transformative" virtues as risk-taking, civic courage, social justice, critical discourse, and liberation. Far from being "antivirtue" thinkers, I believe they are proud practitioners of what I would metaphorically call the "martial virtues." They are ready to take up moral arms against the "oppressor" in behalf of emancipation and large-scale social change. Some consider themselves to be "critical insurgents" battling a "predatory culture" (McLaren, 1995). Others are nomadic "border crossers" who willingly leave the safety of their comfortable social spaces and "journey" to different zones of scholarship, cultural and class locations, and ideologies, in order to achieve "solidarity" with "oppressed" peoples (Giroux, 1994). Some are "warriors" within the schools working to create a new "public sphere" by exposing the class biases of the "hidden curricula" and advocating "open resistance" (Giroux, 1983). Critical pedagogues "teach against the grain" (Kanpol, 1994), "live dangerously" (Freire, 1994b; Giroux, 1993), and challenge "official knowledge" (Apple, 1993).

All of this is noble, well intended, and, in some cases, even necessary, but, in the end, most of my students are left to ask, in the words of Elizabeth Ellsworth (1989), a liberationist ally, "Why doesn't this feel empowering"? Increasingly, even "friendly" critics are beginning to charge critical pedagogy with a number of "transgressions," among them: a thinly concealed sexism; a preference for hyper-rationalist discourse; leaving "relations of domination" untouched in classrooms; positing a one-sided theory of social change and knowledge; "silencing" diverse voices; overlooking the plight of victims of "fat oppression," "ableism," "anti-Semitism," and so forth; stifling "defiant voices"; and hopelessness (see, e.g., Ellsworth, 1989; Kelly, 1991; Portelli, 1991). While they make many valid points, for the most part, I think these "loyal" critics engage in a type of "you're-not-as-liberated-or-as-critical-as-I-am" carping, probably an inevitable hazard of doing critical pedagogy. These writers seem ever on the alert, as critical pedagogues themselves, to up the "counter-hegemonic" ante against other critical pedagogues.

I believe one major reason why critical pedagogy does not feel empowering for most of my students is because many liberationists have inadvertently turned their "transformative" virtues into "deformative" vices. In pursuit of a democracy of contestation, conflict, resistance, and struggle, what I am calling the *martial dispositions*, some liberationists have neglected to develop the softer, more reconciling virtues they will need to justify the radical disruption of people's lives in order to bring about the fundamental social change they seek. Purpel and Shapiro (1995) speak of the need for liberationists to shape an "agenda for educational reform" grounded in moral outrage and a sense of urgency, yes, but also an agenda rich in the virtues of tolerance, diversity, openness, hope, possibility, transformation, humility, compassion, and care. I agree completely that without the moral balance these virtues provide for any revolutionary's agenda, the unanticipated political outcome is likely to be a deformed notion of democracy, or, even worse, a tyranny.

In fact, critical pedagogy fails to connect with many of my students because they reject what they think is its repressive *political* content. They suspect that the liberationist agenda will lead nowhere but to despotism. Although critical pedagogues like to think they have improved upon Karl Marx, their so-called radical critique of capitalism limps in comparison with Marx's vividly grim yet eloquent description of capitalism's impact on society in *The Communist Manifesto*:

> Constant revolutionizing of production, uninterrupted disturbance of all social relations, everlasting uncertainty and agitation, distinguish the bourgeois epoch from all earlier times. All fixed, fast-frozen relationships, with their train of venerable ideas and opinions, are swept away, all new-formed ones become obsolete before they can ossify. All that is solid melts into air, all that is holy is profaned, and men at last are forced to face with sober senses the real conditions of their lives and their relations with their fellow men. (quoted in Van Doren, 1991, p. 263)

Most of my students today refuse to believe that capitalism, in spite of its invidious, internal contradictions, is so irredeemably evil. For the vast majority, capitalism has given them and their families a high standard of living, as well as unlimited hope for the future. In contrast, they look at the revolutions carried out in Marx's name around the world, and they see only misery, oppression, corruption, and radical concentration of power by government bureaucrats and the military. They want no part of any economic or political system that appears to them to breed laziness and mediocrity, as well as fear, loss of freedom, and a crushing despair over life's prospects. They fear, understandably, the liberationists' refusal to be clear about where the revolution is heading, and they do not like leaving it up to the "emancipated" groups to determine this country's political and economic goals. They wonder if the extermination of social classes will lead to the abolition of private property, the loss of personal freedom, and the erosion of a middle-class quality of life they greatly appreciate. This grim prospect, whether realistic or not, is too steep a price for most students to pay for pursuing a utopia of equal outcomes they find morally repugnant.

Notwithstanding these macro fears, however, the liberationists do help my students to understand that democracy and capitalism are a combustible combination whenever capitalism is allowed to gain the upper hand in a society. Certainly, private ownership of capital and a market economy are indispensable for the production of enough wealth to distribute, so that everyone can enjoy a high quality of material life. But, historically, bourgeois capitalist economies tend to betray democratic notions of liberty and equality whenever capital gets concentrated in the hands of a few corporations, and, over time, these institutions accrue disproportionate influence and power outside their appropriate economic sphere (Walzer, 1983). Gradually, this structural inequality produces class conflict, social division, discrimination, and alienation throughout the social order, and chronic destabilization occurs.

At the micro level of everyday life in America, people increasingly experience an erosion of their political power, along with a general sense that the "good life" is becoming more and more difficult to realize for the majority of the poor and the middle class in America. Despite its gloominess, though, this liberationist analysis still rings true for many students, and a few even get roused to action. But, at this point in the discourse, they are stymied. Because the liberationists have not worked on specific pedagogical strategies beyond exhorting teachers to become "transformative intellectuals," bring popular culture into their classrooms, and form solidarity with oppressed peoples, these students are left to ask: Now what? How? Where? When?

Unlike the liberationists, Patricia White (1996) has written insightfully about those "civic virtues" she believes educated citizens will need to function well in a democratic society, and her virtues serve as a powerful counter to the "martial virtues" I discuss above. White's concept of democracy contains both macro *and* micro elements: At the macro level, she thinks of democracy as "the most appropriate embodiment of the values of freedom, justice, and respect for personal autonomy in that context" (p. 1). At the micro level, she puts less emphasis on political principles and more on fostering what she calls the "democratic dispositions." At this level, she characterizes democracy as

> the hope for the maintenance and fuller realization of a way of life in which everyone has a chance at self-creation to the best of his or her abilities, in conditions of peace and adequate resources, within a framework of the usual civic freedoms. (p. 11)

White's micro vision of democracy is, admittedly, minimalist, nonpolitical, and individualistic, and Marxists and sectarian Christians, as well as liberationists, might have a problem marching under its banner. Liberationists would almost certainly contest her belief that, regardless of the institutions in place in a society, everything will be better if people only acquire the pertinent democratic dispositions. They would probably dismiss her "hidden" political agenda as being hopelessly melioristic, insouciant, and system-sustaining. But, for White, regardless of people's ideological differences, it is only at the micro level that teachers, especially, can be most effective in "instantiating" the democratic principles and virtues. And I enthusiastically agree.

What I find highly profitable in White's work for my own thinking about character education are two factors. First, she is willing to formulate an intensive *philosophical* account of those virtues she believes necessary to achieve democracy. The liberationists, as I have pointed out earlier, care little about philosophy and seldom refer, in any explicit way, to the virtues. Second, she names and illustrates the specific dispositions that teachers can model and "instantiate" in the schools. In my estimation, I believe the "martial" virtues of the liberationists would seem far less one-sided to my students if they were accompanied by White's particular set of "civic" dispositions. The virtues she advances are hope, courage, self-respect, friendship, trust, honesty, and decency, and she is convinced that these dispositions are crucial to achieving a "flourishing democratic life." I am as well.

White's approach to civic virtue suggests that before teachers and students can become "transformative intellectuals," they need, first, to *be disposed* to use their understandings and skills democratically. And the formation of a democratic character occurs not just in schools but also in the family and in the pluralistic communities that surround the school. White is also adamant that teachers should both *shape* the appropriate civic virtues and help students to *understand* them. After all, the virtue of self-respect requires that teachers avoid brainwashing or indoctrinating students regarding the "proper" democratic dispositions. From a postmodern perspective, I appreciate White's refusal to ground her virtue agenda in a "grand political narrative" of "oppressors-against-the-oppressed." Rather, she starts with a "local narrative": The need for each person in the classroom to fabricate those moral stories that will serve as "useful fictions" in their everyday lives. And White's teachers constantly encourage students to engage in acts of "self-creation," to freely choose and develop the virtues that will give identity, purpose, and shape to their democratic lives.

Finally, I urge liberationists to take seriously White's (1996) warning that "ideological purity" in the pursuit of sound moral goals is almost always an "obstacle" to "honesty and candor" in democratic settings. In White's perceptive words:

> For some antisexist and antiracist Puritans, however, it is not enough that people recognize the problems, struggle to reorient themselves, adapt to new manners, and help to build new institutional structures. They expect a world of New Men and Women, pure in thought, word, and deed, as of now. Much energy is then spent in attempting to identify the unregenerate racist or sexist behind the "hypocritical facade." But do we want to lock ourselves into the pursuit of purity in this way? (p. 73)

For White, "holier-than-thou," ideological purity in the service of social justice produces dismal moral results: dishonesty, because people are seldom able to live up to impossibly high ideals; hypocrisy; suspicion; and witch hunts. White is saying that, by all means, we should strenuously resist racism and sexism in the schools and colleges. But instead of waiting to pounce self-righteously on people whenever they make mistakes, "we might highlight the more hopeful image of people who have been willing to change their behavior in one context perhaps being prepared, over time, to examine their attitudes and behavior in other contexts" (p. 73).

Too many liberationists appear oblivious to the counterproductive dangers of imposing unrealistically high ideals on people and then expecting immediate personal transformations. Worse, they run the risk not only of denying the existence of human frailty but also of inadvertently running roughshod over the values of many children's families, without doing the necessary groundwork to change these beliefs. For White, shaping virtuous behavior in a democracy will always be a sensitive, difficult activity, and when teachers substitute one vice for another—with the best of intentions—they are actually engaging in the least effective way to shape moral character. I will return to White's formulation of the "democratic dispositions" in the last chapter.

In the following section, I intend to comment on liberationist *language*, the one element in the critical pedagogy agenda that students continually criticize in my classes. I will come at the issues of democracy and virtue from a slightly different vantage point, and I will raise some new questions about how to form the democratic character that I believe critical pedagogues would agree is an important project for schools and colleges.

LIBERATIONIST LANGUAGE

Many students in my course, like C in the earlier imaginary dialogue, cannot wait to criticize the mystifying argot that liberationists employ. They find the terminology "elitist," "technical," and "tedious," and they wonder why liberationist "discourse" has to be so "exclusionary." After all, some students reason, if the goal of critical pedagogy is inclusion of *all* peoples in the common struggle for social justice, how is a jargon-riddled, academic "discourse" going to help matters? Won't this tangled vocabulary merely perpetuate the power differences between the over-class and the underclass, between the educated, the undereducated, and the uneducated? Even two liberationist sympathizers, Purpel and Shapiro (1995), suggest that liberationist writing smacks of "hypercerebralism" and "elitism," and in a very guarded way, they remark that critical theorists do have a responsibility to write clearly.

In my estimation, though, Purpel and Shapiro overlook the "hidden" *moral* message in the "opaque, arid, tendentious, and dense" (p. 122) linguistic style of critical pedagogues, preferring instead to focus on *strategic* difficulties in the critical pedagogy movement itself as the main reason why so many people are put off by the ideas. Certainly, I would agree that the "resistance, fragmentation, and scope" of the critical pedagogy movement are key reasons for not reaching many otherwise favorably disposed readers, but I would reemphasize that something far more important is going on here as well. Often, as I suggested in the previous section, liberationist language is morally arrogant, itself oppressive, and provides an unsettling glimpse of what the "good life" will be like in the "liberated" social order.

First, a few words on the *aesthetic* quality of the writing in critical pedagogy: Personally, I find much of the political prose clotted, repetitive, unnecessarily polysyllabic, and preachy. So, evidently, does the august liberationist himself, Paulo Freire, who observes in *Pedagogy of Hope*

(1994b) that scholarly writing should be both "rigorous" *and* "fine, elegant, and esthetic," a "discourse without sharp edges" (pp. 72–73). But, I also agree with David Hume's stipulation that *De gustibus non disputandum est* ("Matters of taste are not to be disputed" [My translation]). There are times when we must try to get beyond a personal taste for a particular style of writing in order to find the "nuggets" that reside in strange and difficult language. (I always give this advice to those students who find my own peculiar brand of postmodern language utterly incomprehensible.) This is true whether one is reading Shakespeare, a computer-programming manual, a deconstructionist essay, or a critical pedagogy publication. I am more than willing to acknowledge that much liberationist writing is dreadful. What I refuse to concede, however, is that, as a general rule, a woeful writing style ipso facto invalidates the content. My judgment in this instance, though, is that liberationist style and content are so intimately interwoven that *the language* in which critical pedagogues choose to carry on the discourse is ultimately inseparable from the *moral impact* the content is meant to convey. In their case, the political medium *is* the moral message.

Few liberationists actually argue; most tend to declaim, to pontificate. They assume the moral high ground *a priori,* and they proceed to issue a series of self-authenticating, ethical proclamations to the rest of us who inhabit the low ground. They do not demonstrate; they remonstrate. Thus their discourse ends up neither persuading nor convincing most of my students. And when the langugage is effective, I believe it is because it bludgeons some students into guilty submission via the steady drumbeat of powerful, accusatory words. The cumulative impact on students of such guilt-inducing words as *oppression, patriarchy, hegemony, ideology, colonialism, racism, sexism, class interests, capitalism, prejudice, domination, injustice, privilege,* repeated indiscriminately and *ad infinitum* drives home but one point again and again and again: You are either a *bad* person or a *good* person, depending entirely on your skin color, gender, economic status, sexual orientation, social-class membership, politics, and, yes, religious convictions. Never mind who you are as a unique individual, or the content of your incomparable moral character. It is mainly your membership in one or more of these categories that sums up your entire meaning as a human being. And if you do not agree with this harsh diagnosis, then this itself is proof-positive of the accusation: You have been effectively brainwashed, or socialized, or domesticated, or coopted by the hegemonic system to deny your own moral culpability in perpetuating injustice. You are dangerous, or you are oppressed, and you must be reeducated. And because we know what is right for you, we are willing to transform you or to liberate you, whatever is required.

In spite of an occasional empathic aside in the literature that "we are *all* in this together—both oppressed and oppressor"—and that we must *all* unify to achieve a "solidarity," or that we are *all* unjust victims of a "predatory," "rapacious" capitalism, liberationists make it very clear to the majority of my students that critical pedagogy is not an "equal opportunity" movement. Some students, because of the ascendancy and force of the social system, are ineluctably "shaped" to be oppressors, and others oppressed, and that is the fatalistic truth of it. Time and time again, after careful readings of several of the texts I have mentioned above, white women and men will remark in class that they feel "utterly defeated," left in a state of helpless despair and guilt by liberationist authors who are so deterministic.

I regret this, because while many of these students try at least initially to remain open to the readings, they often end up resisting the more penetrating insights in critical pedagogy by becoming numb and shutting down. Worse, a few others adopt (and distort) what they believe to be the liberationist discourse style, and they become converts to the "faith," the true believers. They try to turn the classroom into an arena for combat, featuring *ad hominem* and *ad feminam* attacks; wholesale political indictments of groups, systems, and individuals; and aggressive public "confessions" of their own guilt and shame over some personal or political infraction. I have found that the language of political outrage in critical pedagogy irretrievably shapes the quality of discourse in my classroom and sets the moral climate as well, in spite of my efforts to counter the more deleterious effects of such language.

The "true believers" in my course are quick to conclude that the "big words" in critical pedagogy equate with "big" moral authority, and so some students become ideologically supercilious. They wield "sharp-edged" (Freire, 1994b) words as rapiers in order to "cut" down retrograde political opponents and heretics. They make overly facile distinctions between good and evil, and, in doing so, they oversimplify and elide moral responsibility. Formulaic "praise words," such as *oppressed, counter-hegemony, emancipation, critical discourse, cultural capital, resistance, struggle, critical theory,* and *social justice,* and "blame words" such as the ones I have cited earlier, serve mainly as verbal bombast and obscure the genuine complexity of moral discourse.

I have additional problems in my course with the highly normative language of critical pedagogy. I have found that one-sided, prosecutorial nomenclature generally discourages students' efforts to comprehend and apply it, no matter how discerning and accurate the language may be. As a result, some students reject this language outright. Some parody it. And others spend all their time sniping away at it without ever coming to terms with its important insights. As a general rule in my course, I find that moral language *without a sense of its own fallibility* ceases to be a force for truth, because it inevitably invites students to become deconstructionists: to expend disproportionate amounts of their energy looking for the language's internal distortions, contradictions, and disguised self-interests and hypocrisies. Finally, I have found that the language of the *political* "prophet," no matter how eloquent or penetrating, rarely inspires my students, because, at heart, most students are political skeptics who, sooner or later, will attempt to drive false prophets out of the land. In my experience, language tinged with a little humor and humility can go a long way in blunting such student cynicism.

I must point out, to be fair, that lately some liberationist authors have attempted to write in a more felicitous prose style without forfeiting the "rigor" they believe critical theory must bring to complex social analysis. Some of their writing is more personal, confessional, and narrative in its construction. Thus Paulo Freire in *Pedagogy of Hope* (1994b) can reminisce in some very poignant ways on what has happened to his life since the American publication in 1971 of *The Pedagogy of the Oppressed.* Michael W. Apple can spend the last two chapters of *Official Knowledge* (1993) sharing how he manages to keep his spirits up during the dark days of the "conservative restoration." Even Henry A. Giroux (1992, 1994), a veritable publishing industry all by himself, is becoming somewhat self-referential in his latest works, almost as if to counter his public image as a disembodied intellectual who spends every free moment churning out one highly theoretical book after another. And, intriguingly, many of these authors (e.g., Apple, 1993; Freire, 1994b; Giroux, 1994) have come up with a new self-disclosing twist in their books: They allow people to interview them as quasi-celebrities, and then they append these interviews to their books as final chapters. Although one can argue that these self-referential developments merely accelerate the highly narcissistic, arrogant trajectory already present in liberationist writing, I prefer to put the best construction on these events.

One troubling disclaimer, however: I have noticed that as some liberationist writing gains in clarity, self-revelation, and stylistic flair, the absolute moral certainty quotient actually intensifies. For example, what might a dissenting student make of this "prophetic" statement by Purpel and Shapiro (1995):

> Life in the United States at this time has become so painful, alienating, ethically compromised, and spiritually impoverished, that education must speak first and foremost to this human and social crisis. . . . The crisis

> reaches into the very corners and crevices of our society, producing the pau-
> perization of some and the miseration of many. (p. 143)

Is there any way a student could honestly disagree with the black-and-white, apocalyptic nature of this rhetoric, echoic of the "moral decline" of the neo-classicals, without being dismissed by the authors as morally backward, deluded, or an oppressor?

Moreover, Purpel and Shapiro (1995) can warn against "demonizing" the enemy ("the Right"), "fighting fire with fire" and, instead, advocate using "warmth" and "compassion" and "understanding those who differ with us" (p. 160). But, throughout the same book, the authors can continue to "binarize" (a liberationist "snarl word" for setting up false dualisms) the world into allies and foes. For example, conservatives are said to "worship" the "capitalist marketplace"; they are "selfish," unlike folks like Purpel and Shapiro who are "open, loving, and caring" (p. 138). It is the "power elite," the "oppressive class," who dominate the society and leave "us culturally voiceless, politically powerless, and psychologically maimed" (pp. 107, 117). Unfortunately, notwithstanding their own caveats against the "dangers of self-righteousness and moral zealotry" (p. 156), the authors' polarizing rhetoric, whether intended or not, may indeed be the language of what the authors call "prophetic pragmatism" (p. 211), but it is a long way from the language of the healer.

Peter McLaren (1994) also understands that prophetic moral language needs to be "spiritually restorative" as well as "politically transformative" (p. 281). He rightfully acknowledges that there are "languages" of emotions, desires, and self-transcendence, and any movement that remains exclusively conceptual and political in its use of language is unlikely to deliver full human emancipation. McLaren appears to have learned the lesson that political and economic revolutions alone will never sustain the human spirit over a long period of time. Moreover, he believes that too much polarizing language tends to reduce to a series of "vestigial cliches," and, if critical pedagogy is to become truly transformative and responsive to all peoples, it must insist on a "revisionist literacy consisting of new terminologies" (p. 281).

But McLaren is still unwilling to compromise on the issue of whether liberationist language ought to become more "accessible." In his own brand of "liberationistspeak," he declares that, unfortunately, "common sense" language can "usher in a new dictatorship of pre-theoretical nativism in which experience supposedly speaks for itself . . . such a form of binary thinking would reduce [the] language of analysis to white, hegemonic forms of clarity" (p. 282). The meaning here for students is that "common sense" language is immoral (hegemonic) and what McLaren has come to call "metacritical" language (p. 283) is moral (counter-hegemonic). Thus, even within the context of his fine insight regarding the need for "spiritually restorative" language, McLaren continues to draw the battle lines sharply, separating whom he considers the trans-gressor ("white hegemony") from the transgressed (the "black experi-ence"). Once again, sadly, the ultimate casualty appears to be *tikkun*.

The challenge for liberationists, as I see it, is to continue to make their powerful critique of one-sided capitalist discourses but learn to be much more sensitive to the richness and variety of *all* ideologies, includ-ing the ideology of the Right. The problem with any overly rational, mu-tually exclusive political discourse, whether of the Right *or* Left, is that it squeezes the variety and richness of political ideologies into an artificial homogeneity. In its vehemence, an oppositional discourse runs the risk of obliterating difference, otherness, and nuance. In my classes each se-mester, I have "capitalists" who work at IBM, and other corporations, who cannot be characterized as economic oppressors. Neither are most of my fundamentalist, white Christian believers likely to be racists, or homophobes, or anti-abortion zealots. And neither are the majority of those students who are less well off, regardless of color or social class, willing to think of themselves as "oppressed." In fact, those students who, in any given semester, might be on welfare, out of work, or just "down on their luck" are the very ones who resist what they feel are "elitist," "patronizing" labels that make them appear "victims"—utterly power-less vis à vis their own resources to deal with their predicaments.

One of Michel Foucault's (1977) excellent insights is that "Truth" is a fabrication, an ideology, and when it gets "encoded" in public discourse and circulated in social "narratives," it then becomes an instrument of control and power by those who do the encoding. If Foucault is right, then in many ways critical pedagogy, like free-market ideology, is a "fic-tion," "a system of ordered procedures" that produces and sustains a particular "regime" of power. Like Foucault, I believe the appropriate project of the liberationist scholar, and the college teacher, ought to be to subject *all* "fictions," including postmodernism, critical pedagogy, neo-classical character education, and communitarianism, to continual cri-tique. I submit that this leveling of the ideological playing field is highly egalitarian in that it "privileges" a *process* rather than a particular "truth," "advantages" dialogue rather than doctrinal pronouncements and con-demnations, and strives for otherness and difference instead of universal-ity and sameness. The trick, of course, for us in the classroom, is to learn to engage in a "compassionate" critical discourse whose starting point is nothing more or less than mutual, respectful understanding of our *philo-*

sophical differences. This philosophical understanding, I maintain, must always be preliminary to the resolution of our political, religious, gender, and racial differences in the larger society.

With due respect to this kind of discourse, however, there are serious difficulties. In postmodern terms, for Foucault (1981), there is a determinate "meaning *outside* the text," in the sense that there is an objective power structure in place and its selective "truths" always "privilege" those who control knowledge and disadvantage those who do not. For Jacques Derrida (1978), however, the only meaning resides *"inside* the text itself,"* in our own unique interpretations of the "order of things." In theory, the "truth" of these "unique interpretations" is infinitely variable, because our own individual languages are so uniquely different and our meanings are constantly shifting. "Critical" liberationists, of course, line up with Foucault. "Conservative" postmodern hermeneutes side with Derrida. Richard Rorty (1982), although respectful of both thinkers, looks neither to Foucault nor to Derrida for the final "truth" about knowledge, ideology, and power. For him, there is no ultimate starting or ending point for discourse, because each of us is embedded in a contingent, temporal reality. Thus we can only be sure that each of our interpretations is partial, there can be no universal authority to which we can unanimously appeal, and it is rare that we can ever rise above our individual communities of truth to find a "transcendent" Truth.

As a classroom teacher, I am strongly drawn to Richard Rorty's "reading" of the way things are. I, too, believe that each of us—my students and myself—is a product of many interpretive communities and that these will always be the starting and ending points for our various conversations. In Rorty's (1982) compelling words: "In the end . . . what matters is our loyalty to other human beings clinging together against the dark, not our hope of getting things [finally] right" (p. 157). My own pedagogy is predicated on experimenting with ways for my students to talk to one another that will lead them to some kind of nonviolent, democratic connection, some kind of "clinging together against the dark." I refuse to settle on a political discourse that promotes only perpetual contestation and confrontation. While I certainly appreciate the pedagogical utility of contestation and struggle in any kind of classroom conversation, I also aim toward other outcomes.

The overall goal of my own pedagogy, both inside and outside the classroom, is not to uncover the definitive truth about politics, religion, or economics but to stimulate and sustain a mutually respectful, democratic conversation among all the holders of the differing ideologies that surface in every course I teach. This requires, I believe, finding a language, a discourse, that is accessible and interpretable to everyone, one that is solicitous of *all* views, whose eventual end is understanding and reconciliation rather than rancor and rupture. This, then, is my own "fiction," and, as a teacher, I will continue to remain silent not only on what I believe to be the final "truth" of human existence but also on who I consider to be the "enemies" of the good life. Like Richard Rorty (1989) and Reinhold Niebuhr (1952), I prefer the language of "irony, contingency, and solidarity" in my classroom discourse on moral education. I intend to discuss this type of discourse in the next two chapters. But, for now, I wish to close with Niebuhr's striking words regarding the ironies of finitude, contingency, love, dignity, and moral truth. I believe the liberationist initiative has much to learn from Niebuhr's (1952) understanding of the limits and possibilities of human agency:

> Nothing that is worth doing can be achieved in our lifetime; therefore, we must be saved by hope. Nothing which is true or beautiful or good makes complete sense in any immediate context of history; therefore, we must be saved by faith. Nothing we do, however virtuous, can be accomplished alone; therefore, we are saved by love. No virtuous act is quite as virtuous from the standpoint of our friend or foe as it is from our standpoint. Therefore, we must be saved by the final form of love which is forgiveness. (p. 63)

CONCLUSION

In the last two chapters, I will continue the argument for the "democratic dispositions" made by Patricia White (1996). I will focus expressly on some postmodern conceptions of private and public virtue, with the purpose of developing a rationale for the practice of a type of public, ideology-free dialogue, one that might get us beyond our political and economic differences in a secular pluralist society. In particular, I will discuss a kind of classroom discourse, what I call the "moral conversation," and I will propose a number of "civility protocols" as a way of dealing with difficult issues. I believe that Richard Rorty and others can be very helpful to those of us who are teachers in fostering the kinds of democratic dispositions necessary for civic life in America, a country that has traditionally harbored an "incredulity toward metanarratives" (Lyotard, 1984).

CHAPTER 8

A Personal Interlude:
A Morality of Conversation

The [moral conversation] that might take place between people with divergent attitudes . . . is more likely to continue if we can imagine the world from the other side of the barricade. Standing among "the enemy" for a moment, we might be able to see similarities between them and us, not some common "human nature" or some ineffable "essence" shared by all men, but the fact that we are all bundles of opinions and beliefs, of theories and prejudices about how we and our world are or ought to be. . . . To explore these possibilities, you have to understand more about the intellectual source of your moral conflict, listen a little harder to the other side of the story. [In one sense] morality is a continuing conversation about how we can keep from stomping on one another's special projects of self-improvement.

—*Edward Tivnan*, The Moral Imagination: Confronting the
Ethical Issues of Our Day, 1995

Listening to others does not require that we give up . . . our own point of view. . . . What is called for is an acknowledgement that all of our truths are partial, that all of our understandings are incomplete, that we are always in process. . . . While avoiding confrontation may not always be possible or desirable, there does seem to be considerable benefit in a model that alters our conversations about moral choices in ways that encourage an exchange of viewpoints, that offers possibilities for building relationships rather than erecting barriers between people. . . . Making others more like us in the continuing conversation is not the only reason for interacting with them.

—*D. Don Welch*, Conflicting Agendas: Personal Morality
in Institutional Settings, 1994

Many people seem compelled to jump into a heated argument the moment they sense a different opinion. . . . This tendency may be natural, but it need not be controlling. We can learn to acknowledge, without feeling threatened, the value of ideas that do not fit our system. . . . [When I acknowledge the other] I am simply offering to that person the dignity, support, and encouragement that I myself need as I inch my way along the path. In short, we can choose to act as effective catalysts and staunch supports for one another or we can make [conversation] even more difficult and painful by fueling the fires of self-doubt in ourselves and others.

Elizabeth Z. McGrath, The Art of Ethics: A Psychology
of Ethical Beliefs, 1994

I intend for this brief interlude to be a more personal departure from what has preceded it. An interlude is an intervening space set between the parts of a longer narrative for the purpose of providing a contrast with what goes before and after. Here, in this space, in order to set the stage for the chapter to follow, I intend to talk about moral education mainly from the standpoint of my own seminar teaching in a college of education. That is, what constitutes *my* micro world—my classroom, my teaching method, my students—will be the point from which I look at the macro world of character education, the virtues, and democracy. Neo-classical, communitarian, and liberationist languages inform some of what I have to say in these last chapters, but the worldviews they represent are far too large, monolithic, and prescriptive for my purposes here. In general, my own moral language is a collection of postmodern odds and ends, put together to serve my particular goals. Jeffrey Stout (1988) calls this language of odds and ends a *moral bricolage,* a kind of normative *Esperanto.* And at a time when moral truth claims in the United States are up for grabs everywhere, Stout believes this is exactly the language a secular pluralist society requires. I agree.

We need a public moral language that is *nonfoundational* (a language not grounded in particular, self-evident principles that all must accept), *multifunctional* (a language useful to many individuals and interest groups, regardless of their competing conceptions of the good), and *nonexclusionary* (an inclusive language that "retrieves," "selects," and "re-configures" relevant content from a number of diverse, sometimes conflicting, moral languages). I believe a nonfoundational, multifunctional, and nonexclusionary public moral language is a key in promoting reconciliation and eschewing division not just in a classroom, but in a democracy as well. In the words of Edward Tivnan (1995), in the excerpt that introduces this chapter, I think this type of language is the one best suited to helping us "listen to the other side of the story." Moral bricolage can "keep us from stomping on one another's special projects of self-improvement" (p. 250) because it is open-ended and because it regards morality as a "continuing conversation," without an ultimate trump, or a "final," unimpeachable, high ground.

Where do we learn how to have these "continuing conversations"? I think the schools and colleges are an ideal location for this kind of moral education, and I offer my version of what might be called a "postmodern classroom dialogue"—a "moral conversation"—in the following pages. I have been practicing and refining this type of discussion in my courses for many years, and I believe it to be a worthwhile technique for doing moral education (Nash, in press). While it is not as content-driven or as prescriptive a moral education as the neo-classical, the communitarian, or the liberationist, I still think the moral conversation has much to contribute to improving the quality of civic life, and moral character, in a secular pluralist democracy.

THE MORAL CONVERSATION

At the beginning of each semester, I write a memo to my students developing a rationale for engaging in "moral conversations" in all my courses, but especially in my moral-education seminars. I do this because, after 30 years of teaching a variety of courses in educational philosophy and applied ethics to undergraduate and graduate students in a professional school, I am convinced that *how* students and professors talk about texts and ideas with each other is as important, in some respects, as *what* they discuss.

A Student's Anonymous Letter to Me

My slowly evolving realization of the significance of mutually respectful conversations about texts in the college classroom reached its turning point when I received an anonymous note (which I still have) several years ago from a student in a moral-education class, after the first meeting of the semester. I have edited the mechanics of the following message but not the basic content:

> Professor . . . , your course looks very interesting, but I am not going to stay in it. I did not like the way we talked to each other during the first class. There was too much one-upsmanship, too many nasty put-downs, and a lot of so-called scholarly name-dropping. I am tired of taking seminars where we treat each other rudely, sometimes even savagely, in order to impress our professors (and each other) in class discussions. I don't know whether you were aware of it, but all we did during the first class was maneuver like a bunch of abusive, high-IQ brats. And you seemed to encourage this kind of behavior by paying the most attention to those students who engaged in it. Students soon got the message from you that the way to make points was to show off their intelligence by attacking someone's point of view, or to be "m.c." (morally correct).
>
> Every author you mentioned, for example, you made it a point to describe as "flawed," or "wrong-headed," in some way. I began to wonder: Does every author always have to be wrong? Are all views, including my own, "flawed," or "wrong-headed"? Is this

what a course in moral education is going to be about? Why can't we talk about what's right in a book, or what's good about each other's ideas? Why can't we all respect each other a little more? I know in some ways I must sound like a wimp who wants the class to be a support group where everybody gets a "smiley face" for a grade. But during the first class, I felt like we were all trying to be "winners" with the most intellectual insults. There must be a better way to talk about books and ideas in a moral education class, don't you think?

Do you really believe you are going to get students to talk freely about controversial stuff when they see each other mainly as competitors for your attention, and for the good grades that come with it? What's the point? I just get defensive and clam up. I don't want to tell you how to do your job, but it seemed to me there were a number of times when you could have intervened and taught some *real* lessons about moral education. But you never did. I can't play these "impress-the-prof" games anymore.

Please understand that I love intellectual give-and-take, and I'm not afraid of occasionally having my ego bruised in heated conversation. And I certainly understand the difference between doing a scholarly *critique* and being *critical* in the negative sense. I'm no insecure adolescent. But I didn't like the intimidating, combative, disrespectful tone of the conversation during the first meeting. And so I'm dropping the course. Sorry.

After swallowing hard, I began to reflect on the painful truth in that student's letter. Because that anonymous student put into words what I had actually been feeling for some time in my teaching—dating back to when I was a graduate teaching fellow—I decided, after considerable thought, to attach a personal memo to my moral-education and philosophy of education syllabuses (Nash, 1997). I have been doing this for the past several years, and, as a result, I believe that the tenor, tone, and even the content of conversations in my classroom have changed for the better. One indication of this is that when I first started teaching, and for years afterward, my student slippage rate after the first few classes in a semester ran a whopping 25%. Since I have been using the moral conversation guidelines outlined in my memo, I rarely lose more than one or two students in a semester. Another indication is that in their final course evaluations most students mention the moral conversation as one of the highlights of their learning. And, most satisfying, some of my colleagues have even asked me to do workshops with them on the principles of my moral conversation, because many of my former students ask them why it is not being used in courses other than my own.

I still maintain what I consider to be very rigorous academic standards in my courses: Readings and assignments are among the most demanding in my college. And I continue to insist on each student's responsibility to engage actively and intelligently in seminar discussion. The difference now, however, is that I put as much emphasis on the *manner* in which we converse about texts as I do on the *meanings* contained in those texts. In what follows, I will present the memo in its entirety. Then, in this chapter and the next, I will analyze and evaluate it, for I think it is one particularly effective tool for improving the overall quality of a conversation in a college seminar, with implications for developing "deliberative competence" and the particular moral dispositions citizens need to function well in a democracy. In my moral-education course, this mode of conversation enables my students and me to discuss the neoclassical, communitarian, liberationist, and postmodern virtue initiatives with what Sara Lightfoot (1983) calls "respectful regard," even though each of these worldviews is highly controversial and has its vehement supporters and detractors in my classes. Finally, in the last chapter, I will issue a few caveats, as well as some words of encouragement, to those who might wish to apply the principles of the moral conversation to their own class discussions.

A Memo to My Students About the Moral Conversation

> Greetings. I wish to set up some ground rules concerning how we will talk with each other about our texts every class. In addition to introducing you to some very important philosophical readings, I am primarily interested in engaging you in what I call a "moral conversation" as one very special way to talk about, and learn from, authors and from each other. The Latin root of the word "conversation" is *conversari*, meaning "to live with, to keep company with, to turn around, to oppose." Thus, for me, a conversation is literally a manner of living whereby people keep company with each other, and talk together, in good faith, in order to exchange sometimes agreeable, sometimes opposing, ideas. A conversation is not an argument, although it can get heated. A conversation is at its best when the participants are not impatient to conclude their business but wish instead to spend their time together in order to deepen and enrich their understanding of an idea, or, in our case, the ideas in a text (Martin, 1985).
>
> The primary purpose of engaging in a moral conversation this

semester is to test, expand, enrich, and deepen our various moral languages through the disciplined examination of significant texts, so that each one of us can arrive at a "fuller" (Richard Rorty's [1989] term for "more complete") moral language than we now speak. So, with the ideal of the moral conversation in mind, I hope we can be genuinely attentive to each other's efforts to work through difficult readings, to find a common classroom language to express our individual interpretations of these readings, and to take conversational risks in constructing a more probing and cogent intellectual "discourse" (a word the liberationists often use, as you will see).

I have found in over a quarter of a century of college teaching that a circle format works best in a course like this, because we are all able to look at each other and speak as equals in one major re- spect: We are each seekers of wisdom, and we are each responsible for making the effort to explain our unique interpretive perspec- tives to others, *face-to-face*. Thus I will not dominate the conversa- tion with lengthy, one-way lectures, because this will call attention only to *my* face and to *my* inequalities (you will all be looking pas- sively at me instead of conversing with each other), and hence the moral conversation will stop before it begins. But neither will I en- tirely surrender my professorial authority. I have been authorized by the university to teach this course on the basis of certain earned credentials. And, as far as I know, I am the only person in the class being paid to teach the course this term. So be ready for more than a little professorial provocation, edification, and even complication when I think the time is pedagogically appropriate. I plan to exer- cise good prudential judgment in that I will try not to talk too much or too little, but because I usually err on the side of the for- mer, please let me know when my attempt at inspiration begins to evoke only your perspiration and exasperation.

I also ask that everyone make an effort to talk during class. If you genuinely do not have anything to present or to add to the moral conversation at any given time, then, please, do not speak. This is reasonable, even merciful, silence. But if you never have any- thing to contribute verbally, I would question why on earth you are taking this course. This is, after all, a moral education *seminar*—"a meeting of students for [the purpose of] exchanging information and holding discussions" (*Random House Webster's College Diction- ary*). I maintain that, in a seminar, making at least one verbal contri- bution each session to the moral conversation is a matter of simple equity, focus, and courage. The *virtue of fairness* demands that each participant in the moral conversation try to play an equal verbal role in contributing to the discussion. If some people always hold back—no matter how valid the reason—then others have to shoulder a disproportionate responsibility to carry the conversation. This is an unjust burden.

Moreover, every participant has an *equal responsibility* to stay focused on what is being discussed. "Spacing out" is frequently a conscious choice to "drop out." Spacing out during the moral conversation sometimes (but not always) is a symptom of laziness, lack of interest, anger, fear, or unpreparedness. I urge you to take responsibility for each of these states of mind, if they apply, and transcend them. In the moral conversation, the *virtue of courage* is the willingness to accept insecurity and to overcome fear. We are all insecure when the time arrives to go public with an idea, because any personal interpretation of a reading, or of someone else's opinion, automatically makes us a very visible minority of one in a group. This can be frightening, to be sure. But, as equal learners, we must summon up a little courage and try to persuade others that our particular reading of a text is at least plausible, if not significant.

You will know that you are engaging in good moral conversation when the following is happening more and more frequently in class discussions:

1. You make an honest effort to read texts and to understand others *on their terms* as well as your own.
2. You acknowledge that while you do indeed "construct" meaning when reading a text and listening to others, you also have biases and blind spots that can be exposed, and reconstructed, by others more objective and wiser than you.
3. You maintain an open-mindedness about the possibility of learning something from both the author and your peers in the conversation.
4. You show a willingness to improve your current moral language, because it may be incomplete.
5. You make a conscious effort to refrain from advancing your own current moral language as the best one.
6. You evidence an inclination to listen intently in order to grasp the meaning of other people's moral languages for expressing their truths.

7. You agree that clarifying, questioning, challenging, exemplifying, and applying ideas are activities to be done in a self- and other-respecting way.
8. You realize that we will frequently get off course in our conversations because a spirit of charity, intellectual curiosity, and even playfulness will characterize many of our discussions. Or as David Bromwich (1992) says: "The good of conversation is not truth, or right, or anything else that many come out at the end of it, but the activity itself in its constant relation to life" (pp. 131–132).
9. You appreciate the fact that it will take time for us to get to know each other, and you understand that eventually we will find ways to engage in robust, candid, and challenging conversation about controversial ideas without being so "nice" that we bore each other to death, or without being so hostile that we cripple each other emotionally and intellectually.

Finally, I have a "code of ethics," what I call "civility protocols," for talking about moral education in a moral way. I offer these protocols to you in a genuine spirit of mutual planning for our conversation this term. Together, let us talk about the protocols, dispute them, amend them, eliminate some, add others, try to reach a consensus. No single protocol is sacrosanct. Each is meant to be a springboard for a cooperative decision as to how we will arrange our lives together during the semester.

1. Recognize that each person in the class has a set of mutual rights and obligations, and these ought always to govern our classroom conversations. The most basic right, of course, is the right to be heard. The most basic obligation is the duty to speak. Among other rights are the rights to privacy, confidentiality, veracity, fair and equal treatment, and respect for liberty. These rights generate correlative obligations: Respect privacy. Keep confidences. Tell the truth. Treat others fairly and equally. Keep promises. Be faithful to the process and purposes of the seminar by exhibiting a "respectful regard" for others, even when challenging, dissenting from, and critiquing their ideas.
2. Commit yourself to the ethical principle *primum non nocere* (first of all, do no harm). Treat each person in the class always as an end and not merely as a means (Kant). After all, this is probably the way you would like to be treated. Read as you would be read (Booth, 1988). Listen as you would be listened to. Question as you would be questioned. Pontificate only if you would be

pontificated to. Do not stereotype each other educationally, philosophically, politically, racially, morally, or religiously. Think of one another as fascinating, unpredictable, moral surprises waiting to occur at any time. Resist enticements to parrot party lines of one kind or another, as well as temptations to insist that others parrot these same orthodoxies. This is called *imposition,* and it is one of the deadliest "sins" anyone can commit in my moral-education seminar. It is a sin because it is tyrannical: It shuts down the moral conversation before it even gets started. It is also boring.

3. Show respect for each other by *initially* finding the truth in what you oppose and the error in what you espouse, *before* declaring the truth in what you espouse and the error in what you oppose. This is an easy aphorism to recite, but most difficult to put into constant practice, as you will see in the days ahead.

4. On the one hand, try to avoid censorship, indoctrination, and politicization of your views, even though you may be right. I do not know of anyone who responds favorably—without fear and with enthusiasm—to coercion. On the other hand, do not always assume a position of moral neutrality. You have both a duty and a right to present, explain, and defend your moral views, no matter how unpopular or controversial. This is a delicate balancing act, to be sure, but there can be no conversation in our class unless you are willing to express your moral ideas, no matter how erroneous, outrageous, eccentric, or enfeebled. I ask only that you not continually play the role of devil's advocate, because, as a minister once said in my class, "the devil already has more advocates than you can count." Remember something John Stuart Mill said in *On Liberty* (1859/1982): "In a democratic society, all opinions must be heard, because some of them may be true. And those that are false must be vigorously, but respectfully, contested."

5. Respect the text. Whether you *de*construct or *re*construct the text, allow always for difference and otherness. To attend to the different as different, and to the other as other, is to acknowledge that otherness and difference can be possible sources of truth as you *con*struct your own text. But remember that while reading a text and talking about it can truly be an intrinsically good thing, it is not the most important objective of this course in moral education, nor is it the ultimate end of life. The most important purpose of reading a number of moral-education texts this semester, and learning how to engage in moral conversation with others

who might hold opposing views, is to prepare for freedom and the construction of a more democratic community for *all* people: one where "books are not burned, libraries are not closed, the search for truth is not repressed, and disinterested leisure is not lost" (Adler, 1940, p. 371).

In closing, please know that at times the moral conversation will be heated, even emotionally upsetting. After all, we will be experiencing a microcosm of democracy for 15 weeks in our little seminar. We are bound to hurt one another's feelings at least a few times during the semester, because we will be discussing important ideas that each of us takes very seriously. Neo-classical, communitarian, liberationist, and postmodern authors can be very intense people, as you will see. And they can provoke some very intense feelings in you. Please do not take misguided attacks on your most precious moral convictions personally. If my past experience in teaching this course is any indication, nobody in the class (especially the instructor) will be fully able to live up to the ideals of the moral conversation. In the words of a famous theologian (Pieper, 1992), our "fat, relentless egos" will take care of that. But even though we will be awkward as we learn how to converse with one another in a morally considerate way, I promise that with your help we will improve each meeting.

Thank you.

THE MORAL ELEMENTS OF LANGUAGE AND CONVERSATION

Upon reading my memo at the start of a semester recently, a student made this statement in class:

> This is the first time I ever heard of a professor making a moral issue out of the requirements to talk in class and listen politely to others. Now it seems I might not only fail the class academically, but I could be a moral failure as well. Talk about the ultimate guilt trip!

The memo often elicits this kind of reaction from students, and I usually begin my defense of it by giving them some rationale for why I believe this approach is valuable (Nash, 1997).

I acknowledge how Gabriel Moran (1987, 1989) has taught me to think about teaching as a moral medium for exchanging languages with one another. For Moran (1987), good teaching has to do with talk about talk, with understanding the languages each of us uses and the meanings these languages carry for us and others. When I make clear to students that a good class discussion is not mainly about dazzling one another with our newfound mastery of the assigned readings, or about wielding recently minted jargon like a weapon in order to destroy someone's ideas, then the conversation starts to take a different turn. Students gradually learn to show respect for one another because they enter discussions with the intention of not rejecting anyone's language outright. They begin to understand that, in Moran's (1987) words, a conversation becomes a way of "putting language on a table between us" (p. 157) so that larger truths might emerge. This is what it means for a conversation to be "interesting" (L. *inter*—between; *est*—is): to put different languages before a conversational group ("between us") so that individual languages can be tested, expanded, and enriched. This implies that each seminar member acknowledge that everyone has some portion of the truth. And, what is more, no single person has a totally adequate language to express that truth. The purpose of the moral conversation, then, is to arrive at a "fuller" (more complete) language than each now speaks.

Moran (1987, 1989) goes on to make many sensible and helpful suggestions about moral classroom teaching, especially when he talks about texts. I have learned from him that a moral conversation grounded in textual analysis is disciplined and purposeful, but it is not always opinion-free. Neither is it always unemotional. In my moral-education classes there are generally few students who do not have very strong opinions about every moral topic we discuss. And many students are willing to pull out all the emotional stops in arguing for one particular position over another. In a recent conversation on the liberationist initiative, for example, one highly agitated student erupted this way:

> My wife works for General Motors. She has a Ph.D. in engineering and an M.B.A. in management. She worked damned hard for those credentials, coming from a very poor, working-class background, and she makes a lot of money. But I don't know why these authors we've been reading see her as the enemy. According to them, she's a racist, a capitalist, and a member of the "ruling elite." Well, they're crazy. My wife is a deacon at our church, works at the downtown soup kitchen twice a month all day, and is a volunteer for our community's emergency rescue unit. This sometimes keeps her up all night. Who the hell are they, in the cozy confines of their ivory towers, to call her names? I mean, they make some good points, but they ought to be going after the real culprits: the drug dealers, the white-collar criminals, the corrupt feds, the deadbeat

dads, the adult men who get teenage girls pregnant, the ganglords, the tobacco companies, the chronically unemployed, the welfare cheats. The people who speak the loudest to me are these communitarians we read. They know that charity begins at home in the smaller communities, and they don't indict business. Why some of the neo-classicals we read even talk glowingly about a work ethic and "corporate benevolence". I'm sorry, but these liberationists turn me off. I think they're immoral.

After the outburst, several students sided with the speaker. Others, however, reacted angrily to what they thought was a total misrepresentation of the liberationist position. They resented the speaker's emotional rejection of the entire liberationist initiative and used his attack as evidence that even well-intended people get coopted by a hegemonic system. For them, the speaker's wife per se was not evil; the system was and needed changing. They charged him with ignoring the system's role in causing and promoting many of the abuses he catalogued in his outburst. And they accused him of special, privileged-class pleading. Finally, some other students attacked the speaker for dismissing an entire ideology with the word *immoral,* charging him with the same kind of name-calling he deplored when the liberationists did it.

At times like these, when the moral conversation threatens to fall apart, and students end up sniping at each other and assuming intractable moral or political positions, I remind students that opinions and feelings are to be respected, but they do not constitute the primary subject matter of the course. *The core content is the fullest understanding of the meanings provoked by conversation with others through the text.* I emphasize for students that good moral conversation therefore starts with mastery of the text, progresses to an acute awareness of one's biases, culminates in an open-mindedness about the possibility of learning something from both the author and others in the conversation, and ends up with a willingness to improve (enrich and expand) one's moral language.

In the above example, I asked the angry speaker, his adversaries, and his supporters to return to the original sources, the liberationist texts. For the next meeting we each did a careful rereading of these texts from different perspectives. I asked the speaker to find possible errors in the position he espoused, and truths in the liberationist position. I also requested that the other students look for possible truths in the speaker's position and errors in the texts, depending on their initial positions in the debate. In order to keep the moral conversation going, everybody agreed to go "back to the drawing boards," albeit some very reluctantly.

In time, most students in the seminar were able to talk with one another in a more decorous way about the liberationist perspective. They "tried on" liberationist language, and the speaker's language as well, and they explored the worldviews each of the languages represented. They made an honest effort to interpret the world as each of the protagonists might. Subsequent discussions were just as lively, but now there was less yelling and more respectful listening and questioning. Some conversationalists grew more secure, and thus less defensive, in their use of language to express their most fundamental beliefs. They worked very hard to improve the quality of their discourse. And some saw the value in refusing to force premature closure on two such complex and controversial ways of viewing the strengths and weaknesses in American life. As always, a few students remained miffed that we were unable to reach a consensus that favored their own particular positions on the liberationist initiative.

I also specify for students that the moral conversation is not to be construed as merely a "feel-good" activity. A few students each semester always hope to find a kind of therapeutic healing in the moral conversation whereby the bolstering of individual self-esteem becomes the ultimate group objective, and nobody leaves at the end of the semester any the worse for psychological wear. In contrast, David Tracy (1987) has helped me to understand the importance of insisting on an *intellectually rigorous* and demanding moral conversation:

> Conversation is a game with some hard rules: Say only what you mean; say it as accurately as you can; listen to and respect what the other says, however different or other; be willing to correct or defend your opinions if challenged by the conversation partner; be willing to argue if necessary, to confront if demanded, to endure necessary conflict, to change your mind if the evidence suggests it. (p. 19)

In Tracy's paradigm, a conversation is very much like an interaction between two or more demanding and attentive friends, similar to what often takes place in Plato's dialogues. In the dialogues, there are times when Socrates is graciously sensitive to the questions of his colleagues, even while he proceeds to dissect their reasoning. (See, for example, the *Euthyphro, Crito,* and *Phaedo.*) At other times, occasionally in the same dialogues, Socrates can be arrogant, patronizing, even disdainful, especially with the Sophists. When Socrates is at his best, though, as he can be in the *Republic,* he frequently allows the questioning itself to take over, and he gives in to its logic, its demands, and its rhythms, but always in a way which encourages conversationalists to "exchange their narratives, expose their hopes, desires, and fears" (Tracy, 1987, p. 19). In his more humble moments, Socrates regularly belittles his own erudition by refusing to take his intellectual achievements seriously. He is acutely aware that his students are not so much his disciples as they are his friends whom he loves and appreciates. Whatever his style, though, Socrates remains fixed on a central purpose: the rigorous, uncompromising pursuit of truth, even though his friends might sometimes feel "bad."

Finally, I also mention that Wayne Booth (1988) wants us to consider the intriguing possibility that even an author might want to be a reader's friend. Many students have been conditioned by years of schooling to experience an author as an abstraction whose insights they must either accept or reject, or, at the very least, whose ideas they must master in order to "ace" papers and exams. I have found that students appreciate my telling the author's personal "story" before, during, and even after our analysis of the text. Most students are hungry for authorial context, for precious glimpses into a writer's private life. They want to get as close as they can to the "person" whose ideas they are reading and discussing.

For Booth (1988), in a sense, because the author is meeting a reader to share a story, a very special relationship takes shape. The author becomes a friend, and, as for Aristotle (1976), friendships come in many forms. Some are for pleasure, some are for utility, and some are for the sharing of virtues—the sharing of "aspirations and loves of a kind that make life together worth having as an end in itself" (Booth, 1988, p. 174). Booth maintains that the reader must always ask what kind of friendship is to be shared with the author. Does the reader want to be entertained? Does the reader need information, advice, counsel? Does the reader want to be a better person as a result of accepting the author's offer of friendship? According to Booth, the author's text becomes a "classic" when, during the time that reader and author spend together, the reader lives a "richer and fuller life than [one] could manage on [one's] own" (p. 223). Both reader and author truly become friends in the highest Aristotelian sense: The reader becomes a better human being as a result of the contact, and the author gains inspiration from the continuing impact the text has on the reader.

CONCLUSION

A morality of conversation is my own personal alternative to the more grandiose virtue initiatives advanced by the neo-classicals, the communitarians, and the liberationists. In the words of Tivnan, in the excerpt that begins this interlude, a morality of conversation urges students to "imagine the world from the other side of the barricade" and "listen a little harder to the other side of the story." And, in the spirit of Welch (1994), another excerpt contributor, a morality of conversation emphasizes less the elements of confrontation and intellectual victory and more the possibility of achieving genuine relationships among people rooted in mutual understanding of opposing viewpoints. And, finally, McGrath's (1994) excerpt reminds us that moral conversation appreciates the need each participant has for "dignity, support, and encouragement" in "inching" along the path of self-discovery. In the next chapter, I attempt to make the direct link between the moral conversation and the fostering of democratic virtues.

CHAPTER 9

A Postmodern Alternative: Cultivating the Democratic Dispositions

Henceforth, my dear philosophers, let us be on guard against the dangerous old conceptual fiction that posited a "pure, will-less, painless, timeless knowing subject"; let us guard against the snares of such contradictory concepts as "pure reason," "absolute spirituality," "knowledge in itself." . . . There is only a perspective seeing, only a perspective "knowing"; and the more affects we allow to speak about one thing, the more eyes, different eyes, we can use to observe one thing, the more complete will our "concept" of this thing, our "objectivity" be.
——*Friedrich Nietzsche,* On the Genealogy of Morals, *1887/1989*

These [democratic dispositions] include a preparedness to work with others different from oneself toward shared ends; a combination of strong convictions with a readiness to compromise in the recognition that one can't always get everything one wants; and a sense of individuality and a commitment to civic goods that are not the possession of one person or of one small group alone.
——*Jean Bethke Elshtain,* Democracy On Trial, *1995*

People adept at logical reasoning who lack moral character are sophists of the worst sort. . . . But people who possess sturdy moral character without a developed capacity for reasoning are ruled only by habit and authority. . . . Education in character and in moral reasoning are therefore both necessary, neither sufficient, for creating democratic citizens. . . . In practice, the development of deliberative character is essential to realizing the ideal of a democratically sovereign society.
——*Amy Gutmann,* Democratic Education, *1987*

In this chapter, I talk about the postmodern virtues and democracy. I agree with Amy Gutmann (1987), in the excerpt above, that the ability to engage in a continuing conversation about morality or politics necessitates a certain type of moral character, or else mere sophistry rules the day. Thus, in the tradition of Jurgen Habermas (1983/1993), I advocate a kind of "deliberative competence" or "communicative action" for all citizens of a democracy. I believe, with Gutmann (1987), that this disposition is essential if we are to realize the "ideal of a democratically sovereign society." Also, in the matter of the virtues, I am prepared to go beyond Gutmann's and Habermas's "thin" notion of democracy as deliberation only and advocate what Jean Bethke Elshtain (1995), in the above excerpt, calls the "democratic dispositions." These include the virtues of self-discipline, obligation, tolerance, fairness, and generosity, and they enable us to work with others who are different from us, to compromise when necessary, and to realize that no single person or group can get everything they want all the time.

Finally, I am ready to add to these democratic dispositions what I am calling the "postmodern virtues." In the pages ahead, I talk about the need to have, among other virtues, a sensitivity to the realities of incommensurability, indeterminacy, and nonfoundationalism; dialectical awareness; and hermeneutical awareness. I take the position that postmodernity need not be nihilistic or antireligious. In fact, I believe that it is only when we learn to communicate with one another without the need to impose moral certitudes that we can carry on genuinely fruitful democratic conversations across our doctrinal enthusiasms.

THE CONVERSATIONAL VIRTUES AND
THE DEMOCRATIC DISPOSITIONS

I believe the "conversational virtues" I try to encourage in my moral conversation are precisely those dispositions necessary for living well in a democracy. I return here to Patricia White's (1996) treatment of the "democratic dispositions" that I mentioned in a previous chapter. Beyond the "bedrock" liberal virtues of fairness, tolerance, and personal autonomy—obviously important "thin" qualities that make moral conversations and democracies work more effectively—White considers the "thicker" dispositions to be equally essential for democratic life. And I do as well. Like her, in my teaching, I try to foster a *hope and confidence* in conversational processes and purposes. Citizens, too, need to feel hopeful about democratic values and confident that, in the end, ideological differences can be adjudicated peacefully, fairly, and compassionately. Also, as I mention in the previous chapter, I try to promote displays of *courage* in the moral conversation. I want my students to take conversational risks, to stand up for what they believe, in a way that does not suppress others' views. For White, only courageous action on the part of citizens, with a self-confidence in their "deliberative competence," will assure the advancement of social justice and the protection of basic liberties whenever these are threatened.

Moreover, I try to encourage my students to develop *self-respect* by taking responsibility for the conversational process, by participating in group decision making, and by understanding that each person has a set of fundamental rights and obligations that are binding on everyone, without exception. In this sense, as White (1996) reminds her readers, self-respect is also a sine qua non for the practice of democratic citizenship. Furthermore, the virtues of *friendship and trust,* as I have delineated in the previous chapter, both in the Socratic and Aristotelian contexts, are fundamental elements in the realization of good moral conversations. For White, friendship as "mutual well-wishing" and "well-doing," out of genuine concern for one another, is what gives relationships among democratic citizens an element of mutuality and sustainability. And, in some cases, friendship may offer enough reason even to override obligations to the larger democratic community.

Friendship is also the basis for *trust,* and, in class, when students gradually learn to trust the moral conversation, the process improves remarkably. So, too, in a democracy; White shows how social trust in democratic institutions must begin in the schools where students learn that formal procedures can be helpful when applied fairly and when children from different racial and ethnic groups can interact around common interests free from the stigmas of prejudice and stereotype. White also observes that *distrust* is appropriate at times in a democratic society if citizens are to expose political corruption, and thus the schools have a role to play here as well. They must be willing to listen and respond to valid student criticism without taking such "distrust" personally. In White's words, "Distrust is democracy's chief protective device, and there is no reason to exempt the school from its searchlight" (p. 64).

The personal qualities of *honesty* and *decency* are also fundamental to the success of the moral conversation. When people of integrity, trustworthiness, and candor engage in mutual give-and-take around moral issues that are value-loaded and emotion-packed, the results can be advantageous for everyone. In contrast, the practice of deceit, fraud, and hypocrisy can be as destructive to moral conversations as they are lethal to a democracy. And yet, as White (1996) points out, students must understand that democratic adversarial politics does not always have to give way to dishonesty, cynicism, and personal attack. In the moral conversation, students sometimes shift between being advocates in advancing their own views and adversaries in challenging those of others. In either case, though, the most successful conversationalists are able to refrain from cynicism, hyperbole, and personal attack. Despite the fervor of their views, they remain trustworthy and respected by the rest of the group. Other students continue to respect them as people of integrity and honor.

Finally, I am in full agreement with White (1996) that philosophers have, for too long, underrated the virtue of moral *decency*. For me, moral decency—civility; goodwill; reaching out; being respectful, obliging, and willing to put the "best construction" on things—nicely characterizes the ethos I am trying to create in the moral conversation. In my classes, a code of decency (the civility protocols) is the minimal requirement for creating a bond among people of differing temperaments, values, ideals, and convictions, and that is why I spell out my expectations in a memo. Sadly, however, in my experience, when the moral conversation founders, in spite of the group's many supererogatory efforts to rescue it, it is usually because students are lacking in basic moral decency. As in a democracy, this is not an easy disposition for me to cultivate unless it is present in individual members at the outset at least in some vestigial form. Aristotle's (1976) observation that we can only induce goodness in a suitably receptive character is sound:

> It is a regrettable fact that discussion and instruction are not effective in all cases. . . . Therefore, we must have a moral character to work on that has some affinity to virtue; one that appreciates what is noble and objects to what is base. (p. 337)

The sectarian communitarian Mark R. Schwehn (1993), to whom I refer in a previous chapter, discusses what he calls the "spiritual virtues" as a way to advance classroom conversations. In some respects, Schwehn's virtues resemble White's, except that he is primarily concerned with furthering these dispositions in what he calls "communities of *higher* learning," as am I. He also gives his virtues a religious gloss. For Schwehn, the virtue of *humility* ought to take the form of a presumption: There is wisdom and authority in an author, and, regardless of how discordant an idea might at first appear to a student, there is always a possibility to learn something from a writer. I would add to Schwehn's insight that his presumption should also hold for *all* the participants in a moral conversation. Each person—author, instructor, and student—has a piece of truth to convey, no matter how tiny. Furthermore, the virtue of *faith* ought to compel us to trust the work of others, even while we criticize their ideas. In Schwehn's words, trust and faith motivate us to "believe what we are questioning and at the same time question what we are believing" (p. 49).

According to Schwehn, the virtue of *self-denial* is the capacity to "surrender ourselves for the sake of the better opinion" (p. 49). Self-denial requires that, at times, we must be prepared to abandon our most sacrosanct assumptions in the pursuit of truth. And, finally, for Schwehn, the greatest of the spiritual virtues is *charity,* a disposition to find a way to understand other points of view, especially when the initial temptation is strong for us to ridicule or to dismiss views we consider inferior. In a spirit of charity, Schwehn believes that students should become "more cautious in appraisal, more sympathetic with human failings, less prone to stereotype and caricature" (p. 51).

While Schwehn's analysis of the virtues of "spirited inquiry" parallels my own in several respects (he seems to like the work of Parker Palmer [1983], Richard Rorty [1979], and Jeffrey Stout [1988] as much as I do), our basic differences are nevertheless pronounced. While I enthusiastically endorse his first "commandment" for "spirited inquiry"—"Put the best construction on everything" (p. 51)—I am highly reluctant to think of his "virtues" as *distinctively* Christian, or even as spiritual. On the two occasions I have used his book, *Exiles from Eden: Religion and the Academic Vocation in America* (1993), in my course, students, for the most part, have reacted with indignation. They complained that his Christian characterizations tended to make his virtues appear rigidly prescriptive, exclusivist, "precious," and bound up with a theological tradition that not everyone shared.

Also, Schwehn's observation that whenever we practice these virtues, we are actually living off "a kind of borrowed [Christian] fund of moral capital" (p. 53) infuriated several of my students. They found it to be both denigrating and inaccurate. As I observed in an earlier chapter, for most of my students, these virtues, if they are to be worthwhile, must be valid in their own right—because they are good, or useful, or uplifting. Few of them know, or care about, the religious foundations of these dispositions. In fact, in the view of many, religion has been responsible for the *degradation* of these virtues in American life, and, whether the stereotype is true or not, no amount of counterevidence convinces these students otherwise.

I believe that if the virtues of humility, faith, self-denial, and charity are to have any functional utility in secular educational institutions, and in a democratic society, then they have to be "decoupled" from their religious roots and secularized. Indeed, we should teach students to understand, and respect, the virtues' origins in the traditional religions. But we ought to deemphasize the fundamental *Christian* nature of virtues that, I contend, can stand on their own. Schwehn's way of talking about education and the virtues is simply too triumphalistic and foundationalist for most students in my classes. And they become even more resistant to his excellent insights when, for example, he ranks "religious piety" over "secular piety," because the former is more "robust." For too many students, the human chronicle has been amply bloodied by "robust" expressions of "religious piety" run amuck (Haught, 1990).

In summary, Schwehn (1993), like White (1996), has much to offer me by way of thinking about, and fostering, the conversational virtues. It is easier for me to "put the best construction" on Schwehn's insights, however, when he talks about *how* to teach the virtues. He thinks there are two stages: exemplification and organization. I concur. I try continuously to exemplify the conversational virtues in the moral conversation, and whenever I falter, I talk about these lapses with my students, ask for their help to get back on track, and proceed a bit more humbly than before. I also call attention, in an undramatic way, to particular student instantiations of the virtues. Moreover, I try to organize my classroom in such a way as both to promote the conversational dispositions and to subject them to rigorous analysis as an ongoing intellectual activity. Thus the moral conversation becomes a process to be practiced for its own sake as well as for the intellectual benefits it produces as an object of scholarly inquiry. One of these intellectual *and* practical benefits, as I have tried to argue in this section, is that the moral conversation can provide a basis for encouraging those dispositions that are the heart and soul of democratic life. It is these "thick" dispositions, I contend, that best lay the groundwork for a citizen's informed voting, decision making, and civic service.

POSTMODERN CONCEPTIONS OF TRUTH AND VIRTUE

After reading my memo, included in the previous chapter, some students will always ask:

> Is the truth of a text or a discussion always relative to the way we will talk about texts? How will we know which text, or which person's insights, are truer than others'? How will we ever be able to criticize the readings, and each other, without clear and distinct truth criteria? How will we know which virtues are good and which are vices? Does it all depend on context and conversational style? Where's the objective content, or isn't content important? Will we ever be able to arrive at a point where we can say definitively that one of the virtue initiatives—neo-classical, communitarian, liberationist, or postmodern—is better than the others?

I make it a point whenever these questions are raised to talk of the "truth" of texts in a relational language that strikes some of my students as highly unusual (Nash, in press). I rarely talk about moral truth by using propositional or metaphysical vocabulary until I am well into a course. In my experience, many undergraduate and graduate students who are new to seminar conversations—even though they tend to be relativists or constructivists on personal (moral and religious) matters—still think that the purposes of formal seminar conversations in a moral-education course are to uncover verifiable or indisputable facts in texts, to find the "right answers," and to identify the author's fundamental "message" beyond the vagaries of personal opinions or interpretations. Although I agree with students that these purposes certainly have their proper place in any discussion about morality, many fledgling seminar participants think they ought to occupy the *only* place, because this is how they tend to think of "truth" when they first begin to discuss books and ideas without the assistance of systematic, propaedeutic lectures.

In response, I frequently distinguish between "big-*T*" Truths (Truths that are seen to exist apart from, and to transcend, an author's or reader's perceived experience) and "little-*t*" truths (truths that are seen to be relatively noncontroversial, that are personally constructed, and that do not require a major leap of faith for anyone to accept them). I warn students that while I respect and even encourage big-*T* Truth talk, I will insist that the conversation stay with the little-*t* truths, at least until we learn how to carry on a moral conversation with one another that is not lethal. During the early stages of a moral-education seminar, I have found, unfortunately, that those students who believe they are in the possession of big-*T* Truths are often more tempted to *impose* their views on others. Conversely, those who hold to small-*t* truths are more inclined to *propose* their views. I have also, of course, found several exceptions to this huge covering principle.

In fact, big-*T and* little-*t* truth-seekers come in many shapes and sizes in my moral-education seminars, but, *at the extremes,* both types can be "fundamentalists" in the worst sense, because of their unwavering conviction of certitude and self-righteousness and because of their inclination to debunk and convert (Rauch, 1993). Both sets of truth-seekers, at the extremes, strictly adhere to a particular set of basic ideals or principles, and they can be especially disruptive to a moral conversation. *Neoclassicals* can be fundamentalists whenever they insist that because the "right" virtues have been "canonized" in a set of classical moral writings and traditions, they must become normative for everyone. *Communitarians* can be fundamentalists whenever they dismiss out-of-hand the "virtues" of liberal individualism, because these are said to be inferior to those of fraternity, solidarity, harmony, belongingness, and the common good. *Liberationists* can be fundamentalists whenever they grant an *a priori* advantage to the "virtues" of persons in historically "oppressed" classes and a disadvantage to the "virtues" of persons in historically "privileged" classes. And *postmoderns* can be fundamentalists whenever they "deconstruct" the virtues of each of the three initiatives on the grounds that because they lack unimpeachable foundations, they are morally incommensurable and indeterminate, and therefore of arbitrary worth.

I have come to be particularly wary of those big-*T* seekers who might be libertarians, Rush Limbaugh/Patrick Buchanan conservatives, born-again Christians, neo-Marxists, literary "canonists," environmentalists, multiculturalists, gender feminists, and science absolutists, among others, who rarely miss an opportunity to insist on the ultimate perfection and rightness of their own beliefs and to point out the dubious worth of the opposition's. I am also apprehensive about those little-*t* seekers who might be doctrinaire relativists or skeptics, holding strictly to the belief that because values differ from society to society and from person to person, then all attempts to arrive at universally applicable norms or principles are merely arbitrary and authoritarian impositions. These are the cynics—many pride themselves on being members of Generation X—and they can "smell" the infliction of a moral prescription at the first mention of a personal conviction in a conversation. They, too, are ready to do battle at a moment's notice. I am less concerned with the *content* of these various fundamentalisms, however, as I am with the tendency of their adherents to enter the moral conversation with their minds already made up and their languages intact and inviolate. Fundamentalism at its worst precludes every attempt at moral conversation because it is simply uncharitable: It is smug, closed-minded, imperialistic, and other-denigrating.

I cannot emphasize enough the danger of political stereotyping: I believe that nothing can destroy the ideal of the moral conversation as fatally as when participants become ideological zealots. It does not take long for everyone in the class to get typecast, and soon the element of predictability replaces spontaneity and freshness in a discussion. Whatever the topic, after a while, some students speak only as militant liberationists who see victimization and oppression everywhere. Others pigeonhole themselves as radical libertarians or conservative communitarians who perceive ubiquitous government threats to individual freedoms and property in every textual assertion. Others narrowly categorize themselves as radical egalitarians because they translate all their interpretations into the language of social justice or equality. And, metaphysically, still others straitjacket themselves into assorted theistic, agnostic, or atheistic categories.

I make it a point to propose in the very first class that while each of the aforementioned ideological positions is eminently defensible, even laudable, in some respects, it is better if we emphasize that each participant in the conversation—instructor, student, and author—has a prior nonpartisan integrity. This will require, I contend, that we scrupulously listen for the truth in other views, without rigid political preconceptions, and that we ruthlessly challenge the taken-for-granted truth we always assume in our own views. This will therefore obligate us to "try on" a variety of moral perspectives during the semester, if for no other reason than to become less transparent, and less tiresome, to each other.

Richard Rorty's Postmodern "Truth"

What does it mean to find a "fuller truth" in the moral conversation? Does a text exist only to provoke questions, to enrich and challenge languages? Or does it also contain certain "truths" that make a claim on readers to reconsider, maybe even to change, their own moral truths? Is the only truth to emerge from the moral conversation the principle to treat each other respectfully as friends?

In order to respond to these types of questions, I turn to Richard Rorty (1979, 1989, 1991), perhaps America's leading philosopher today (Borradori, 1994; Edmundson, 1993; Hall, 1994). I have been greatly influenced by his work. Rorty, who once characterized himself as a "postmodernist bourgeois liberal pragmatist" (1991, p. 201), argues that objective truth is unknowable, and therefore any systematic effort to know such a truth is to play God. For Rorty, the world is an "alien" place and is essentially unfathomable, except as we attribute our attitudes and descriptions to it. There is no "unshakeable foundation" to knowledge. At best, there is only an "airtight case" (1979, p. 157). For Rorty, the best metaphor to use in the pursuit of knowledge is not *vision* but *conversation*. An "objective truth" is knowledge consensually agreed upon through conversation—nothing more, nothing less.

Rorty is very critical of what he calls "systematic philosophy," the attempt to find self-evidently true beliefs, because he believes this is a futile attempt to transcend the accidents of time, place, and language. For Rorty, in contrast, "edifying philosophy" is much less interested in finding foundational truths to knowledge than in "participating in a conversation" (1979, p. 371). Participants in a conversation hope to achieve, at best, a kind of "authenticity" in their quest for knowledge, because they realize that certainty is impossible and that they must strive to bear up under the burden of choice. In a later work (1989), Rorty maintains that we ought to attempt to be "liberal ironists" in the moral conversation: people who want to avoid cruelty and who are committed to the struggle against injustice (liberals); but also people who know their most fundamental beliefs and desires are always "contingent" on particular times and places, and hence never certain (ironists). Anyone who thinks that there is an ultimate answer to the question "Why should I not be cruel?" is, for Rorty, "in his heart a theologian or a metaphysician," occupations Rorty holds in low esteem (p. xv).

I believe that Rorty makes a strong case for the kind of conversation that must occur in a secular pluralist society, wherein no single person has an irrefutable corner on moral truth and the ideal is to settle intellectual differences without resorting to metaphysical or political absolutes. For Rorty, the exchange of opposing points of view in a free and open encounter best allows the truth to emerge, even though the emergent truth may always be less than we would like. Rorty is unrelenting in his insistence that we learn to live with the fact of plurality without demanding absolute validity in our conversations with each other. And, so, the task for everyone in the moral conversation is to pursue some kind of meaning in a pluralistic world where many views predominate and where no single view can ever be metaphysically validated as true for all times and places.

Each of the virtue initiatives I examine throughout this book has important truths to convey about morality and life, but there is nothing especially sacred about any of the views. Certainly there is no rational warrant in any of the views for the use of force (psychological or physical) in imposing a particular view of the good life on us. In fact, according to Rorty, the best that we can do in a postmodern world is to "decry the notion of having a view while avoiding having a view about having views" (1979, p. 371). Or, better still, as Reinhold Niebuhr (1937) observed: "Every philosophy is under the illusion that it has no illusions because it has discovered the illusions of its predecessors" (p. 223). For Niebuhr, as for Rorty, any particular view of the good life is illusory, because from some other view, that view, too, is nothing more than an illusion.

Is Rorty's postmodern take on truth therefore relativistic or nihilistic? I do not believe it is either. At various times, critics have accused him of being "frivolous," "confused," "conservative," "aphoristic," "utopian," "smug," "subjective," "poetic," "narrativist," "romantic," and "antidemocratic" (Hall, 1994). Rorty rejects most of these criticisms, preferring to think of himself as "liberal" and "humanitarian." He clearly eschews relativism, because, in his own words, he does not believe that "every moral view is as good as every other" (Edmundson, 1993, p. 44). What Rorty is saying about the "final" truth of one way of life as against another way of life is that there are no "unwobbling pivots" (p. 44), no neutral common ground that would allow opponents to argue out their differences as to what particular moral, political, or economic alternative is *objectively* valid. For Rorty, the search for objectivity and certainty is a matter of securing as much "intersubjective agreement" as possible. Intersubjective agreement renders the question of relativism or absolutism null and void.

In practice, Rorty is convinced that democratic institutions alone, among all the other alternatives, have the potential to "increase equality and reduce suffering" (quoted in Edmundson, 1993, p. 46). But, as he says over and over, there will never be an airtight connection between people's political views and their views on metaphysical matters. There is simply no way in a secular pluralist world to "hold reality . . . morality, and political responsibility . . . in a single vision" (p. 48). "Ultimate determinants" are notoriously contingent. Rorty states definitively that he is not the person

> to come to if you want confirmation that the things you love with all your heart are central to the structure of the universe, or that your sense of moral responsibility is "rational and objective" rather than "just" a result of how you were brought up. (p. 49)

Rorty is adamant that it is possible to reject "grand narratives" and "metanarratives" (philosophical, political, or religious "stories" that contain all-encompassing truths) and still believe in something worth fighting for. Tony W. Johnson (1995), an educational philosopher, has recently attacked Rorty for engaging in "playful, therapeutic criticism" and for "debunking" the past without providing a more "robust" alternative political vision for educators to pursue (p. 90). Johnson wants Rorty to be more like John Dewey, Rorty's putative mentor, and promote a "thick" conception of democracy, one that emphasizes solving large social problems and promoting grand "visions." For Johnson, Rorty is nothing more than a "bourgeois liberal" whose "edifying philosophy" of conversation is a prescription for "impotence in effecting educational change" (p. 92).

While I like much of what Johnson says about the potential of educational philosophy to "reconstruct" our educational system, and while I agree that John Dewey still speaks powerfully to educators today, especially when he talks about democracy, I think Johnson unfairly severs Rorty's thinking from Dewey's. Johnson appears upset because Rorty is not a "prophet," or a change agent, or a Foucauldian. But this, I believe, is precisely Rorty's point in rejecting the philosopher's and the theologian's projects. His own project has been to discover the best way to leave people's private lives alone, to refrain from imposing a particular "visionary vocabulary" on them, while still trying to prevent suffering and cruelty, and maximizing equality in the society at large (Rorty, 1989). Rorty goes about this work not as a neo-classical philosopher, or as a liberationist, or even as a communitarian, though he maintains it is in our individual communities where we must begin to construct moral lives for ourselves.

Contra Johnson, I believe Rorty is actually a utopian thinker, someone who has much in common with his hero, John Dewey. While Rorty obviously picks and chooses from Dewey's work what suits his purposes, and while he thinks of himself as a "neo-pragmatist" without Dewey's scientific method, both thinkers are left-leaning liberals in their politics. Rorty and Dewey are antifoundationalists who abhor metaphysical dualisms. Both are pragmatists in the sense that they share a faith in the promise of science and technology to decrease human suffering and to replace religious and Enlightenment claims to certainty (Hall, 1994). Both would agree strongly that "the moral prophets of humanity have always been poets, even though they spoke in free verse or parable" (Dewey, 1920/1958, p. 348). And both place great faith in the power of education to prepare people for an enriched democratic life (Diggins, 1994).

Ideologically, Rorty and Dewey have been attacked by the political right as "anarchistic" and by the left as "conformist" and "counter-revolutionary." Both have been charged with overemphasizing a laissez-faire approach to change and with promoting an apolitical philosophy of self-expression and personal growth. Both assume that the extravagance of power will correct itself once freedom prevails in the private sphere, or, in Dewey's case, in the school and in the economy. Both remain convinced that virtue cannot be taught as a body of rules or by grounding moral authority in any transcendental source. For Dewey, students become good to the extent they develop the "power of trained judgment" (Dewey, 1909). For Rorty (1989), people become good when they allow themselves to experience pain and remorse in the presence of others' humiliation and suffering. And, lest we forget, it was John Dewey who said that "democracy begins in conversation" (quoted in Diggins, 1994, p. 461), a statement that could very well encapsulate Rorty's entire political ethic—and my own as well.

This last assertion is especially important, I believe, because while both men share a similar view of democracy, I would argue that Rorty pays much more attention than Dewey to the *kind* of public dialogue he believes will get us there. Even though he would disagree with the following observation, I think Rorty provides a pragmatic "method" for effecting the kind of social change Dewey sought throughout his life. For Rorty, only "edifying" conversations can get us to the point where people in a pluralist democracy can talk about what they have in common, including their suffering, without obliterating their differences. I believe that Rorty and Dewey would concur that democracy should be a process whereby people can attain an appropriate combination of unforced agreement with tolerant disagreement. Rorty's is a thoroughgoing utopia of cultural pluralism, and, I would argue, this tolerance of difference is what makes constitutional democracies possible. But, as yet, Rorty refuses to compromise on his central conviction that democratic institutions, *and* philosophers, must remain neutral, or at least agnostic, on the ultimate questions of morality, meaning, and the truth of human existence.

Tony W. Johnson (1995) ends his critique of Rorty with the caustic words: "Richard Rorty: You are no John Dewey." In an unintended sense, of course, Johnson is right, but not because Rorty lacks Dewey's grand "vision." First, Rorty is a wonderful writer—accessible, poetic, and lucid, a kind of "public intellectual" whom nonphilosophers can read and enjoy. In contrast, Dewey's writing style is very turgid, once prompting Oliver Wendell Holmes to remark about Dewey's "cosmic prose": "how God would have spoken had He been inarticulate but keenly desirous to tell you how it was" (quoted in Diggins, 1994, p. 346). Second, and more important, though, Rorty lives in an age that no longer accepts Dewey's illusions that science is always a redemptive force, or that progress is inevitable, or that the scientific method is the ideal for solving complex, social problems. Although both men put democracy before philosophy, Rorty is a late-twentieth-century thinker who, unlike Dewey, turns to language and conversation—rather than to schooling, science, reason, and active political participation—in order to improve the quality of democratic life in America.

The ultimate ideal for Rorty is *solidarity*, and the way to get there is through conversation, narration, and respect for alterity and individual self-expression. For Rorty, who possesses a late-twentieth-century hindsight that Dewey, of course, lacked, grand political visions have historically produced societies marked by compliance, contestation, conformity, and suffering. In opposition to "grand visions" and "master narratives," Rorty argues that it is only through extensive conversation that people in secular pluralist democracies will ever come to agree on common convictions. At this particular time in American history, I would contend that it is indeed good that Richard Rorty is no John Dewey. Moreover, I believe that if Dewey were alive today, he would find much in Richard Rorty's morality of conversation to support, including many of the postmodern virtues I elaborate below.

The Postmodern Virtues

Early on in my moral-education course, I assign Parker Palmer's *To Know as We Are Known: A Spirituality of Education* (1983). Palmer reminds us that "truth" comes from the Germanic root *troth*, which has to do with the virtues of faith and trust, betrothal and engagement. Hence, for Palmer, the search for truth involves virtue—the disposition to enter a faithful and trusting relationship whereby we might become part of one anothers' lives. I find Palmer's equating of truth with faithful relationship to be an excellent way to prepare students to deal with Rorty's (1989) unique truth language. While Rorty does not talk about truth and relationships using Palmer's vocabulary, he does remind us that we can read *nonfiction* texts as moral narratives with their own unique vocabularies. Some vocabularies are, of course, richer than others. Some stories are more suggestive, persuasive, or "edifying" than others. There can never be a "final" vocabulary or story, never a "best" ideal or "ultimate" moral principle, only a "better" one. In Rorty's sense, a text contains "truth" only when it produces a virtuous response in readers, only when it has helped us to risk ourselves in the world more courageously and to choose our actions more wisely. Additionally, in the spirit of Palmer's notion of truth as relationship, Rorty believes a text is true to the extent it has helped us to recognize one anothers' common humanity and need for solidarity and only when it has helped each of us in the individual task of "self-creation."

For Rorty, one lives a life of truth whenever one accepts the responsibility to create an authentic personal existence in a society that can never conclusively demonstrate that one must work to reduce cruelty and injustice in people's lives, or even that one must be moral. I also refer in class to Booth (1988), and I ask his master moral question: Has the text enabled the reader to become a better (more virtuous) person than before it was encountered? And I repeat Moran's (1989) query as well: Has the text allowed the reader to construct a fuller, richer language with which to express a particular truth to others?

In my experience, students gradually come to understand that what Palmer, Rorty, Booth, and Moran have in common is that their conceptions of truth are neither excessively subjective nor objective and that they are ultimately connected to virtue. These authors agree that truth is never final. They also concur that some truths are more complete and richer than others according to how well they have helped us to construct a cogent language to express what is important to us. They understand that truth is both personal and communal in the sense that the act of "self-creation" goes hand-in-hand with the moral responsibility to reduce cruelty and injustice in people's lives. They believe that author, text, and reader have an integrity of their own, and, therefore, in Gadamer's (1984) words, each of us has a moral responsibility to "encounter the Other as Other within a hitherto unknown horizon that invites not observation but listening" (p. 179). To my way of thinking, Palmer, Rorty, Booth, and

Moran agree that the best way for author, text, and reader to communicate with one another is through a "moral conversation" featuring mutually regardful dialogue, challenge, and personal transformation.

Postmodern conceptions of truth like those of Rorty, Palmer, and Booth entail a particular set of dispositions—what I call the "postmodern virtues"—and I contend these are a necessary precursor to the development of the democratic dispositions I discussed earlier. Teaching these virtues presents a formidable challenge, because students must learn a whole new way of thinking about morality, truth, and communication. I will briefly summarize what I consider to be the pivotal postmodern virtues and put them into a context of moral conversation.

1. A CRITICAL SENSITIVITY TO THE POSTMODERN REALITIES OF INCOMMENSURABILITY, INDETERMINACY, AND ANTIFOUNDATIONALISM. Most postmodern writing assumes the absence of a common moral standard by which to evaluate competing moral vocabularies, traditions, and frameworks (incommensurability). It also assumes that no authority can ever determine, or settle in advance, what ought to be the "final" word on truth or morality (indeterminacy). Moreover, no authority can justify a moral assertion once and for all by tracing it back to first principles, self-evident truths, something bedrock, or some antecedent reality (antifoundationalism). As I have tried to show in previous chapters, neo-classicals, communitarians, and liberationists all suffer from the same hubristic flaw: Each attempts to advance a particular moral vocabulary as the "final" or "highest" moral standard, the ne plus ultra of virtue talk. And while their first principles or self-evident truths may differ, their end is similar: to terminate the conversation at some point by postulating the "final" moral language.

Richard J. Bernstein (1993) discusses the strengths and weaknesses of the incommensurability, indeterminacy, and antifoundationalism triad in a way I have found to be very helpful in my work with the moral conversation. While a critical sensitivity to these concepts does serve to keep the moral conversation open-ended and to discourage moral one-upsmanship and conversation-stopping "high grounds," I have found it does not necessarily have to end up in relativism or subjectivism, as the neo-classicals, communitarians, and liberationists would charge. I believe that students, with a renewed humility and caution, can compare and contrast incommensurable moral languages in a number of ways, but especially from the vantage point of determining those virtues that are most likely to encourage a better quality of democratic life for everyone. In this way, students can learn to work with, and integrate, a number of conflicting moral languages with their rival pluralistic values and traditions in order to advance one major democratic goal: the common good.

Also, incommensurable moral languages do overlap at times, and it can be the conversational task to find those points of overlap and criss-cross to determine what might fruitfully lead to common moral ground. This is what the philosophers of public conversation James Davison Hunter (1991, 1994) and Edward Tivnan (1995) are trying to do in foster-ing a nationwide dialogue around such issues as abortion, capital punish-ment, and physician-assisted suicide. Moreover, while it is true that no moral language can ever be determinate or final in a pluralistic democ-racy, I believe people can still agree, at least provisionally, on those moral criteria and standards that they politically admire. As a minimum, the moral conversation requires that people give examples of those virtues they consider exemplary or normative and then try to convince others of their worth. Thus conversation and persuasion can replace imposition and indoctrination, along with the guilt-mongering and politicization that often accompany the latter.

2. A CAPACITY FOR DIALECTICAL CONVERSATION. The postmod-ern dialectic differs substantially from the neo-classical, communitarian, and liberationist forms, all of which are essentially "destructive" in their approach to discourse. The neo-classical dialectic proceeds by trying to destroy "relativistic" assumptions about what constitutes the virtuous life by positing a set of objective moral principles that require individual compliance. In the Platonic ideal, the neo-classical conversation culmi-nates in the apprehension of Ultimate Moral Truths as located in the Western heritage, or in "great books," or in cultural traditions, or in a set of "core values."

The communitarian dialectic proceeds by trying to destroy liberal assumptions about the good life premised on a belief in autonomy, rights, and personal liberty. In the ideal, the communitarian conversation culmi-nates in an awareness that because the individual is actually an embed-ded and embodied social person, morality must begin with the culti-vation of such social virtues as reciprocity, trust, sharing, mutual responsibility, and communal caring. The communitarian conversation, whether sectarian, postliberal, or civic liberal, proceeds from a dialectic of conformity whose ultimate goal is submersion of the individual into a group cohesion.

And the liberationist dialectic proceeds by trying to destroy assump-tions about the presumed "goodness" of political and economic life in the United States. In the ideal, the liberationist conversation culminates in the awareness that capitalism is oppressive, struggle is liberating, and knowledge is actually power that conceals and advances special class interests. The liberationist conversation is based on a dialectic of contestation whose major purpose is emancipation, achieved through radical social transformation.

In contrast to these three "destructive" dialectics, my notion of the postmodern dialectic is inspired by Hans-Georg Gadamer (1984), who thought of dialectic primarily as nonmanipulative, "undominated" conversation that resists presumptions in advance of what counts as good and true. Hence, in the spirit of Gadamer, I think of the moral conversation as free-flowing, in the sense that all moral assertions are open to critical discussion and negotiation. And because the dialectic is non-manipulative, "undominated" conversation, the objective is not merely to assert a moral viewpoint or to exact agreement from other conversationalists. Rather, the major safeguard against conversational "hegemony" is to listen to others in a spirit of mutuality and self-criticism in order for personal transformation to occur. However, as Gadamer recognized, in the end, the conversational dialectic carries with it no metaphysical guarantees that either personal transformation or reconciliation of contrasting moral views will occur, or that a "best" moral truth will result, or that radical social transformation will take place (Gallagher, 1992).

3.   HERMENEUTICAL SENSITIVITY.   Shaun Gallagher (1992) has written what I consider to be a magisterial account of hermeneutics and education, and what I have to say here has been profoundly influenced by his work. I consider myself a "moderate" hermeneute, to use his designation, rather than a "conservative," "radical," or "critical" one. My own hermeneutic, as I have already said, eschews using the moral conversation to locate objective truths, or to play word games by deconstructing languages, or to engage in the construction of grand political narratives that promise deliverance from exploitation and oppression. In the few paragraphs that follow, my own account of hermeneutics will be far briefer than Gallagher's, and my language and purposes will be fundamentally different from his as well. I am primarily concerned with looking at hermeneutical sensitivity as a virtue and linking it to my use of the moral conversation.

Hermeneutical sensitivity has to do with an awareness that people always interpret and translate texts into their own idioms. As Nietzsche says in the excerpt that introduces this chapter, there is only a "perspective seeing," only a "perspective knowing". The Greek *hermeneuein* means "to make clear and understandable, to interpret, to give expression to." This is what Hermes in Greek mythology did to the cryptic messages of the gods so that mortals could understand them. And this is what readers do to any text, because, whether they know it or not, they are constantly interpreting and translating the words of others through the mediation of their own "perspectives," including their vocabularies, historical situations, and background beliefs. A hermeneutical sensitivity recognizes and respects the principle that reality is endlessly interpretable.

The goal of a hermeneutical understanding of morality is to determine what traditional and contemporary moral teachings actually mean in light of the everyday lives each of us leads. Thus a postmodern embrace of virtue and character starts with an intention to reach moral self-understanding, progresses to an ability to express oneself publicly in an intelligible and defensible moral idiom, and, ideally, eventuates in actual virtuous behavior. The master hermeneutical question is: What can I take and use from a cultural moral system that predates me, that to a large extent exists outside of me, and that will most likely survive me long after I am gone? Jurgen Habermas (1983/1993) warns that people must become aware of the various particularities and ideological distortions that prevent them from understanding each other whenever they engage in moral discourse. This is why I insist in the moral conversation on getting the authors', along with my own and students', ideological biases on the table early with the hope that we can at least begin to expose pieces of our hermeneutical frameworks to each other at the beginning of the semester.

Do all these different interpretations and perspectives on morality therefore mean that the most we can ever say about virtue or moral character is that it all depends on the individual's hermeneutic? Are the neo-classicals, communitarians, and liberationists correct when they charge postmodernists with a dead-end subjectivity, or, worse, with a moral Babel that ends in anarchy? I think not. Gadamer (1984) claims that behind the chaos of individual perspectives is a *shared* moral reality. As he puts it: "The purpose of my investigation . . . is to discover what is common to all modes of understanding and to show that understanding is never subjective behavior toward a given 'object,' but toward its effective history" (p. xix). In other words, the *object* of truth should never be the central question. Because nobody can discover a "truth" independent of significant interpretive variables, it is only in a mutual sharing of partial perspectives that people can arrive at some common understanding of the "given object." This is Gadamer's way of avoiding the Scylla and Charybdis of two perilous extremes—relativism and objectivism.

In a larger sense, Gadamer is saying that we all live in the same world, experience similar basic needs and drives, and rely on the medium of language to communicate these needs and drives. Consequently, Gadamer (1984) believes it is possible for individuals to achieve a "fusion of horizons" through a particular type of conversation in which the conversationalists engage in dialogue in which, for example, they share their various interpretations of a text or an idea. They question texts and one another, listen carefully, and try to "reach behind" the texts whenever possible, and, when everything goes well, conversationalists are able to reach a kind of "communion" in which they undergo fundamental changes.

In Gadamer's sense, I believe the hermeneutical virtues are demanding. If "shared understanding," or "full rapport," is the objective of hermeneutical dialogue, as he proposed, then conversationalists need to develop the virtues of openness to otherness, respect for plurality, patience, tolerance, and empathy (Thiselton, 1995). I would add to Gadamer's list of hermeneutical virtues Rorty's (1989) sense of irony and humor, as well as a compassion in the presence of suffering with an antipathy toward violence of any kind. And I would also include Schwehn's (1993) capacity for faith, hope, love, and humility in the face of shifting and elusive conceptions of reality, goodness, and truth. Unlike the neoclassical hermeneutic of compliance, or the communitarian hermeneutic of conformity, or the liberationist hermeneutic of contestation, a conversational hermeneutic is one of trust and optimism rather than suspicion (Gallagher, 1992).

POSTSCRIPT

Students raise several questions about the moral conversation, postmodernism, and my approach to doing moral education. In this postscript, I intend to respond briefly to a number of these questions as a way to summarize my own approach to imparting virtues in my moral-education course.

Question: I think I understand the rationale for encouraging a moral conversation in a college classroom. But what does the moral conversation have to do with democracy?

Response: Earlier I mentioned a philosopher of "public conversation," James Davison Hunter (1991, 1994). I think he makes the connection between moral conversation and democracy very effectively. Hunter, who writes a great deal about what he calls the "culture wars," claims that what Americans need today is a "new *unum,* capable of binding together a *pluribus* that seems ever more fragmented" (1994, p. 228). In confronting our deepest differences as a nation over such volatile issues as abortion, Hunter argues for an *unum* "generated from the bottom up." This requires a new kind of "public argument," where people engage in "civil but principled engagement" (p. 238).

I believe Hunter's guidelines for conducting civil public debate are highly compatible with my "civility protocols," which I developed in the previous chapter. Hunter's rules are: Debate civilly. Criticize, but only if you are willing to accept the responsibility to comprehend. Try to influence, but do not inflame. Try to persuade on the basis of what is best for the common good. And remember—not only is realism required in public debate but modesty as well. Hunter realizes that *how* we contend over our moral differences as a nation is as significant as the *content* of our differences. For him, and for me, *the manner* of contention is what democracy is about.

You should also read Amy Gutmann (1987), hardly a postmodernist, but someone, I believe, who would be very comfortable with moral conversation. For Gutmann, a "democratic education" should train students in "deliberative competence." She has two principles she believes ought to "constrain" every public conversation in a democracy: nonrepression and nondiscrimination. According to her, *all* citizens, without discrimination, should be educated to participate in the democratic process, and *no* view should be repressed. For Gutmann, the most important "democratic virtue" is the "ability to deliberate, to participate in conscious social reproduction" (p. 46). And Gutmann urges that citizens must learn to carry on their public conversations without needing to rely upon a "closed system of self-evident axioms, an original position, or a neutral dialogue" (p. 47). I think Gutmann, a democratic political theorist, very nicely captures the spirit of my conversational intentions.

Question: But isn't this naive? What do you do when moral differences are irreconcilable in this country? Have you heard the contentious national debates lately on same-sex marriages, abortion, capital punishment, affirmative action, social justice, welfare, and physician-assisted suicide, to mention just some?

Response: I am not naive, just tired of the same old acrimony, media soundbites, and self-righteousness whenever we talk publicly about these highly volatile moral issues—and others as well. This is why I like Richard Rorty's approach to public conversation. Isaiah Berlin once said: "We can discuss each other's point of view, we can try to reach common ground, but in the end what you pursue may not be reconcilable with the ends to which I find that I have dedicated my life" (quoted by Tivnan, 1995, p. 234). Now what? To which Rorty is likely to answer: Then we've either got to change the subject, or we've got to change the language we use to talk about these inflammatory subjects, or we've got to get beyond the need to appeal to an "objective truth" hiding in some "sacred" text in order to defend our views and to justify imposing them on others.

For Rorty, and for me as well, the alternatives to moral conversation are undemocratic: verbal authoritarianism, political intimidation, imposition, indoctrination, and violence. I can only agree once again with John Dewey, Rorty's mentor: "The task of future philosophy is to clarify men's ideas as to the social and moral strifes of their own day" (quoted by Tivnan, 1995, p. 239). And Rorty would add: This clarification of controversial ideas must begin with an awareness that our moral vocabulary is always a product of our "customs, traditions, and values." Clarity requires self-reflection, informed awareness, and public dialogue. And I would say: A good start is right here in the classroom, practicing the moral conversation.

At least two advocates of multicultural education agree with me. Judith Renyi (1993) argues for a kind of classroom conversation around cultural diversity, even at the elementary school level, that approximates my own conception of the moral conversation. Also, Harlon L. Dalton's book, *Racial Healing: Confronting the Fear Between Blacks & Whites* (1995), is an excellent model of using some of the principles of the moral conversation in getting blacks and whites to speak honestly and openly to each other about their racial beliefs. In his words: "We should simply put everything on the table. Own up to the tension. Acknowledge the risks. When somebody inevitably screws up, rather than beat a hasty retreat, we should seize the opportunity to deepen the dialogue" (p. 224). Dalton, an African American Yale University law professor, believes that racial engagement in this country requires a public conversation that is candid, willing to take risks, forthcoming about self-interests, and open about fears and desires. For Dalton, trying to understand different racial languages is the first step in getting blacks and whites to connect with each other as equals, by becoming equally vulnerable. For me, moral conversation is about this kind of equal vulnerability and hence equal strength.

Question: Postmodernism is grim. What's left to believe in? Can you really be so hopeful, so optimistic? How do you avoid falling into the traps of relativism and nihilism? I'm a believer in God. What's to become of folks like me?

Response: Postmodernism is a slippery, all-purpose term that is frequently used as a "purr" word or a "snarl" word, depending on your particular hermeneutic. For me, the word purrs more than it snarls. Again, I quote Rorty: "It is useless to ask whether one vocabulary rather than another is closer to reality. For different vocabularies serve different purposes, and there is no such thing as a purpose that is closer to reality than another purpose" (quoted in Grenz, 1996, p. 155). Rorty captures the nub of postmodernism, as I understand and use the term. Mainly, postmodernism is about language, functionality, purposes, tolerance, humility, mutual respect, and, above all, conversation.

In the context of this course in moral education, *my* moral vocabulary is the "tool" I use to solve my moral problems. Often, I use different vocabularies to solve other kinds of problems: religious, political, educational, recreational, relational, emotional, professional, and so forth. It is unlikely I will ever find a "metavocabulary" to cover all these problems. And so I do the best I can with the flawed languages I've got. And I assume you do as well. In principle, I can't prove to you that any single one of *my* languages is the one that will give *you* everything you need to solve your own problems. But I can respect your languages. I can try to understand them. I can practice empathy when I do not understand them. I can challenge them in a nonviolent way. And, on occasion, I can even "redescribe" them in my own vocabulary. I have faith that you can do the same with me. Perhaps we will someday find a way to help each other.

In a liberal, secular pluralist democracy, I can't imagine how else we might carry on peaceful and productive conversations with each other. With Rorty, I am hopeful that if we make an honest effort to converse in this fashion, we might be able to achieve some kind of human "solidarity," some way to stop inflicting pain and humiliation on each other whenever we display our different vocabularies. The central purpose of the moral conversation is to surface as many moral vocabularies as possible in order for us to learn how to speak different languages and to enrich and deepen our own "native" moral language. I am no relativist or nihilist, if by these words you mean that I think all moral languages are equivalent or that moral languages are unnecessary. For me, moral languages are all we've got to talk with each other about how we should live our lives, both as individuals and as people who must somehow forge some common agreements with each other (R.J. Nash, 1996). And, for me, the "best" moral language is the one that encourages respectful engagement, peaceable and productive problem solving, nonviolence, fairness, individual liberty, justice, creativity, and the unrestrained opportunity to pursue excellence in our chosen spheres.

Can you be a theist and still function as a postmodernist in the classroom, and maybe even in the world outside? I think you can be, and so do a number of respectable theologians (Grenz, 1996; Thiselton, 1995; Tracy, 1994), but only if you look for what theists and postmodernists have in common. Granted the fit will always be a tenuous, often disturbing, one, but I think mutually beneficial coexistence is possible at some level (Armstrong, 1997). It seems to me that both you and the postmodernists are aware of the limits of twentieth-century reason, science, technology, and political ideology to produce metaphysical certainty and the guarantee of a good life. And you both are rightly skeptical of those political "grand narratives" that promise deliverance from suffering and injustice but, throughout this century, have managed to end up as justifications for totalitarianism and tyranny. And you both are keenly aware of the historicity and contingency of human life and the fact that our situated experiences color, and flaw, all of our interpretations. Thus you both understand that human knowledge is always incomplete and partisan.

I agree with the theologian David Tracy (1994) that, ironically (a useful postmodern term, by the way), postmodernity has ushered in the "strange return of God" (p. 42). Tracy says:

> "Let God be God" becomes an authentic cry again. This God reveals God-self in hiddenness; in cross and negativity, above all in the suffering of all those others whom the grand narrative of modernity has set aside as non-peoples, non-events, non-memories, non-history. (p. 43)

What Tracy is urging theists to consider is that postmodernism need not be a threat to belief at all. Rather, it can stimulate a search for different and alternative ways to think about theology. At the very least, according to Tracy, this is a time to wonder at the "overwhelming mystery of God," as some postmodern physicists and cosmologists are doing in very creative theologizing (Davies, 1983, 1992; Polkinghorne, 1996).

Question: What are the risks for educators in adopting the postmodern alternative? What is worrisome about this "initiative" in doing moral education?

Response: Epistemologically, postmodernism is worrisome to me because some of its proponents tend to emphasize only its more nihilistic, despairing elements: Knowledge, at best, is fragmented and indeterminate. There is no ultimate justification for truth, no unimpeachable *telos* or *logos,* so truth claims must always be suspect. This greatly disturbs the neo-classicals. Furthermore, some "radical," political postmodernists, the liberationists, send the message that *all* knowledge is corrupt, because, at best, it is ideology and it disguises power interests on behalf of the privileged. Thus, they wonder, what is the point of trusting any authority?

This loss of hope, this all-pervasive hermeneutic of suspicion, the communitarians remind us, collapses every human relationship into a contest of power interests, characterized by alleged sexism, heterosexism, racism, or capitalistic competition. Genuine community, therefore, eludes us. Thus people either become doctrinaire converts to a particular political orthodoxy, or else they become doctrinaire skeptics committed mainly to discrediting orthodoxy. I worry that a view of knowledge based entirely on a hermeneutic of suspicion and contestation will ultimately devastate the democratic process and return us to Thomas Hobbes's (1651/1962) "war of all against all," if it hasn't done so already. I also worry about a creeping anti-intellectualism and the loss of a "deliberative competence" that citizens will increasingly need to govern themselves intelligently and peaceably.

Politically, the postmodern, conversational perspective I am advocating is problematic as well. Because I hope to place the moral conversation "beyond ideology," I am vulnerable to the liberationist charge that I am merely "producing or reproducing" a new hierarchy in the form of a more dangerous, dominating ideology. In other words, my ideal of open-ended, mutually respectful conversation, in the hope of reaching some type of peaceable consensus, actually serves destructive, ideological ends. My concealed "metanarrative" is bourgeois liberal individualism, and my "democratic" virtues are precisely what a capitalist system needs to continue its domination. Moreover, as liberationists might point out, my commitment to a popularly constituted government and to the principles of diversity and social justice appears to be in irreconcilable conflict with my belief in a wide range of individual opportunities, a market economy, and a constitutionally protected sphere of privacy and individual rights.

I respect the concerns behind these charges, and I can offer no defense of my own views that will be entirely convincing to those who speak a different moral language from mine. The most that I can say to those who use neo-classical, communitarian, or liberationist vocabulary is that I hope students (and citizens) will continue to come together in *goodwill* to learn and to solve their problems and that what constitutes objective truth, group solidarity, and emancipation to each of these initiatives frequently lies in the hermeneutic of the individual beholder, in Nietzsche's "perspective seeing." I am well aware of the risks in moral conversation at the classroom level, but I am not convinced that the answer lies in keeping conversation more in line with the putative "truths" of neo-classical, communitarian, or liberationist ideologies. I do agree, however, with Gallagher (1992) that conversation must become more "playful" in order to balance the "agonistic [argumentative], paralogical [illogical], and deconstructive" elements of the ongoing classroom dialogue. I would also add that conversation must help students become more self-aware, so that conversationalists fully understand the impact of their own ideological self-interests in directing the conversation one way over another.

For my part, I will continue to put neo-classical, communitarian, liberationist, and postmodern languages in conversation with one another in my moral-education classes, not so we can get to the "bottom of things" or arrive at a factitious sense of communal well-being, but so we might find out what our opposing languages have in common, if anything, and what we might be able to agree on by way of solving our common problems. And I will do this knowing full well that I operate under my own "illusions" that people often act out of goodwill, that words can be persuasive, and that conversation can replace creed as a way to move students, and citizens, to self-reflection and action.

Question: Do you have any practical tips for actually carrying out moral conversations in the classroom?

Response: I'll try to be brief. I'll talk here about the *college* classroom, because this is where I work, but I believe the principles are generalizable (Nash, in press).

1. Keep a sharp intellectual focus in moral conversations, along with clearly understood textual purposes, or else they can become nothing more than encounter groups or bull sessions. Insist on particular textual themes for discussion foci, frequent references to "proof-texts" in the readings, rigorous "unpacking" of an author's concepts, and continual student rephrasing of each other's observations and interpretations. Don't "throw" reading assignments at students unless you intend to spend time publicly unpacking them in class. An unpacked text is like an unread text: It is a missed opportunity for the possibility of "fusing horizons," to use Gadamer's arresting phrase.
2. Be prepared for the unpredictable "conversation bombs" that sometimes explode during discussion: the dumb bomb, the hostility bomb, the self-interest bomb, the personal grievance bomb, the subversive bomb, the agenda-grabbing bomb, the humor bomb, the "totally off-base" bomb, and so forth. Use good judgment when trying to "defuse" the bombs, because they can easily blow up in your face (Christensen, Garvin, & Sweet, 1991).
3. Establish a powerful presence as a leader in the moral conversation by projecting a sense of ease, unflappability, poise, and self-assurance. Be dignified and informed without being intimidating. Be compelling without being controlling. Be superbly prepared but also spontaneous.

Be conspicuously in charge without being arrogant or unwilling to surrender authority when appropriate.

4. Avoid indoctrination. Always maintain the element of ideological surprise. Respond "out of political character" to questions and issues, and do this often.

5. Trust the process. First, realize that in the moral conversation things will most likely go wrong before they go right. When everything is falling apart, when the "bombs" are dropping, the only recourse may be to mutter something incomprehensible. But have faith. The process is self-correcting in time, especially if everyone is committed to it. Second, resist the temptation to rescue conversationalists whenever they stray into unchartered conversational territory. Well-meaning rescue actions frequently deliver the message that students are too brittle and unable to handle candor, challenge, or criticism. Expect to have to handle all of these yourself. In fact, encourage students to challenge you. One sign that your group has engaged in genuine moral conversation is when conversationalists welcome conflict because they feel safe enough to handle it. And third, at strategic intervals, stop teaching and telling, and start listening and learning. Ask for feedback on the conversational process. *Practice the virtues you want others to emulate.*

6. Finally, ask a variety of questions. Rainer Maria Rilke asks that we "love the questions. . . . I want to beg you, as much as I can, to be patient toward all that is unsolved. Try to love the questions themselves. Do not now seek the answers which cannot be given you because you would not be able to live them. Live the questions now. Perhaps you will then gradually, without noticing it, live along some distant day into the answer" (quoted in Christensen, Garvin, & Sweet, 1991, p. 163). Avoid a surfeit of factual *who, what, when,* and *where* questions. Ask these types of conversational questions instead: *Why* do you use the particular moral vocabulary you do? *Why* do you think the author uses the particular moral vocabulary he or she does? *How* has the text affected your own life? *How* might people live together more virtuously after having read the text? *What* do you mean? *In what sense* do you think the author means that? *How* would you "unpack" this particular proof-text? *What moral story* is the author telling? *What moral story* is the author living? *How* is the *author* "redescribing" previous authors' moral insights? *How* do *you* choose to "redescribe" the author's key moral insights? *In what senses* have you "rewritten" the author's text? These types of questions, and others like them, are more likely to elicit the hermeneutical responses that I believe to be crucial in a moral conversation (Christensen, Garvin, & Sweet, 1991).

A LAST WORD ON THE *MENO*

In the *Meno,* a Platonic dialogue I referred to in Chapter 1, Socrates ends up asserting that we can only learn to be virtuous by "divine inspiration." Anytus, Socrates' friend, believes, in contrast, that the best way to teach virtue is by exemplification and modeling. The Sophists and skeptics throughout the Platonic dialogues sometimes argue that moral character is innate and thus unteachable. The neo-classicals, communitarians, and liberationists in the preceding chapters have in common the view that virtue can, indeed, be taught and that the schools and colleges must play a principal role in imparting the desired dispositions. In general, the post-moderns are not so sure, although moderates such as Richard Rorty believe conversation is a good place to start practicing his desired virtues.

In my own view, virtue and moral character have little to do with checklists of individual qualities, or bags of particular habits or dispositions, or reading the "virtue books," or even exemplary modeling, although I acknowledge the latter to be an important determinant in character formation (Damon, 1988). While I profoundly respect the views of the various virtue initiatives I have critically examined in the previous chapters, I remain something of a minimalist when it comes to teaching virtue. I believe that grand moral visions, whatever the content, are, in the end, potentially dangerous. Niebuhr (1935) reminded us that because master moral visions are "accustomed to a telescopic view of life and history, [they do] not adjust [themselves] as readily to the microscopic calculations and adjustments which constitute the stuff of the moral life" (p. 102). And Martin Luther King, Jr. (1958) taught that radical political visions too often give way to violence. For King, "Violence is immoral because it thrives on hatred rather than love. It destroys community and makes brotherhood impossible. It leaves society in monologue rather than dialogue" (p. 213).

I do not want to lose the individual in a grand moral or political scheme. Neither do I wish to run the risk of choosing inconsistent (coercive) means to bring about laudable moral ends. It is my hope that somehow the schools and colleges can do their part to help us respond to our problems, pursue our particular goals, and learn to live harmoniously with one another by teaching us how to engage in moral conversations together. I am, admittedly, an optimist, I know, because schools and colleges must first learn, and practice, the art of moral dialogue in their own internal transactions. Nevertheless, I remain hopeful, for when the public conversation ceases, when we begin to speak to one another only in "monologues rather than dialogues," then, in the words of Martin Luther King (1958), we are tempted to "humiliate the opponent rather than win his understanding; to annihilate rather than to convert" (p. 213). Meanwhile, I will continue to teach each of the virtue initiatives I have presented here not as a "minister" of morality or as a "virtuecrat" but as a moral conversationalist. I sincerely believe that, in spite of their excesses and deficiencies, neo-classical, communitarian, liberationist, and postmodern languages can help us to enrich, deepen, and extend the democratic dialogue.

References

Adler, M. J. (1940). *How to read a book: The art of getting a liberal education*. New York: Simon & Schuster.

Adorno, T. W., & Horkheimer, M. (1972). *Dialectic of enlightenment* (J. Cumming, Trans.). New York: Continuum.

Angeles, P. A. (1992). *The HarperCollins dictionary of philosophy*. New York: Harper-Collins.

Apple, M. W. (1979). *Ideology and curriculum*. Boston: Routledge & Kegan Paul.

Apple, M. W. (1993). *Official knowledge: Democratic education in a conservative age*. New York: Routledge.

Aristotle. (1976). *The ethics of Aristotle: The Nicomachean ethics* (J. A. K. Thomson, Trans.). New York: Penguin.

Armstrong, J. P. (1997). *Postmodernism and higher education: A new openness for Christian faith*. Unpublished master's thesis, University of Vermont, Burlington.

Aronowitz, S., (1992). *The politics of identity*. New York: Routledge.

Aronowitz, S., & Giroux, H. (1985). *Education under siege*. South Hadley, MA: Bergin & Garvey.

Aronowitz, S., & Giroux, H. (1991). *Postmodern education: Politics, culture, and social criticism*. Minneapolis: University of Minnesota Press.

Attitudes and characteristics of freshmen. *The Chronicle of Higher Education almanac*. Washington, DC: The Chronicle of Higher Education.

Audi, R. (1995). (Ed.). *The Cambridge dictionary of philosophy*. New York: Cambridge University Press.

Barber, B. (1992). *An aristocracy of everyone: The politics of education and the future of America*. New York: Ballantine.

Barnes, J. (1982). *Aristotle*. Oxford, England: Oxford University Press.

Bates, S. (1993). *Battleground*. New York: Holt.

Beauchamp, T. L., & Childress, J. F. (1994). *Principles of biomedical ethics* (4th ed.). New York: Oxford University Press.

Bellah, R. N., Madsen, R., Sullivan, W. M., Swidler, A., & Tipton, S. M. (1985). *Habits of the heart: Individualism and commitment in American life*. Berkeley: University of California Press.

Bennett, W. J. (1988). *Our children & our country*. New York: Simon & Schuster.

Bennett, W. J. (1992). *The de-valuing of America: The fight for our culture and our children*. New York: Summit.

Bennett, W. J. (1993). *The book of virtues: A treasury of great moral stories.* New York: Simon & Schuster.

Bennett, W. J. (1995). *The moral compass.* New York: Simon & Schuster.

Berlak, A. (1994). Antiracist pedagogy in a college classroom: Mutual recognition and a logic of paradox. In R. A. Martusewicz & W. M. Reynolds (Eds.), *Inside/out: Contemporary critical perspectives in education.* New York: St. Martin's.

Berlin, I. (1992). *The crooked timber of humanity.* New York: Vintage.

Bernstein, R. J. (1993). *The new constellation: The ethical-political horizons of modernity/postmodernity.* Cambridge, MA: MIT Press.

Berryman, P. (1987). *Liberation theology.* New York: Pantheon.

Beyer, L. E., & Apple, M. W. (Eds.). (1988). *The curriculum: Problems, politics, and possibilities.* Albany: State University of New York Press.

Bloom, A. (1987). *The closing of the American mind.* New York: Simon & Schuster.

Bloom, H. (1995). *The Western canon: The books and school of the ages.* New York: Riverhead.

Booth, W. (1988). *The company we keep: An ethics of fiction.* Berkeley: University of California Press.

Borradori, G. (1994). *The American philosopher.* Chicago: University of Chicago Press.

Bowers, C. A. (1987). *Elements of a post-liberal theory of education.* New York: Teachers College Press.

Bowles, S., & Gintis, H. (1976). *Schooling in capitalist America.* New York: Basic Books.

Brameld, T. (1956). *Toward a reconstructed philosophy of education.* New York: Holt, Rinehart & Winston.

Brameld, T. (1965). *Education for the emerging age: Newer ends and stronger means.* New York: Harper & Row.

Bromwich, D. (1992). *Politics by other means: Higher education and group thinking.* New Haven, CT: Yale University Press.

Bruffee, K. A. (1993). *Collaborative learning: Higher education, interdependence, and the authority of knowledge.* Baltimore: Johns Hopkins University Press.

Budziszewski, J. (1995). The problem with communitarianism. *First Things, 51,* 22–26.

Burke, E. (1960). *Reflections on the revolution in France.* London: Dent. (Original work published 1790)

Carter, S. L. (1993). *The culture of disbelief: How American law and politics trivialize religious devotion.* New York: Basic Books.

Chazan, B. (1985). *Contemporary approaches to moral education: Analyzing alternative theories.* New York: Teachers College Press.

Christensen, C. R., Garvin, D. A., & Sweet, A. (Eds.). (1991). *Education for judgment: The artistry of discussion leadership.* Cambridge, MA: Harvard Business School Press.

Coles, R. (1993). *The call of service: A witness to idealism.* Boston: Houghton Mifflin.

Collins, M. (1990). *Marva Collins' way.* New York: Putnam.

Counts, G. (1932). *Dare the school build a new social order?* New York: Day.

Cox, H. (1965). *The secular city: Urbanization and secularization in theological perspective.* New York: Macmillan.

Dalton, H. (1995). *Racial healing: Confronting the fear between blacks & whites.* New York: Doubleday.

Damon, W. (1988). *The moral child: Nurturing children's natural moral growth.* New York: Free Press.

Davies, P. (1983). *God and the new physics.* New York: Simon & Schuster.

Davies, P. (1992). *The mind of God: The scientific basis for a rational world.* New York: Simon & Schuster.

Delpit, L. (1995). *Other people's children: Cultural conflict in the classroom.* New York: New Press.

Dennis, L. J., & Eaton, W. E. (Eds.). (1980). *George S. Counts: Educator for a new age.* Carbondale: Southern Illinois University Press.

Derrida, J. (1978). *Writing and difference* (A. Bass, Trans.). Chicago: University of Chicago Press.

Dewey, J. (1909). *Moral principles in education.* Boston: Houghton Mifflin.

Dewey, J. (1916). *Democracy and education.* New York: Macmillan.

Dewey, J. (1958). *Reconstruction in philosophy.* Boston: Beacon. (Original work published 1920)

Dewey, J. (1959). *Dewey on education: Selections.* New York: Teachers College Press.

Diggins, J. P. (1994). *The promise of pragmatism: Modernism and the crisis of knowledge and authority.* Chicago: University of Chicago Press.

Dionne, E. J., Jr. (1991). *Why Americans hate politics.* New York: Simon & Schuster.

Eagleton, T. (1996). *The illusions of postmodernism.* Cambridge, England: Blackwell.

Edmundson, M. (Ed.). (1993). *Wild orchids and Trotsky: Messages from America's universities.* New York: Penguin.

Ellsworth, E. (1989). Why doesn't this feel empowering? Working through the repressive myths of critical pedagogy. *Harvard Educational Review, 59,* 297–324.

Elshtain, J. B. (1995). *Democracy on trial.* New York: Basic Books.

Etzioni, A. (1993). *The spirit of community: Rights, responsibilities, and the communitarian agenda.* New York: Crown.

Fine, M. (1991). *Framing dropouts: Notes on the politics of an urban public high school.* Albany: State University of New York Press.

Foucault, M. (1977). *Discipline and punish: The birth of the prison.* New York: Pantheon.

Foucault, M. (1979). *Power, truth, and strategy.* Sidney, Australia: Feral.

Foucault, M. (1981). *Power/knowledge.* New York: Random House.

Fox, R. (1985). *Reinhold Niebuhr: A biography.* New York: Pantheon.

Freire, P. (1971). *Pedagogy of the oppressed.* New York: Herder & Herder.

Freire, P. (1973). *Education for critical consciousness.* New York: Seabury.

Freire, P. (1985). *The politics of education: Culture, power, and liberation.* South Hadley, MA: Bergin & Garvey.

Freire, P. (1994a). *Paulo Freire on higher education: A dialogue at the National University of Mexico.* Albany: State University of New York Press.

Freire, P. (1994b). *Pedagogy of hope: Reliving pedagogy of the oppressed.* New York: Continuum.

Frost, S. E., Jr. (1962). *Basic teachings of the great philosophers.* New York: Dolphin.

Fukuyama, F. (1992). *The end of history and the last man.* New York: Free Press.

Gadamer, H. G. (1984). *Truth and method* (G. Barden & J. Cumming, Ed. and Trans.). New York: Crossroad.

Gaddy, B. B., Hall, T. W., & Marzano, R. J. (1996). *School wars: Resolving our conflicts over religion and values.* San Francisco: Jossey-Bass.

Gallagher, S. (1992). *Hermeneutics and education.* Albany: State University of New York Press.

Gardner, J. (1991). *Building community.* Washington, DC: Independent Sector.

Gates, H. L., Jr. (1992). *Loose canons: Notes on the culture wars.* New York: Oxford University Press.

Geuss, R. (1981). *The idea of a critical theory.* Cambridge, England: Cambridge University Press.

Giroux, H. (1983). *Theory and resistance: A pedagogy for the opposition.* South Hadley, MA: Bergin & Garvey.

Giroux, H. (1988). *Schooling and the struggle for public life: Critical pedagogy in the modern age.* Minneapolis: University of Minnesota Press.

Giroux, H. (1992). *Border crossings.* New York: Routledge.

Giroux, H. (1993). *Living dangerously.* New York: Peter Lang.

Giroux, H. (1994). *Disturbing pleasures: Learning popular culture.* New York: Routledge.

Glendon, M. A. (1991). *Rights talk: The impoverishment of political discourse.* New York: Free Press.

Glendon, M. A., & Blankenhorn, D. (Eds.). (1995). *Seedbeds of virtue.* Lanham, MD: Madison.

Graff, G. (1992). *Beyond the culture wars: How teaching the conflicts can revitalize American education.* New York: Norton.

Gramsci, A. (1971). *Selections from prison notebooks* (Q. Hoare & G. Smith, Ed. and Trans.). New York: International.

Grant, G. (1985). Schools that make an imprint: Creating a strong positive ethos. In J. H. Hunzel (Ed.), *Challenge to American schools: The case for standards and values* (pp. 127–146). New York: Oxford University Press.

Grenz, S. J. (1996). *A primer on postmodernism.* Grand Rapids, MI: Eerdmans.

Griffin, R. S., & Nash, R. J. (1990). Individualism, community, and education: An exchange of views. *Educational Theory, 40*(1), 1–18.

Gutek, G. L. (1988). *Philosophical and ideological perspectives on education.* Englewood Cliffs, NJ: Prentice-Hall.

Gutierrez, G. (1973). *A theology of liberation.* Maryknoll, NY: Orbis.

Gutmann, A. (1987). *Democratic education.* Princeton, NJ: Princeton University Press.

Habermas, J. (1993). *Moral consciousness and communicative action* (C. Lenhardt & S. W. Nicholsen, Ed. and Trans.). Cambridge: MA: MIT Press. (Original work published 1983)

Hall, D. L. (1994). *Richard Rorty: Prophet and poet of the new pragmatism.* Albany: State University of New York Press.

Hare, R. M. (1982). *Plato.* New York: Oxford University Press.

Hart, H. L. A. (1983). *Essays in jurisprudence and philosophy.* New York: Oxford University Press.

Hauerwas, S. (1981). *A community of character: Toward a constructive Christian social ethic.* Notre Dame, IN: University of Notre Dame Press.

Hauerwas, S. (1988). *Against the nations: War and survival in a liberal society.* New York: Harper & Row.

Hauerwas, S. (1991). *After Christendom?* Nashville, TN: Abingdon.

Hauerwas, S., & Westerhoff, J. H. (Eds.). (1992). *Schooling Christians: "Holy experiments" in American education.* Grand Rapids, MI: Eerdmans.

Haught, J. A. (1990). *Holy horrors.* Buffalo, NY: Prometheus Press.

Hegel, G. W. F. (1977). *The phenomenology of spirit* (A. V. Miller, Trans.). Oxford, NY: Oxford University Press. (Original work published 1821)

Herron, J. (1988). *Universities and the myth of cultural decline.* Detroit: Wayne State University Press.

Hersh, R. H., Miller, J. P., & Fielding, G. D. (1980). *Models of moral education: An appraisal.* New York: Longman.

Hobbes, T. (1962). *Leviathan* (M. Oakeshott, Ed.). New York: Macmillan. (Original work published 1651)

Hollinger, A. F. (1995). *Postethnic America: Beyond multiculturalism.* New York: Basic Books.

Holmes, A. F. (1975). *The idea of a Christian college.* Grand Rapids, MI: Eerdmans.

Holmes, S. (1993). *The anatomy of antiliberalism.* Cambridge, MA: Harvard University Press.

Honderich, T. (1995). (Ed.). *The Oxford companion to philosophy.* New York: Oxford University Press.

Honig, B. (1987). *Last chance for our children.* Reading, MA: Addison Wesley.

hooks, b. (1994). *Teaching to transgress: Education as the pratice of freedom.* New York: Routledge.

Hughes, R. (1993). *Culture of complaint: The fraying of America.* New York: Oxford University Press.

Hunter, J. D. (1991). *Culture wars: The struggle to define America.* New York: Basic Books.

Hunter, J. D. (1994). *Before the shooting begins: Searching for democracy in America's culture war.* New York: Free Press.

Johnson, T. W. (1995). *Discipleship or pilgrimage? The educator's quest for philosophy.* Albany: State University of New York Press.

Jung, P. B. (1992). A call for reform schools. In S. Hauerwas & J. H. Westerhoff (Eds.), *Schooling Christians: "Holy experiments" in American education* (pp. 115–128). Grand Rapids, MI: Eerdmans.

Kanpol, B. (1994). *Critical pedagogy: An introduction.* Westport, CT: Bergin & Garvey.

Katchadourian, H., & Boli, J. (1994). *Cream of the crop: The impact of elite education in the decade after college.* New York: Basic Books.

Katz, M. B. (1968). *The irony of early school reform: Educational innovation in mid-nineteenth century Massachusetts.* Cambridge, MA: Harvard University Press.

Kaus, M. (1992). *The end of equality.* New York: Basic Books.

Kelly, U. A. (1991). From text to textuality: Reading McLaren's life in schools. *Journal of Education, 173,* 8–14.

Kilpatrick, W. (1992). *Why Johnny can't tell right from wrong: Moral illiteracy and the case for character education.* New York: Simon & Schuster.

King, M. L. (1958). *Stride toward freedom.* New York: Harper & Row.

Kirst, M. W. (1984). *Who controls our schools? American values in conflict.* New York: Freeman.

Knight, M. K. (1995). *Building community in a public high school: Theory and practice.* Unpublished doctoral dissertation, University of Virginia, Charlottesville.

Kohl, H., & Greer, C. (Eds.). (1995). *A call to character: A family treasury.* San Francisco: HarperCollins.

Kozol, J. (1991). *Savage inequalities: Children in America's schools.* New York: Crown.

Kymlicka, W. (1995). Liberalism. In T. Honderich (Ed.), *The Oxford companion to philosophy.* New York: Oxford University Press.

Lasch, C. (1995). *The revolt of the elites: And the betrayal of democracy.* New York: Norton.

Lehman, D. (1992). *Signs of the times: Deconstruction and the fall of Paul de Man.* New York: Simon & Schuster.

Leming, J. S. (1993). In search of effective character education. *Educational Leadership, 51,* 63–71.

Lickona, T. (1991). *Educating for character: How our schools can teach respect and responsibility.* New York: Bantam.

Lightfoot, S. L. (1983). *The good high school: Portraits of character and culture.* New York: Basic Books.

Lyotard, J. F. (1984). *The postmodern condition: A report on knowledge.* Minneapolis: University of Minnesota Press.

MacIntyre, A. (1984). *After virtue.* Notre Dame, IN: University of Notre Dame Press.

MacIntyre, A. (1990). *Three rival versions of moral enquiry: Encyclopaedia, genealogy, and tradition.* Notre Dame, IN: University of Notre Dame Press.

Males, M. A. (1996). *The scapegoat generation: America's war on adolescents.* Monroe, ME: Common Courage.

Marsden, G. M. (1994). *The soul of the American university: From Protestant establishment to established nonbelief.* New York: Oxford University Press.

Marsden, G. M., & Longfield, B. J. (Eds.). (1992). *The secularization of the academy.* New York: Oxford University Press.

Martin, J. R. (1985). *Reclaiming a conversation: The ideal of the educated woman.* New Haven, CT: Yale University Press.

Martusewicz, R. A., & Reynolds, W. M. (Eds.). (1994). *Inside/out: Contemporary critical perspectives in education.* New York: St. Martin's.

Marty, M. (1985). *Pilgrims in their own land: 500 years of religion in America.* New York: Penguin.

McBrien, R. P. (1987). *Caesar's coin: Religion and politics in America.* New York: Macmillan.

McGrath, E. Z. (1994). *The art of ethics: A psychology of ethical beliefs.* Chicago: Loyola University Press.

McLaren, P. (1994). *Life in schools: An introduction to critical pedagogy in the foundations of education.* New York: Longman.

McLaren, P. (1995). *Critical pedagogy and predatory culture: Oppositional politics in a postmodern era.* New York: Routledge.

Meier, D. (1995). *The power of their ideas: Lessons for America from a small school in Harlem.* Boston: Beacon.

Mill, J. S. (1982). *On liberty.* New York: Penguin. (Original work published 1859)

Moran, G. (1987). *No ladder to the sky: Education and morality.* San Francisco: Harper & Row.

Moran, G. (1989). *Religious education as a second language.* Birmingham, AL: Religious Education Press.

Murray, J. C. (1960). *We hold these truths: Catholic reflections on the American proposition.* New York: Sheed & Ward.

Nagel, T. (1986). *The view from nowhere.* New York: Oxford University Press.

Nash, M. (1996). *A dialogue of ideas between Thomas Lickona and David Purpel.* Unpublished manuscript.

Nash, R. J. (1988). The revival of virtue in educational thinking: A postliberal appraisal. *Educational Theory, 38,* 27–39.

Nash, R. J. (1996). *"Real world" ethics: Frameworks for educators and human service professionals.* New York: Teachers College Press.

Nash, R. J. (1997). Fostering moral conversations in the college classroom. *Journal on Excellence in College Teaching, 7*(1).

Nash, R. J., & Griffin, R. S. (1987). Repairing the public–private split: Excellence, character, and civic virtue. *Teachers College Record, 88,* 549–566.

Neuhaus, R. J. (1987). *The Catholic moment: The paradox of the church in the postmodern world.* New York: Harper & Row.

Neuhaus, R. J. (1996). The Christian university: Eleven theses. *First Things, 59,* 20–22.

Niebuhr, R. (1932). *Moral man and immoral society: A study in ethics and politics.* New York: Scribner's.

Niebuhr, R. (1935). *An interpretation of Christian ethics.* New York: Seabury.

Niebuhr, R. (1937). *Beyond tragedy: Essays on the Christian interpretation of history.* New York: Scribner's.

Niebuhr, R. (1943). *The children of light and the children of darkness: A vindication of democracy and a critique of its traditional defense.* New York: Scribner's.

Niebuhr, R. (1952). *The irony of American history.* New York: Scribner's.

Nietzsche, F. (1989). *On the genealogy of morals* (W. Kaufmann & R. J. Hollingdale, Trans.). New York: Vintage. (Original work published 1887)

Nisbet, R. (1982). *Prejudices: A philosophical dictionary.* Cambridge, MA: Harvard University Press.

Nisbet, R. (1983). *The social philosophers: Community & conflict in western thought.* New York: Washington Square Press.

Noblit, G. W., & Dempsey, V. O. (1996). *The social construction of virtue: The moral life of schools.* Albany: State University of New York Press.

Noll, M. A. (1994). *The scandal of the evangelical mind.* Grand Rapids, MI: Eerdmans.

Nord, W. A. (1995). *Religion & American education: Rethinking a national dilemma.* Chapel Hill: University of North Carolina Press.

Oldenquist, A. (1986). *The non-suicidal society.* Bloomington: Indiana University Press.

Palmer, P. (1983). *To know as we are known: A spirituality of education.* San Francisco: Harper.

Pelikan, J. (1992). *The idea of the university: A reexamination.* New Haven, CT: Yale University Press.

Pellegrino, E. D., & Thomasma, D.C. (1993). *The virtues in medical practice.* New York: Oxford University Press.

Pieper, J. (1992). *Abuse of language: Abuse of power.* San Francisco: Ignatius.

Pincoffs, E. L. (1986). *Quandaries and virtues: Against reductivism in ethics.* Lawrence: University Press of Kansas.

Plato. (1956). *Great dialogues of Plato* (W. H. D. Rouse, Trans.). New York: Mentor.

Pojman, L. P. (1995). *Ethics: Discovering right and wrong.* Belmont, CA: Wadsworth.

Polkinghorne, J. (1996). *Quarks, chaos & Christianity: Questions to science and religion.* New York: Crossroad.

Portelli, J. P. (1991). From text to textuality: Using McLaren's *Life in Schools. Journal of Education, 173,* 15–27.

Pratte, R. (1988). *The civic imperative: Examining the need for civic education.* New York: Teachers College Press.

Purpel, D. E. (1989). *The moral & spiritual crisis in education: A curriculum for justice & compassion in education.* Granby, MA: Bergin & Garvey.

Purpel, D. E., & Shapiro, S. (1995). *Beyond liberation and excellence: Reconstructing the public discourse on education.* Westport, CT: Bergin & Garvey.

Rauch, J. (1993). *Kindly inquisitors: The new attacks on free thought.* Chicago: University of Chicago Press.

Ravitch, D. (1983). *The troubled crusade: American education 1945–1980.* New York: Basic Books.

Ravitch, D. (1984). *The schools we deserve: Reflections on the educational crises of our time.* New York: Basic Books.

Reich, R. B. (1992). *The work of nations.* New York: Basic Books.

Renyi, J. (1993). *Going public: Schooling for a diverse democracy.* New York: New Press.

Rippa, S. A. (1992). *Education in a free society: An American history.* New York: Longman.

Roof, W. C. (1993). *A generation of seekers: The spiritual journeys of the baby boom generation.* San Francisco: HarperCollins.

Rorty, R. (1979). *Philosophy and the mirror of nature.* Princeton, NJ: Princeton University Press.

Rorty, R. (1982). *Consequences of pragmatism.* Minneapolis: University of Minnesota Press.

Rorty, R. (1989). *Contingency, irony, and solidarity.* New York: Cambridge University Press.

Rorty, R. (1991). *Objectivity, relativism, and truth.* New York: Cambridge University Press.

Sacks, P. (1996). *Generation X goes to college: An eye-opening account of teaching in postmodern America.* Chicago: Open Court.

Said, E. (1993). *Culture and imperialism.* New York: Knopf.

Sandel, M. J. (1982). *Liberalism and the limits of justice.* New York: Cambridge University Press.

Sandel, M. J. (1996). *Democracy's discontent: America in search of a public philosophy.* Cambridge, MA: Harvard University Press.

Schwehn, M. (1993). *Exiles from Eden: Religion and the academic vocation in America.* New York: Oxford University Press.

Shapiro, H. S. (1990). *Between capitalism and democracy: Educational policy and the crisis of the welfare state.* Westport, CT: Bergin & Garvey.

Shor, I. (1986). *Culture wars: School and society in the conservative restoration 1969–1984.* Boston: Routledge & Kegan Paul.

Sichel, B. A. (1988). *Moral education: Character, community, and ideals.* Philadelphia: Temple University Press.

Simon, R. (1992). *Teaching against the grain: Texts for a pedagogy of possibility.* New York: Bergin & Garvey.

Simonds, R. L. (1994). A plea for the children. *Educational Leadership, 51,* 12–15.

Sommers, C. H. (1984). Ethics without virtue: Moral education in America. *The American Scholar, 53,* 111–118.

Stout, J. (1988). *Ethics after Babel: The languages of morals and their discontents.* Boston: Beacon.

Tarnas, R. (1991). *The passion of the Western mind: Understanding the ideas that have shaped our world view.* New York: Harmony.

Taylor, C. (1989). Cross-purposes: The liberal–communitarian debate. In N. L. Rosenblum (Ed.), *Liberalism and the moral life* (pp. 159–182). Cambridge: Harvard University Press.

Taylor, C. (1992). *The ethics of authenticity.* Cambridge, MA: Harvard University Press.

Thiselton, A. C. (1995). *Interpreting God and the postmodern self: On meaning, manipulation, and promise.* Grand Rapids, MI: Eerdmans.

Thomson, J. J. (1990). *The realm of rights.* Cambridge, MA: Harvard University Press.

Tipton, S. M. (1982). *Getting saved from the sixties: Moral meaning in conversion and cultural change.* Berkeley: University of California Press.

Tivnan, E. (1995). *The moral imagination: Confronting the ethical issues of our day.* New York: Simon & Schuster.

Tocqueville, A. de. (1988). *Democracy in America* (G. Lawrence, Trans.). New York: Harper & Row. (Original work published 1848)

Tracy, D. (1987). *Plurality and ambiguity: Hermeneutics, religion, hope.* New York: Harper & Row.

Tracy, D. (1994). *On naming the present: God, hermeneutics, and church.* Maryknoll, NY: Orbis.

Tyack, D., & Hansot, E. (1982). *Managers of virtue: Public school leadership in America, 1820–1980.* New York: Basic Books.

Ulich, R. (1968). *History of educational thought.* New York: American.

Van Doren, C. (1991). *A history of knowledge: Past, present, and future.* New York: Ballantine.

Walzer, M. (1983). *Spheres of justice: A defense of pluralism and equality.* New York: Basic Books.

Warren, K. L. (1997). *Education as the means to freedom: A critical analysis of oppression.* Unpublished master's thesis, University of Vermont, Burlington.

Weaver, M. J., & Appleby, R. S. (Eds.). (1995). *Being right: Conservative Catholics in America.* Bloomington: Indiana University Press.

Weiler, K. (1988). *Women teaching for change: Gender, class & power.* New York: Bergin & Garvey.

Welch, D. D. (1994). *Conflicting agendas: Personal morality in institutional settings.* Cleveland, OH: Pilgrim Press.

Westerhoff, J. H. (1992). Fashioning Christians in our day. In S. Hauerwas & John H. Westerhoff (Eds.), *Schooling Christians: "Holy experiments" in American education* (pp. 262–281). Grand Rapids, MI: Eerdmans.

White, P. (1996). *Civic virtues and public schooling: Educating citizens for a democratic society.* New York: Teachers College Press.

Willimon, W. H., & Naylor, T. H. (1995). *The abandoned generation: Rethinking higher education.* Grand Rapids, MI: Eerdmans.

Wilson, J. Q. (1995a). Liberalism, modernism, and the good life. In M. A. Glendon & D. Blankenhorn (Eds.), *Seedbeds of virtue* (pp. 17–34). New York: Madison.

Wilson, J. Q. (1995b). *On character.* Washington, DC: American Enterprise Institute.

Wojda, P. J. (1995). Liberation theology. In R. M. McBrien (Ed.), *The HarperCollins encyclopedia of Catholicism* (pp. 768–769). New York: HarperCollins.

Wuthnow, R. (1988). *The restructuring of American religion: Society and faith since World War II.* Princeton, NJ: Princeton University Press.

Wuthnow, R. (1993). *Christianity in the 21st century: Reflections on the challenges ahead.* New York: Oxford University Press.

Wynne, E. A., & Ryan, K. (1993). *Reclaiming our schools: A handbook on teaching character, academics, and discipline.* New York: Macmillan.

Index

About the Author

Robert J. Nash is a professor in the College of Education and Social Services, University of Vermont, Burlington, specializing in philosophy of education, ethics, moral education, and higher education. He holds graduate degrees in English education, theology, liberal studies/applied ethics, and educational philosophy. He administers the Interdisciplinary Master's Program, and he teaches courses in applied ethics and moral education. He has published more than 110 works in such journals as *Harvard Educational Review, Teachers College Record, Phi Delta Kappan, Journal of Teacher Education, Journal of Thought, School Review, Educational Theory, Journal of College Student Development,* and *Journal on Excellence in College Teaching.* His book *"Real World" Ethics: Frameworks for Educators and Human Service Professionals* was published by Teachers College Press in 1996.